Competitive Intelligence

FOR

DUMMIES

A Wiley Brand

by Jim Underwood

FOR

DUMMIES

A Wiley Brand

Contents at a Glance

Table of Contents

Part II: Gathering, Confirming, and Organizing Relevant Data 79

Chapter 5: Gathering Intelligence from Internal Resources 81

Chapter 6: Exploring External Sources for Valuable CI Information 99

Introduction

* * *

Business is war. The losers are the organizations that fail to adapt to the ever-evolving marketplace, and the winners are those that continually capitalize on momentary advantages the losers don't foresee.

Competitive intelligence (CI) can help your organization win the war. It essentially hands you a crystal ball that serves as your window into the future. With CI, you can predict where a market or sector is headed, which technologies are likely to drive changes in your industry, and how your competitors and their CEOs are likely to respond in any given situation. CI enables you to spot opportunities and threats months or even years down the road. It informs the decision makers and acts as an early-warning system to help your organization navigate the minefield that will sink your unwary competitors.

To put competitive intelligence to work for you, you need an experienced guide to tell you where to find the most illuminating and publicly available information, how to analyze that information to convert it into actionable intelligence, and how to convince your organization's leadership to put that intel into action. Welcome to *Competitive Intelligence For Dummies*. In this book, I reveal the secrets of CI that took me nearly 20 years to discover and the wisdom I've gained by supervising more than 200 graduate consulting projects for Fortune 500 companies and through hundreds of my own private consultations. I equip you with multiple skills and tools you can put to practical use, including see-mean-do (SMD) analysis and observe-orient-decide-act (OODA) loops. I also walk you through how to profile your competitors and their CEOs, forecast market trends, and interpret nonverbal communication so you can tell what someone is really saying and when they're probably trying to mislead you.

About This Book

My objective in this book is threefold: to give newbies a leg up on becoming solid CI contributors and analysts, to equip seasoned CI practitioners with some fresh ideas and advanced tools, and to help convince CEOs and other executives of the value of CI and the importance of implementing CI initiatives.

You can find plenty of books on the market that explain what competitive intelligence is and why it's an essential component of any organization's future success, but few, if any, of these books explain *how* to conduct competitive intelligence and overcome resistance to change within an organization. That's what makes this book stand out. Here, you not only discover the four steps to conducting intelligence but you also find out *how to* perform those steps:

- ✔ How to build a competitive intelligence function within your organization and staff it with the right people, even if you're operating without additional funding

- ✔ How to collect data and which sources to scour for the most valuable information and insight

- ✔ How to conduct competitive intelligence legally and ethically to stay out of trouble and protect your reputation as a fair player

- ✔ How to validate the data you've collected so you're certain that it's accurate and that it has the breadth, depth, and relevance to be useful

- ✔ How to analyze raw data and transform it into actionable intelligence that provides insight into future opportunities or threats

- ✔ How to profile competitors and their CEOs so you can accurately predict what they're going to do in any given situation

- ✔ How to overcome the barriers standing in the way of change so you can convince your organization to implement the changes that lead to growth and increased profit

One last thing: Although, I'd love for you to read every word I wrote, you're welcome to skip over the sidebars. You'll still be able to understand the key how-tos and explanations without them.

Foolish Assumptions

If you're reading this book, I assume that you're the person charged with conducting CI for your organization, someone who's pursuing a career in competitive intelligence, or a business owner or executive who wants to find out what CI is all about and how it can benefit your organization.

The only other assumption I made while writing is that you're committed to improving your organization and ensuring that it survives and thrives for the foreseeable future. The only way you and others in your organization can accomplish that goal is to build a competitive intelligence function and use it to drive creativity and innovation. Otherwise, your organization is destined, like most, to devolve into a calcified bureaucracy headed for extinction.

Speaking of assumptions, I *don't* assume that your organization is populated with like-minded people who have a similar commitment to identifying and capitalizing on potential future opportunities. In fact, I assume that you're probably going to encounter quite a bit of resistance to any innovations or changes you propose, which is why I devote an entire part of this book to explaining various ways to overcome resistance to change.

Icons Used in This Book

Throughout this book, the following icons appear in the margins to clue you in to different types of information that I present. Here's a breakdown of what each icon stands for:

 This icon marks absolutely critical information. If you happen to forget everything else you read in this book, at least remember what I tell you in these paragraphs.

 This bull's-eye indicates that you're about to read an insider insight. When you're looking for a better, faster way to do something, check out the information flagged with this icon.

 "Danger, Will Robinson, danger!" This icon alerts you to situations that call for extra vigilance or professional help.

Beyond the Book

In addition to the abundance of information on competitive intelligence that I provide in this book, you also get access to more help on the web. I provide a free Cheat Sheet at www.dummies.com/cheatsheet/competitive intelligence that you can check out from any web-enabled device. It provides a rundown of basic CI principles, a list of CI benefits (in case you need to convince someone, including yourself, that CI is worthwhile), tips on good CI sources, and advice on how to stay future focused to keep your organization in the lead.

Where to Go from Here

Think of this book as an all-you-can-eat buffet. You can grab a plate, start at the beginning, and read one chapter right after another. Or you can dip into any chapter and pile your plate high with the information it contains.

If you want a quick overview of competitive intelligence, check out the chapters in Part I. To get started on a shoestring budget, head to Chapter 3. For the bare-bones basics of conducting analysis, visit Chapter 10. And don't miss the list of top-performing companies' values in Chapter 15. Wherever you choose to go, you'll find plenty of useful information and guidance.

Part I
Brushing Up on the Basics

getting started
with

competitive
intelligence

Visit www.dummies.com for free content that helps you learn more and do more.

In this part . . .

- ✔ Grasp the basics of what competitive intelligence (CI) is and what it's not. (Hint: It's *not* about spying on your competitors!)

- ✔ Wrap your brain around the CI process of planning, gathering, analyzing, and executing — which ultimately leads to more planning, gathering, analyzing, and executing.

- ✔ Discover what *information advantage* is, why you want it, and how to get it.

- ✔ Convince yourself and the decision makers in your organization of the value of CI by considering its many benefits.

- ✔ Pick up some strategies for conducting CI on a shoestring budget by using resources already at your disposal.

- ✔ Find out how to stay squeaky clean when gathering intel so you don't ruin your organization's reputation or get into a legal mess.

Chapter 1

Gaining Information Advantage

*W*henever you're preparing to embark on a journey, it helps to look at a map and plot your route from point A to point B. And even though competitive intelligence is a journey with no end, this chapter serves as your map to understanding the process of gathering and using information to the benefit of your organization. I provide a bird's-eye view of what competitive intelligence is and what it involves. After reading this chapter, you'll have a general idea of where you're going and a framework on which to hang the details presented in the remaining chapters of this book.

Defining Competitive Intelligence and Information Advantage

Every field of study has its own terminology. The two key terms you need to know in this field are *competitive intelligence* and *information advantage*. If you can wrap your brain around these two puppies, you're well on your way to understanding how knowledge in business truly is power. In the following sections, I define these two terms, distinguish *competitive* intelligence from *competitor* intelligence, and offer some general guidance to help you take the first steps toward gaining the information advantage.

Understanding competitive intelligence

Competitive intelligence is the process of legally and ethically gathering, analyzing, and acting on information about an organization's market environment, competition, and other forces that may impact its future success. Done well, CI reveals future opportunities and serves as an early-warning system to help companies steer clear of organizational disasters.

Here are some key points to keep in mind about competitive intelligence:

- ✔ **CI isn't spying.** Professionals don't participate in or condone the use of illegal or unethical means of gathering intelligence about competitors. I recommend a standard of *integrity above reproach.* (See Chapter 4 for details.)

- ✔ **The CI process involves four essential steps: planning, gathering, analyzing, and executing.** If any step is missing or performed poorly, the value of the CI is compromised or nonexistent. For more about these steps, see "Knowing What It Takes: Information-Advantage Essentials," later in this chapter.

- ✔ **CI is service oriented.** Think of CI as a product and your organization's leaders as clients. To be useful, CI needs to be tailored to the type of intelligence the organization's decision makers need in order to gain a competitive edge. Successful CI makes the higher-ups look like geniuses, and for CI to succeed, the higher-ups must promote CI as essential to the organization's future survival and vitality.

- ✔ **Successful CI requires the right combination of process and people.** The process ensures that all four steps — planning, gathering, analyzing, and executing — are completed efficiently. The people involved in CI ensure that each step is performed correctly. CI must team up with the decision makers during the planning stage to identify the types of information needed and what it will ultimately be used for. Planning ensures that CI is able to gather high-value information that's targeted to answer a question, solve a problem, avoid a costly mistake, or identify opportunities or threats. Analysts must convert that raw information into meaningful intelligence. Executives and managers then need to put that intelligence into action. Failure at any stage is failure overall.

By understanding decision makers and other influential individuals and groups within the organization, their intelligence needs, and the involvement of executives, the CI team can markedly improve the ability of an organization to execute on important information.

You're already doing it!

Your organization is already performing CI to some degree. Here are a few CI activities that may be similar to what you're already doing:

✔ Sales people hear comments from customers about a competitor's next big product.

✔ Your CEO hears a speech by a competitor CEO that talks about a change in strategy.

✔ One of your company's drivers reports seeing a new type of distribution equipment on the back of a competitor's truck.

✔ Your sales manager hears a story about your largest competitor's pending merger with an industry supplier.

✔ You just noticed that your top competitor has changed its mission statement on its website to appeal to a new segment of the market.

✔ A trade journal features an article about a new technology that can reduce manufacturing costs by 50 percent.

✔ You hear it through the grapevine that two of your top competitors have laid off their entire information technology (IT) departments.

All these pieces of information are competitive intelligence. In fact, your organization is probably swimming in a sea of information about competitors, technologies, strategies, legislation, and other factors that affect your industry overall and perhaps your organization specifically. If you're acting on that information, good for you. But if your organization is like most, it's probably not analyzing the info or executing responses, which are two of the essential steps of the CI process. In fact, 80 percent of the time, valuable CI is wasted; leadership simply fails to put that intelligence into action.

Getting up to speed on information advantage

Simply put, *information advantage* is what an organization achieves when it uses competitive intelligence (which deals with external factors) to gain strategic insight into internal analytics (in other words, it's an understanding of what the numbers mean). You can look at it as a formula:

Internal analytics + External competitive intelligence = Information advantage

Information advantage can help you answer key competitive questions, such as: "Why did sales of product X decline last quarter?" and "Why did sales of our product mix change in the United Kingdom last month?"

When you're operating with information advantage, it's sort of like taking a road trip with the assistance of a GPS device. CI constantly monitors where you are and provides feedback so you can correct your course and remain on track as your competitors lose their way. With information advantage, you use people and technology, internally and externally, to continuously create preemptive business strategies to boost profits and win market share.

If you don't gain information advantage, you're at information *disadvantage* in relation to any competitor who's engaging in competitive intelligence and using it to shed light on its internal analytics.

Note that in the context of the term *information advantage, information* is the product of CI and internal analytics, such as sales trends; it's the insight gained through the careful analysis of facts. When I use the term *information* outside the context of information advantage, I'm talking about raw, unprocessed information. In general discussions, you need to understand the distinction between data, information, and intelligence:

- **Data:** Unprocessed facts or figures outside of a context that would make them meaningful. For example, if your company sold 50,000 bouncy balls last year, that's data. But without anything to compare that number to, it's not meaningful.

- **Information:** Facts or figures in a meaningful context. For example, if your company sold 50,000 bouncy balls last year and 100,000 the previous year, that's information. It has some meaning: Sales of bouncy balls declined by 50 percent.

- **Intelligence:** Insight that can lead to better decision making. For instance, your sales of bouncy balls declined by 50 percent last year because the market was saturated with bouncy balls. You now know the reason and can plan accordingly.

Distinguishing competitive intelligence from competitor intelligence

Another key distinction to make is between competitor and competitive intelligence:

- **Competitor intelligence:** *Competitor intelligence* focuses solely on what competing firms are up to. If you're focused solely on the competition, you'll never be a market leader. You'll always be at least one step behind, and you'll never be able to take the initiative to seize opportunities. In addition, you'll be more prone to engaging in industrial espionage, which runs counter to CI principles.

> ✔ **Competitive intelligence:** *Competitive intelligence* analyzes everything that could possibly affect your market, including emerging technologies, legislation, industry regulations, customer sentiment, changes in the industry and the economy, and dozens of other factors, as well as what competitors are up to. Competitive intelligence provides the insight you need to gain a first-mover advantage.

Don't get hung up on the competition. Opportunities are more likely to arise from what the competition *isn't* doing to serve customers than from what it *is* doing. That's how Steve Jobs managed to kill the competition for over ten years.

Making the Case for Competitive Intelligence

Organizations often fail to engage in CI for a variety of reasons. Some don't see the point. Others can't justify the cost, because CI's impact on profits flies below their radar. Others are too bogged down by size and bureaucracy to be open to the idea of making positive changes. Some executives are arrogant; they think they already know everything that's worth knowing. Some may even perceive CI as a threat to what they do or as another source of useless reports they need to read and process.

If you have any reservations about engaging CI, you've arrived at the right place. In the following sections, I describe the reasons why CI is crucial, explore specific potential benefits to your organization, and put the cost of conducting CI in perspective.

Noting the role of intelligence in success

You can usually figure out why certain companies succeed and others fail by looking at two factors: intelligence and action. The first company to discover a new idea, product, or technology and act on that discovery usually wins. Of course, intelligence itself isn't an idea, a product, or a technology, but intelligence usually inspires creative thinkers to recognize opportunities. To remain on the leading or bleeding edge of your industry or marketplace, your organization must continually gather and analyze relevant information and act on it.

The problem is that most people miss the true role that intelligence has in creating an advantage for companies. During the 1980s, *Fortune* magazine featured a number of articles about all the brilliant breakthroughs in the computer industry at the Xerox PARC research lab. PARC invented the mouse, the what-you-see-is-what-you-get (WYSIWYG) text editor, a graphical user interface (the ancestor of the Microsoft Windows Desktop), and other high-tech innovations. The only problem is that Xerox let the ideas get away. It failed to act and to capitalize on its information advantage.

While Xerox was struggling with internal issues, its competitors, recognizing how important those innovations were, reaped the rewards of what should have been Xerox's information advantage. They took these incredible products to market and built their success on the failures of Xerox.

The Xerox of today stands in contrast. The company has morphed into a leading-edge organization because of its ability to use CI and information advantage to continually grow and profit.

Striving to be more than just a learning organization

Over time, as the role of information in corporate success became more obvious, the idea of a *learning organization* developed. However, over the years people figured out that learning alone isn't enough. To gain the information advantage, you have to learn (through the process of gathering and analyzing information) and then transform and perform (by executing change initiatives based on what you've learned). You must put intelligence into action.

To become more than just a learning organization, leadership needs to promote CI throughout the organization and collaborate closely with the CI team to formulate and execute strategies.

Ditching the notion of a sustainable competitive advantage

Businesses often rise by doing one thing very well. Perhaps your organization made its mark by developing cutting-edge products, by streamlining production to manufacture products at a lower cost, or through creative advertising. Organizations with this kind of success are often lulled into thinking that they have a sustainable competitive advantage. They may be leading their industries in profits and market share and foresee no serious threats from their competitors.

However your organization has achieved its current success, you should celebrate it . . . and then forget it. The world is constantly changing. Inventors and entrepreneurs are always pushing the limits of technology and innovation. Competitors are always developing new products and services and devising strategies to claim a bigger share of the market. They undoubtedly know what you've done in the past to achieve success and have probably adapted as a result. Customers are always looking for superior products and services and lower prices. Changes in legislation often give rise to new opportunities and mark the end of traditional practices. Suppliers raise or lower prices, change the way they do business, or go belly up. Competitors may acquire new businesses or be bought out by others. What matters now is not the past but the future. So what are you going to do tomorrow and next month and next year to build on your prior success? As strategist J. K. Lindsey said, "All competition takes place in the future."

Because the landscape is constantly changing, you need to give up on the notion that you have a sustainable competitive advantage. To maintain your lead, you need to develop new strategies with the help of competitive intelligence.

Capitalizing on momentary advantages

To maximize success, your organization must look past any historic competitive advantage it may have had. It must strive to continually take advantage of opportunities and respond to potential threats in ways that incrementally increase profits and market share. It must begin to operate with a *momentary-advantage mindset* — an awareness that the playing field is in a constant state of change that continually produces new opportunities and threats.

One of the keys to success is to think of an organization as a system. Every facet of an organization is subject to forces that drive its evolution. Change isn't isolated to product development, sales, or marketing. It can also affect human resources, manufacturing, distribution, shipping, receiving, and other departments. If an organization's context changes, it must strategically realign every aspect of itself to meet new and more complex challenges. CI makes this realignment possible by monitoring the changing conditions, identifying potential opportunities and threats, and providing insight on how to adapt to and even capitalize on changes.

To grasp the importance of operating with a momentary-advantage mindset, answer the following five questions about how your competitors will operate over the next three years:

- ✔ Will they be the same as today?
- ✔ Will they offer the same products as today?
- ✔ What technologies will emerge in products in the future?
- ✔ Will they use the same marketing approach as they do today?
- ✔ Are any technologies emerging that could possibly trigger revolutionary change?
- ✔ Will they seek to keep their market share at the same level as today?
- ✔ Will they be content to maintain their current product portfolio instead of attempting to discover the next big thing?

Obviously, the answer to all those questions is a resounding "No!" Your competitors' goal is or should be to gain market share at your expense, and you need to return the favor by working toward gaining market share at their expense through CI.

Recognizing specific potential benefits

You can't always assign a dollar figure to CI in terms of cost or benefits. Gauging the value of a process that improves decision making is difficult, because decisions tend to have a cumulative value measured in overall success. Because of this, successful companies don't weigh the costs of CI against its benefits. Instead, they approach CI as an essential component of their overall success. But some people still need convincing, so here's what CI can help your organization do:

- ✔ **Make smarter decisions.** Well-informed decisions are generally better decisions.

- ✔ **Spot opportunities.** By monitoring the forces that impact your business, you become more in tune with customer needs, growing trends, and other factors that reveal opportunities for new products, services, and ways of doing business. While some of these may be small wins, a succession of small wins can keep you in the lead.

- ✔ **Gain first-mover advantage.** Continually collecting and analyzing targeted information enables you to spot opportunities that your competitors may not anticipate because they're either not gathering the right information or not acting on it.

✔ **Avoid costly mistakes.** If you're about to make a major investment, acquire a business, change suppliers, introduce a new product, or engage in any other costly endeavor, CI can help you assess the risk and potential upside and avoid making a serious mistake.

✔ **Avoid nasty surprises.** Good CI is all about being proactive versus reactive. When you're continually monitoring what's likely to impact your business, you're less likely to be surprised by competitor innovations, cost-cutting technologies, changes in industry regulations, disruptions from suppliers, and so forth.

✔ **Anticipate competitor moves.** One key aspect of information advantage involves analyzing competitors and predicting their future strategies. Developing intelligence about a competitor's goals, its ability to achieve those goals, and its customers, suppliers, and partners enables you to see where the company is going and why and develop your own strategies in response.

✔ **Detect new or potential competitors.** CI can be a great early-warning system for the strategic planning team, detecting the new kids on the block and finding out what they're up to.

✔ **Predict changes in the industry.** Changes in production, materials, distribution, and other factors can significantly affect the way you do business or should be doing business. Organizations on the leading edge of these changes fare well. Those that lag behind fail. CI delivers the intelligence you need to lead your field.

✔ **Size up candidates for acquisitions or mergers.** CI can help your organization perform its due diligence before committing to an acquisition or merger, again helping you avoid costly mistakes.

✔ **Plan for changes in legislation or regulation.** In certain industries, changes in legislation can have a significant impact on products and services and how consumers access them. (The telecommunications industry and banking and other financial sectors, for example, are majorly affected by regulations!) Knowing what's around the bend can help your organization navigate the turns without becoming the next train wreck.

✔ **Identify customer needs.** CI can "listen in" to what customers say online, over the phone when speaking with customer service representatives, and even in discussion forums hosted by competitors to identify unmet needs that may lead to ideas for new products and services.

✔ **Gauge customer sentiment.** An organization's reputation can have a significant impact on sales. CI can tune in to what the media and the masses are saying about your organization and provide valuable feedback for sales and marketing to respond constructively.

- ✔ **Learn from other companies' mistakes.** CI can monitor other companies' actions and how the market responds and provide valuable insight into the market's expectations.

- ✔ **Improve your organization internally.** Benchmarking your procedures and processes against the best in the business can significantly improve efficiency and quality.

- ✔ **Scope out prime real estate for expansion.** CI is crucial when you're planning to move your company or expand. Intelligence can tell you which locations are most tax friendly, which of them have the highest concentration of the expertise you need, which are best for efficient and reliable shipping and receiving, and much more.

- ✔ **Stay competitive when a product becomes a commodity.** When a product becomes a commodity, you need to find new ways to differentiate yourself from the competition. Information advantage gives you insight into how customers perceive you in the marketplace; how you stack up against the competition; what your customers expect in terms of price, quality, and customer service; and a host of other factors you need to consider.

- ✔ **Discovering cost-saving technologies, products, and processes.** History shows that the first competitor in any industry to take advantage of an emerging technology tends to gain a competitive advantage. Your CI team can give you a heads up on emerging technologies, products, and processes that can save you time and money.

  Of course, early adopters often get burned, too. They invest in emerging technologies, and when superior technologies hit the market, they're too heavily invested in what they already adopted to make the switch. To avoid this pitfall, during its high-growth years, Dell would patiently watch multiple new technologies until they could determine which one would be the winner. Then it would pounce on the new technology and use it as the foundation for superior growth.

Intelligence is key to making well-informed decisions. Everyone in the company needs to know about emerging technologies in order to think creatively about how to apply those technologies to streamline operations, connect with customers, improve products and services, and reap other benefits.

Considering the costs

CI can cost as little or as much as you decide to invest in it, but remember that the entry fee may be next to nothing. All you need to do is formalize what you're already doing — decide which information is necessary, gather it, analyze it, and send the analysis to the decision makers. In Chapter 3, I offer guidance on how to conduct CI on a low budget.

Costco: Embracing automation to control costs and boost profits

Few companies can afford to compete on price alone. Costco is an exception. This hugely successful retailer has gained a competitive edge by focusing on reducing and improving efficiency in *transactions* — the number of times a product is touched by human hands from the time it leaves the factory to the point at which the customer picks it off the shelf and drops it in her shopping cart. Costco has achieved unmatched efficiency through the use of vendor partnering, packaging, and process design. Although this type of innovation may seem simple, it adds millions of dollars to Costco's bottom line.

Only through careful analysis can you discover the secrets of how certain organizations achieve success. Without analysis, Costco's competitors would never know its secret; they would need to figure it out on their own or miss the opportunity altogether.

When you begin to see positive results from this shoestring-budget approach, you'll probably want to invest more in CI, perhaps by hiring a professional analyst or having a talented employee receive some formal training. You may even decide to invest in specialized software, fee-based data services, expert panels, interview services, and more.

Don't concern yourself so much with the cost of conducting CI. Think about the cost of *not* engaging in it. If your competitors are successfully engaged in CI, not doing it is already negatively affecting your profit.

Knowing What It Takes: Information-Advantage Essentials

To gain information advantage, you must engage in a continuous four-step process that involves planning, gathering information, analyzing the information, and formulating and executing strategies, as shown in Figure 1-1.

As strategies are developed and implemented, additional intelligence is required to fine-tune the strategies, address any issues that arise, and constantly monitor ever-changing conditions for new opportunities and threats. In the following sections, I describe each step in greater detail and explain what I mean by operating with an *information-advantage mindset*.

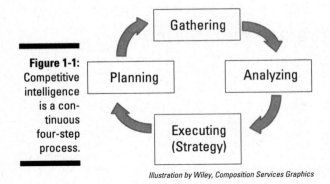

Illustration by Wiley, Composition Services Graphics

Figure 1-1:
Competitive intelligence is a continuous four-step process.

Planning

Planning involves determining the intelligence that's needed in order to make well-informed decisions and identifying the sources where you're most likely to find the best information. Planning enables you to target your search and narrow the scope so the information you gather is more relevant to its intended purpose.

Every CI assignment is different. During the initial planning stage, you're usually trying to find out who the final client is (often the CEO or a department head), the urgency of the project (if the client is the CEO, then urgency is usually high), the projected impact of the issue under study, and the funding available for the project. The upfront understanding of the key issues behind the project is very important because these key issues usually drive the project's design.

During the planning phase, the CI team needs to understand the decisions executives will be making and consult with decision makers to determine the type of intelligence they need. Their needs may be general; for example, the managers responsible for product development may want CI to monitor the industry for any emerging technologies that are likely to drive future innovations. Managers may also have specific needs — a question they need answered or a problem they're trying to solve.

During the planning stage, everyone involved must also address which information sources are most relevant. If CI is tasked with monitoring developing technologies, for example, it may be looking at patent applications, trade magazines, newsgroup discussions, and other sources to pick up on any buzz about new technologies. If the industry is heavily regulated, CI may be asked to monitor relevant legislation and lawsuits that may pose challenges or open new opportunities.

When planning to gather CI, the team also needs to consider deadlines in respect to the time required to tap certain resources. For example, if a manager has a three-week timeline for making a decision, and a freedom-of-information request is likely to take two months or longer to produce the required intelligence, then the CI team needs to explore other sources. For more about laying the groundwork for CI, see Chapter 2.

Gathering and organizing valuable information

Without good information, the organization can have no information advantage, but what constitutes good information? The following benchmarks enable you to answer that question for yourself (and you can check out Part II for more detail on gathering information).

Volume

The volume of information required varies according to the question you're trying to answer or the problem you're trying to solve. You can't measure it in megabytes or gigabytes or pages worth of documentation. The only real gauge is subjective: Are you confident that you have enough information to move forward?

The volume of available information is often determined by *scope* — how narrow or broad the question or problem is. If your scope is global, the volume of information needed is obviously much larger than if you're focusing on a local or regional issue. In Chapter 5, I explain how to define your scope before proceeding to collect information.

You really can't have too much information, as long as the information can be sorted by date and other criteria. An overabundance of information becomes a problem only when the database is polluted with outdated, irrelevant content that can't be filtered out.

Time relevance

Although you can learn great lessons from history, the most useful information for intelligence is that which results in future-focused and predictive analysis. If you're looking back at what a competitor did in the past or at what customers are shopping for right now, you're missing future opportunities. You must think three or four moves ahead, and to do that, you need information that helps you predict your competitors' decisions, your customers' needs, and market conditions months or years down the road.

A great way to think about this is to assume you're in the notebook computer business for a moment. You already know what your competition is doing today, but that really doesn't help you prepare a strategy for tomorrow. You need to assess the future needs of your users and consider processor speed, new software, internal memory requirements, social-media demands, new wireless technologies, and numerous other factors. Your future success hinges on your ability to accurately assess the potential of emerging technologies and how you can tap that potential to invent new products that meet consumers' needs and capture their interest.

Steer clear of the common and most serious trap of focusing on information that merely provides insight into the present. Information that focuses on the present or the past is a tempting target because so much of it is readily available, but information that serves as a window to the future is much more valuable. Always ask yourself, "Is our information future focused and predictive?"

Accuracy

Not all information is relevant or even accurate. When you're collecting information, part of your job is to filter out what's useless, incorrect, misleading, or obtained illegally or unethically. Here are some CI methods of separating good information from bad:

- **Source ranking:** Certain sources are more reliable than others; for example, a newspaper or magazine article is more likely to contain accurate information than something you heard through the grapevine.

- **Triangulation:** Checking a source against other sources can help validate the information or call it into question.

- **Ethical queries:** Questioning whether the information was obtained legally and ethically is essential in determining whether you can use the information. For example, if the information is publicly available, it's fair game. On the other hand, if it was obtained from an inside source during a private conversation, it can't be used without the organization's approval.

See Chapter 4 for additional details regarding legal and ethical issues. For more about validating information, see Chapter 9.

Beware of deception, a tactic that's been in practice since the first relatively complex organisms evolved on planet Earth. Competitors who are wise to CI may try to use deception against you by leaking false information and tempting you to squander resources in pursuit of phantom opportunities. Always cross-check your intel against information from other reliable sources.

Quality

Quality of intelligence is measured in depth and clarity:

- **Depth:** Depth comes from understanding motives, leader tendencies, mission, and even an organization's research focus so you can understand the information in context. To achieve depth of intelligence, ask plenty of open-ended questions, such as who, what, when, where, why, and how. For example, if you happen upon an intriguing observation or insight, try to identify the individual who shared it and question the person's motives for sharing it in the context in which it was shared. If you discover that the original source of the information was a competitor bragging about his business in a trade journal in which he advertises, some of the claims may be exaggerated. However, if that same information came from an unbiased analyst, you may have greater reason to trust it. Having as much depth as economically feasible is always important.

- **Clarity:** The most valuable information usually applies to the future, which is often fuzzy. Information that facilitates future-focused analysis tends to be vague or fragmented, so use cross-checks, ask questions, and consult additional sources to fill in the gaps.

As your CI team collects information, it needs to ask itself, "Does our information provide sufficient depth and clarity for effective analysis?"

Collecting high-quality information not only results in superior CI but also improves efficiency. During an intelligence assignment, an interviewer discovered 1 expert out of over 20 who seemed to have more quality information than the other 19 combined. In other words, 1 competent analyst is more valuable than 19 clueless ones.

Value

Value is a metric that's tough to pin down. It relies heavily on a metric described previously in this chapter — time relevance. Generally, the value of information rises as its relevance moves along the time continuum from past to future focused:

- Historical information has very little value.

- Information that provides insight into current conditions has limited value.

- Information that sheds light on a potential threat or opportunity in the future has a very high value.

But value goes beyond time relevance. Value is really measured by the opportunities that the information has the potential to reveal or the pitfalls it helps you avoid. When evaluating your information's value, ask the question, "Does our information enhance our ability to achieve our strategic goal or avoid a potentially costly mistake?" If you can honestly answer yes to that question, you have high-value information.

Organization

Anyone who has a cluttered garage, attic, or apartment knows that if you can't find a tool when you need it, the tool is useless. The same is true for information. Organizing information is the key to using it and maximizing its value. In this age of technology, organization calls for storing information electronically and cataloging it so you can extract information selectively according to your intelligence needs. For example, you may consider indexing information by competitor, technology, product, geographical market, customer, strategic sector, and date. If you need to analyze some aspect of a competitor's strategic goals, you can then extract information related to competitors without having to pick through information on products or customers.

As you gather and store information, your CI team needs to ask the question, "Is the information organized and indexed in a manner that facilitates analysis?" If you answer no to this question or you're having trouble finding and using the information you're collecting, then you have a problem with organization. In Chapter 9, I help you solve that problem.

Analyzing information: Converting information into meaningful intelligence

You have a huge database of high-value information. So what? Now that you've acquired the information, how can you use it to create opportunities for profit and growth? The goal of analysis is to transform raw information into meaningful intelligence that guides strategic planning.

After collecting the information, you're ready for the analysis stage, which basically involves the following three steps, which I refer to as *see-mean-do* (SMD):

1. **Observe (see).**

   Ask yourself the question, "What do I see?" Try to summarize the information in a single sentence without reading into it.

2. **Interpret (mean).**

   Ask yourself, "What does this mean?" or "Why?"

3. **Act (do).**

   After you figure out the underlying reasons for a certain event, you need to determine what response is appropriate. You're not actually doing anything here other than coming up with one or more recommendations for a decision maker or executive to follow through on. However, you do need to develop clear and clever recommendations and spend some time developing a pitch to convince leadership of the need to take action.

For additional details about SMD analysis, see Chapter 3. Part III features more in-depth coverage of analysis.

Formulating and executing strategies

Most CI models end with analysis, but I consider that to be only step 3 of 4. If you're part of the CI team, I encourage you to approach your job as though it ends with action. After all, if the intelligence isn't put into action, it hasn't achieved its goal. Of course, you can't force a manager or executive to implement a recommended course of action, but you can and should present the intelligence as convincingly as possible to prompt the necessary action. Following are some strategies to clear the path between analysis and execution:

✔ **Involve everyone in the CI process from beginning to end.** Involving everyone in CI improves intelligence and makes everybody more receptive to the analysis and recommended changes.

✔ **Recruit high-level sponsors.** When your organization's leaders believe in the value of CI, they'll promote CI to the rest of the organization and become more receptive to CI's insight and advice.

✔ **Evaluate the learning styles of your organization's leaders.** Some people may prefer printed reports, whereas others find multimedia presentations more convincing. By catering to each leader's preferred learning style, you increase your chances of having your presentation be understood and accepted.

✔ **Be confident.** If you're recommending a certain course of action, don't waffle. Convince yourself first so you can confidently recommend a course of action. If you're not convinced, ask more questions and gather and analyze additional information to reveal more clearly the best course of action, but don't recommend moving forward until you answer all the relevant questions to increase your own confidence in making the recommendation.

✔ **Produce quality reports and presentations.** Present your information and intelligence professionally so your audience will take it seriously.

For more about getting buy-in for CI, see Part IV.

Operating with an information-advantage mindset

Eighty percent of CI initiatives fail somewhere between analysis and execution. In other words, 80 percent of the time, company leadership simply does not act on the intelligence it has at its disposal. Company size and age are usually the culprits; as an organization grows and ages, its ability to change deteriorates until it becomes a frozen bureaucracy. The most successful companies and their leaders operate with an information-advantage mindset, exhibited by the following qualities:

- **Leaders with intuitive paranoia:** *Intuition* is immediate knowledge not acquired or arrived at through learning or reasoning; you just know something is true. *Paranoia* is suspicion or distrust; you think that people are generally motivated by ill will toward you. A leader with intuitive paranoia has a sixth sense that enables her to immediately recognize potential threats.

- **Leaders with a momentary-advantage mentality:** Your organization's leadership needs to recognize that all opportunities are fleeting and that successful organizations are usually those that continually capitalize on momentary advantages. Leaders need to convey a sense of urgency about future opportunities that ripples through the organization.

- **Confidence in the information's volume, time relevance, accuracy, quality, and value:** To ensure company-wide support for CI, everyone needs to be confident in the information from which inferences are drawn, predictions are made, and strategic initiatives are formulated. You build confidence over time by producing positive results and communicating effectively.

- **Talented, skilled analysts:** To perform effective CI, you need the most talented and skilled analysts available. These are the people who provide the insights on which key decisions are based. Top-notch analysts are often born and trained. They're born curious, observant, and skeptical. They're trained to dig up valuable information, use analytics, process and synthesize large volumes of information, think logically and critically, and trust their instincts.

- **Confidence in the analytical, intuitive, and synthesis capabilities of the analysts:** Regardless of how talented and skilled the analysts are, if leadership lacks confidence in their abilities, those leaders won't be receptive to the analysis or eager to plan and implement recommended changes. Confidence in the entire process is key to success.

- **Use of a systematic approach to ensure the accurate, meaningful interpretation of the information:** One of the not-so-secret secrets to success is to put good procedures in place and hire competent personnel to carry out those procedures. The same is true in CI. Having a system in place ensures that all the required steps are done: information planning, gathering, analyzing, and executing. Failure at any stage is failure overall.

✔ **An emphasis on future-focused analysis:** Data collection must be focused on information that enables analysts to draw inferences and make predictions. If the information leads to conclusions based solely on past or current market conditions, it's useless in formulating future-focused strategic initiatives.

✔ **Use of skeptical questioning and antagonistic thinking in evaluating conclusions:** Confidence doesn't mean blind acceptance of conclusions. Analysts and leaders need to question not only the accuracy of the information but also the reasoning that led to any conclusions or recommendations for change. Ideas need to pass the test of frank and honest debate to ensure that they're worthy of resources, planning, and action.

✔ **Development of reliable inferences and categorization of threats and possible outcomes:** Skeptical questioning and antagonistic thinking should eventually evolve into drawing inferences and considering the endgame. Decision makers need to look at the possible ramifications of making a recommended change, including costs and potential outcomes. What will implementation entail, what are the likely results, and what are the potential downsides?

✔ **Management and executive sponsorship to ensure that critical intelligence is considered and, when appropriate, acted upon:** Simply put, managers and executives need to step up to the plate and exude their confidence in all phases of CI, from information gathering and analysis through the execution of recommended changes. Without highly visible, top-level support for CI, implementation of changes is likely to fall short of the goals.

✔ **Reduction in resistance to change:** Companies, especially larger, older companies, tend to be averse to change. Part of leadership's job is to ensure that change occurs incrementally to reduce resistance.

When an organization is operating with the information-advantage mindset, it's engaged in a never-ending cycle of gathering information and using it to gain first-mover advantages. This cycle has four stages that sort of align with the four stages of the CI process:

1. **Collective:** Gather comprehensive, relevant information about competitors, products, technologies, and trends *before* they impact the organization's bottom line.

2. **Strategic:** Analyze the information and synthesize it into accurate, clear, and meaningful inferences and insights.

3. **Executive:** Communicate results and issue a call to action to influence key decision makers to act on critical intelligence.

4. **Preemptive:** Enable the firm to continually reap the rewards of first-mover advantage by leading the industry in innovation.

To determine whether your organization is properly geared for information advantage, ask whether it's organized in such a way that it can perform CI effectively and act on critical intelligence. In Chapter 2, I explain how to gauge your level of involvement in CI. In Chapter 19, I provide a more comprehensive list of questions to assess your organization's CI readiness.

Playing Fair: Adhering to Legal and Ethical Guidelines

Before you engage in CI, I urge you to establish legal and ethical standards for gathering information. Obviously, planting spies in your competitor's organization and hacking into its network are prohibited, but even more subtle intelligence tactics, such as listening to private conversations, cross the line. In Chapter 4, I provide guidance for establishing ethical standards, but here's a quick test to determine if you can ethically use certain information you collected. Simply answer yes or no to each of the following questions:

✔ **Is the information publicly available?** If the information is public, it's fair game.

✔ **Is the information in plain view?** *Plain view* means that the owners of the information knowingly made it public; their intention was to allow it to become available to outside parties. If you can't be certain that the information was intentionally and knowingly made public, you shouldn't use it in any way.

✔ **Was the information obtained in a manner that was above reproach?** Above reproach means that any reasonable, moral, and ethical human being would consider the way you obtained the information to be fair. If any reasonable person could possibly perceive your actions as unethical, then you're not acting above reproach.

✔ **Was the information obtained from an inside source?** If the information originated from someone inside the organization and it's not publicly available, you can use it only if you have permission to do so from an authorized representative of the company.

These questions are the first line of defense for steering clear of the most common legal and ethical pitfalls of conducting CI. In addition, violations may occur depending on the circumstances.

Don't cheat. You can obtain the information you need legally and ethically. If you try to bend the rules, you may be exposing yourself and your organization to legal action and place your organization's and your own reputation at risk.

Protecting Sensitive Information

Chances are good that you're not the only one interested in finding out what your competitors are up to. Most of your competitors probably want to know what you're up to as well, and some of them may even be willing to breach ethical standards in order to obtain the information they want. Here are a few preventive measures your organization can take to protect your information:

- ✔ **Protect all sensitive corporate information.** Never allow sensitive documents to be left in plain view on a computer screen or on a desk. Never leave sensitive information unattended in meeting rooms.

- ✔ **Warn customer-service and sales personnel to remain on alert for fake customer calls from competitors looking for sensitive information.**

- ✔ **Never forget that all electronic devices can be tapped by the right technology.** Always be suspicious of cameras, microphones, or wires that look out of place. Sinister people really do plant devices in offices and meeting rooms to monitor discussions; this doesn't just happen on TV and in the movies.

For more about defending against competitor intelligence, see Chapter 18.

Chapter 2

Getting Started with CI

In This Chapter

▶ Figuring out what you have and what you need to get started

▶ Assembling a competitive intelligence team

▶ Identifying the information you need and where to find it

▶ Optimizing results — strategies and tips

For competitive intelligence (CI) to be effective, it must be formal, systematic, and continuous. It has to be an integral part of your daily business operations, regardless of your organization's size. However, size does influence what the CI function looks like in different organizations. In a small business with an owner and a handful of employees, the CI function may consist of a weekly or monthly meeting in which employees share information with the owner, who conducts analysis and formulates strategy. A large corporation, on the other hand, may have one or more CI departments that gather information internally and externally, analyze it, and collaborate with the corporation's leadership to formulate strategy.

In this chapter, I explain how to put all the pieces in place to build a CI function within the framework of your existing business. Most of the advice I offer applies regardless of the size of your organization, but some advice is obviously directed toward larger operations. Fortunately, CI is scalable; you can reap its benefits even if you're operating a sole proprietorship and expand operations as your business grows. Approach this chapter with your scale of operations and resources in mind.

Establishing Your CI Starting Point

The first step is always the hardest. Before you start to collect data, make sure you have everything in place to store, organize, analyze, distribute, and act on your intelligence. In the following sections, I lead you through the process of gauging your CI-readiness and describe what you need to get started and how to obtain what's missing.

Gauging your organization's current level of involvement in CI

Your organization is engaged in CI to some degree, but your efforts may be insufficient to make an impact. How can you tell? If your company has no formal process in place for gathering, analyzing, and acting on competitive intelligence, then it probably isn't sufficiently engaged in CI. If your organization does have a formal process in place, then assign a number from 1 to 4 to each of the following statements to gauge your organization's current level of involvement in CI:

1 = Strongly disagree

2 = Disagree

3 = Agree

4 = Strongly agree

_____ My company has an organized approach for gathering information for the purpose of making better decisions and formulating effective strategies.

_____ My company has a team or person who's responsible for receiving and organizing intelligence information for the entire company.

_____ My company has one or more individual(s) responsible for analyzing and interpreting the information that everyone else in the organization gathers and passes along to them.

_____ We have a team of sponsors, including senior executives, who are responsible for reviewing CI and taking it forward for action by the senior executive team.

Total your scores and see where your firm's CI ability is ranked:

4–6 = Problematic

7–9 = Limited

10–12 = Encouraging

13–14 = Fantastic

If you're in the 4–9 range, you definitely need to initiate CI in your organization. If you're in the 10–14 range, you're well on your way, but there's always room for improvement.

Conducting a CI needs assessment

A CI *needs assessment* sheds light on your own internal CI goals and on the investment you need to make in CI to remain competitive:

- ✔ **Investment:** Begin your assessment by looking at your competitors and asking the following questions:

  - • Do they have a formal CI function and the infrastructure in place to put intelligence into action?

  - • What do they do to gather and analyze data?

  - • How much money do they spend on CI?

  Of course, even answering these questions requires CI. (Are you dizzy yet?) See Chapters 6 and 7 for guidance on how to collect data from external sources and tap experts and expert panels for additional information and insights.

- ✔ **Goals:** Ask yourself and your organization's leaders how quality CI could serve the executive team, the marketing/sales team, and even human resources (HR). Think of CI as a customer-service organization. Your customers are your organization's decision makers. Interview executives and managers to find out what sort of information and intelligence they need in order to make better decisions. Your CEO, for example, may want to know what certain competitors are planning to do in the future and whether any competitors would make good targets for future acquisitions. Sales managers may want to know which sectors have the most potential for future sales. Marketing needs to know about potential customers that their message isn't reaching.

After you have an overall assessment, look more closely at what you need in terms of data collection and management, analysis, and execution, as explained in the following sections.

Taking stock of your data-collection resources

CI is valuable on an ad hoc basis; for example, to answer a specific question or solve a problem. But it's more valuable if it's systematic and continuous, when it's used to monitor conditions and predict the likelihood of certain events. The farther into the future your CI can see, the more opportunities your organization has to attain and maintain market leadership.

Effective CI begins with planning (deciding what issues you need to investigate and which sources are likely to have the information you need), but it never ends. Planning leads to gathering, analysis, and execution, but that cycle only leads to more planning. Conditions are always changing, new opportunities and threats are always on the horizon, and you always have room for improvement, so approach CI as a system that continuously generates future-focused intelligence.

To ensure that data collection is systematic and ongoing, you need procedures and technology in place to store, organize, and validate the data. Specifically, your organization must have the following:

- **A *formal* process for gathering data:** Data collection typically involves everyone in the organization, including executives, managers, marketing personnel, sales agents, and customer-service reps. Some data collection can be automated through customer relationship management (CRM) software. In a perfect world, everyone in the organization needs to be trained to recognize the types of data to collect and how to input that data into the system or transfer it over to CI. However, that may not always be possible. Emphasis initially should be placed on individuals with outward-facing roles in the organization, such as sales, marketing, and customer service. You may also have procedures for gathering external data and input from experts and expert panels. The chapters in Part II discuss data collection in greater detail.

- **Technology and procedures for storing and indexing data:** Your organization needs a secure, central database in which all intelligence is stored and accessible to analysts and personnel who use the information. For more about storing and indexing data, see Chapter 9.

- **Procedures in place for validating data:** As you collect data, you need formal procedures to separate fact from fiction, filter out irrelevant and misleading information, and gauge the relative value of data and data sources. For example, you may want to use a triangulation procedure to make sure that any data is backed up by two other reliable sources before it's taken into consideration. See Chapter 9 for additional guidance on how to validate data.

Assessing your data-interpretation expertise

Take a look at existing personnel who you think may be qualified to analyze your CI and ask two questions:

- **Do they have the innate ability to analyze intelligence?** An analyst is naturally curious, observant, skeptical, and of course, analytical. Some folks just don't have what it takes, and training is no substitute.

- **Do they have the training that will make them effective?** This book provides the basic training required. Additional training is available in the form of college-level courses, certification programs, seminars and webinars, conferences, journals and magazines, and web-based resources including websites and blogs. A good place to start looking for additional training and education is at SCIP (Strategic and Competitive Intelligence Professionals). Visit `www.scip.org` to find out what this organization offers.

If you don't have the necessary talent in-house, you may need to outsource analysis to a consulting firm or hire an analyst to fill the position.

Reviewing your strategic readiness

Strategic readiness is the ability to act on intelligence. It's a reflection of four broad areas:

- ✔ Leadership that fosters creativity and discovery
- ✔ A culture that rewards personal initiative
- ✔ Values that focus on integrity, empowerment, and recognition
- ✔ A preoccupation with being exceptional as individuals and as an organization

Strategic readiness doesn't happen overnight. Leaders in the company must make a persistent effort to build a community that's committed to quality and the vitality of the organization. For additional details on performing a strategic readiness assessment, see Chapter 15.

Auditing your execution systems and strategies

Your organization is probably engaged in CI to some degree. But to ensure that you're able to use intelligence to the fullest, you need to be able to confidently answer yes to the following questions:

- ✔ Does the intelligence report from the CI team or one of its analysts describe a clear call to action? CI needs to progress from just showing information and insight to indicating what actions may be taken. Although CI usually lacks the authority to actually execute a strategic initiative, it should offer one or more ways the organization can respond to a perceived threat or opportunity.
- ✔ Is the information communicated in such a way that the reader can quickly understand the level of urgency attached to it?
- ✔ Is your information getting to the right people?
- ✔ Are you observing positive action (execution) in response to the information that's provided?

If you answer no to *any* of these questions, you're probably facing a problem with communication or resistance to change. If you answered no to any of the first three questions, your problem is with communication. See Chapter 17, where I explain how to create an effective prelaunch brief and communicate CI issues to decision makers. If you answered no to the fourth question, then the next section can help you overcome resistance to change. (Chapter 15 covers this topic in greater detail.)

Getting Buy-In for a CI Function

The biggest obstacle to implementing CI in an organization is the internal resistance to it. In certain cases, an organization's leadership simply fails to appreciate the value of CI; they see it as a cost center rather than as a profit center. Some managers may perceive CI as a threat or just another source of reports they already have in excess. Likewise, employees may view their involvement in CI and any additional work that CI initiatives call for as more busywork they're not getting compensated for. A few people in your organization may view CI as unethical. (As explained in Chapter 4, CI, if done properly, is an ethical business practice.)

One of the first and biggest challenges to overcome is to convince your organization's executives and managers that CI is valuable — that it's essential for your organization's survival and will boost future profits and growth. In the following sections, I offer a few suggestions on how to get leadership and staff to buy in to CI.

One of the most consistent realities that organizations face is the 80 percent failure rate of change initiatives and new ideas. CI often falls victim to this reality, which is why I include tips throughout the book on clearing that hurdle.

Creating CI value out of things that keep CEOs awake at night

Fear sells. One way to sell CI to your organization's leadership is to find out what they fear most and offer CI as a solution.

1. **Create and maintain a list of the issues that keep your executive team awake at night.**

   Ask executives and managers to describe key issues that they perceive as threats. Ask them, "What internal or external issues related to the success of our organization keep you awake at night?"

2. **Explore ways that CI can be used to identify potential threats and address existing challenges.**

3. **Keep your organization's leadership posted about perceived threats and opportunities and provide written reports that include recommended changes to give your organization a competitive edge.**

   Prove your value by serving the needs of others.

4. **Continue to provide support as others in the organization formulate and implement strategic initiatives based on the intel you provided.**

   CI needs to prove that it's a team player, serving the needs of others in the organization for the greater good of everyone involved.

Communicating actionable intelligence convincingly

For CI to have impact, it must convince everyone in the company to embrace the changes necessary to capitalize on momentary advantages. Often, nothing is more convincing than a story. When preparing a report that recommends a certain course of action, choose a point in the future and then use CI to tell the story of what that future holds for your organization: "If we take advantage of this particular momentary advantage, here's how our company will benefit. . . ." As you compose your story, stick to the following guidelines:

- ✔ **Establish a realistic timeline for future events.** For example, you may include timelines for your own and your competitor's product-development cycles or a timeline showing changes in government regulations or policies.

  Stay future focused. If you're looking at the past or present, you're already several steps behind your competitors.

- ✔ **Present different scenarios, including best- and worst-case scenarios and what you expect will happen.** Consider possible contingency plans if events fail to unfold as expected.

Discovering pockets of need

Like any customer, your CI customers may not know what they need until you tell them. As a perceptive, intuitive CI professional, you should be well qualified to identify needs. Here are some suggestions to increase your exposure and make you more sensitive to your organization's needs:

✔ **Spend time walking around the organization.** Walking around an organization often enables you to see the big picture, make observations that lead to insights, and speak with people who are on the front lines.

✔ **Ask questions.** As a CI professional, you should be naturally curious. Satisfy that curiosity by asking questions.

✔ **Be a good listener.** Get to know everyone in the organization by listening to what they have to say. Find out what they struggle with at work on a daily basis. What concerns do they have? Ask if they have any ideas for improving the company or their department or a certain product or service.

✔ **Collaborate with department heads to develop a needs map of the entire organization by functional or departmental area.** Managing the needs map puts you in the position of intelligence broker to decision makers throughout the organization. Chapter 5 provides a form that department heads can fill out to describe their needs and sources they have access to.

✔ **Help different departments gain insight into trends they observe.** Often, internal analytics pick up product trends based on sales of specific products or product areas. As experts in intelligence, you can become the research arm for helping departments find the reasons behind those trends.

Gaining sponsorship

To gain respect in the organization, CI needs management and *executive sponsorship* — influential leaders in the company who have the power to raise CI's profile and standing in the company.

The CEO is the best sponsor your CI can have because he's a visible and enthusiastic presence in the company. Get the CEO onboard and ask him to encourage the formation of a small team of executives who will not only work with the CI team in discussing sensitive information but also be willing to show support for the work and the value of the CI team.

The best ways to recruit sponsors are to get them involved in CI and continually demonstrate its value:

✔ Interview executives and managers to determine what intelligence they need to make better decisions and their timetables for making those decisions.

✔ Create periodic intelligence briefings for executives, including the CEO and managers. You need to deliver on the promise of CI by demonstrating its value.

- ✔ Ask influential members of the executive management team who seem supportive to serve as CI sponsors, either formally or informally. (Look for people who show an interest in the information you're collecting and in what you're doing; these are the people who are likely to be most supportive.)

  Don't ask any leaders who seem unsupportive to serve as sponsors. They'll only drag you down.

- ✔ Coordinate all efforts with your intelligence sponsors so they feel engaged in the process and can provide you with valuable information and insight.

Remind sponsors of the importance of sharing credit for CI success. They should feel free to take credit for their decisions, but CI needs to be acknowledged in a high-profile way for its contributions in order to motivate the CI team and encourage all personnel to share data and intelligence and consult CI before making key decisions.

Getting everyone involved

You can get support from reluctant employees in your organization by involving them and by explaining how CI can benefit them. Everyone in your organization is a potential intelligence source. Whether they work in marketing, sales, customer service, manufacturing, or distribution, they have eyes and ears and are engaged in tasks that generate profits and growth. Get everyone involved in CI to tap their brains for information and ideas and motivate them when the time comes to implement changes. Let them know how vital CI is to the very existence of your organization and to their jobs. Reward employees who contribute quality intelligence and those who use it to develop new products, services, and processes.

A fun way to get employees involved and highlight the benefits of CI is to engage in war games to simulate competition. Split employees or a select group of them into two teams, one representing your organization and the other representing the competition. Instruct each team to develop strategies to gain a competitive edge and see which team comes out on top. War games produce several benefits, including the following:

- ✔ Participants have fun while learning to think more analytically.
- ✔ Engaging in simulated competition often promotes innovative thinking.
- ✔ Simulated competition often reveals miscalculations in thinking and assumptions.

Creating and Positioning Your Intel Team

One of the great things about CI is that everyone in the organization makes the team and plays an important role. In large organizations, however, certain team members form a core group to keep CI on track and ensure that all tasks required for effective CI are carried out. This core team may even constitute a separate department that collaborates with other department heads and with the organization's executive leaders to formulate and execute strategies.

In the following sections, I describe the key participants in this core group and tell you where to position the group in the organization for maximum impact.

Recruiting CI team members

Whether you form a separate CI department or recruit personnel to take on extra CI duties, you must fill these key positions on your CI team:

- **Sponsors:** Look for people with the *position power* (that is, influence and authority stemming from their job titles) to help you overcome internal resistance to change. Make sure that they're true believers in the power of CI and are committed to helping CI make a difference. (For more about recruiting sponsors, see the earlier section "Gaining sponsorship.")

- **Planners:** The planning committee should include decision makers and analysts. The analysts ask the decision makers about the intelligence they need to make better decisions, and the decision makers tell them. Planning consists of identifying the intelligence that's needed, the most likely sources to provide it, and decision deadlines.

- **Gatherers:** Recruit everyone in the organization, from the CEO down, to gather information so the analysts have a continuous stream of information that enables them to produce actionable intelligence. If you have a corporate library, the librarian can be a key player in collecting published and web-based information.

- **Analysts:** Analysts are the people who convert raw information into insight and then try to convince decision makers to act on it. Professionals who follow your industry also serve as analysts; develop relationships with them, subscribe to their briefings or newsletters, and (when possible) develop personal relationships with them.

Building your CI team around the five personalities of change

Although CI is a process and parts of it can be automated, it's still primarily a people-driven process; that is, it requires people at every stage to carry it out. To achieve success, you need to have the right mix of people with different personalities. I call them the *five personalities of change,* based on categories developed by Everett M. Rogers (*The Diffusion of Innovations,* The Free Press):

- ✔ **Pathfinders** are the first people to see change coming, yet they represent only about 2.5 percent of the general population.

- ✔ **Listeners** are receptive to what the pathfinders say and have the organizational credibility to move the intelligence forward. Listeners represent 13.5 percent of the population.

- ✔ **Organizers** are the detail-oriented, driven personalities who most often end up as the managers in the firm. They're highly resistant to change, which explains why organizers, who often rise to the rank CEO, frequently lead organizations to failure. Organizers comprise about 34 percent of the population.

- ✔ **Followers** hate pathfinders and resist change, but they're tenacious. Assign them a task, and they'll get it done, even in the face of adversity. Followers are great in roles such as sales, because they can tolerate high levels of rejection. They contribute another 34 percent or so of the general population.

- ✔ **Diehards** fill about 16 percent of the seats and embody a suicidal resistance to change. Given the chance, they'd fire the pathfinders, but they're very faithful to the organization.

To organize CI around the five personalities of change, you need to stack the deck with pathfinders and listeners, especially early in the process. Your CI team should be comprised of at least 50 percent pathfinders and 20 percent listeners. You need to engage organizers in the process because they can help the team develop a reasonable course of action in the later stages, but pathfinders and listeners should outnumber them. (Even though the organizer personality is highly resistant to change, this type usually makes up the leadership team of the company. The unavoidable reality is, you have to get their buy-in as early as possible.)

Don't invite the followers and diehards to be part of CI in the implementation phase. As you move forward and form successive pilot teams, keeping the followers and diehards out of the mix becomes progressively more difficult, but after you involve 25 percent of the organization, change occurs naturally.

Positioning CI to optimize impact

To develop a sustainable, effective intelligence operation, position your CI team at the very center of operations, as shown in Figure 2-1, so everyone in the organization can feed information to CI and access its output. Think of CI as a service provider within your organization.

Having advised you to position CI at the center of your organization, I do realize that all organizations are different and focus CI efforts in different areas. As a result, many organizations attach their CI function to certain positions or departments in the organization. For example, CI may be attached to the CEO or another executive, where it serves as strategic advisor. In some organizations, CI is attached to the legal and regulatory department. Many organizations make CI a function of marketing. However, to ensure that it monitors all factors that can affect the organization, CI really should maintain contact with all departments and decision makers within the organization. In other words, regardless of where it's positioned, it should act as though it's at the center of the organization, pulling data from all areas and serving their strategic needs.

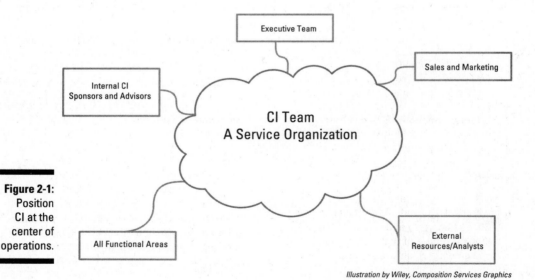

Figure 2-1:
Position
CI at the
center of
operations.

Illustration by Wiley, Composition Services Graphics

Formulating Your Purpose and Scope

Before you start collecting data, you need to know what you're looking for. If you're looking for an answer to a specific question, your purpose and scope are clear; for example, if you want to find out whether acquiring a certain company is a good decision, your purpose is to find out if that company would help yours achieve its strategic goals, and your scope is limited to that company or other companies that may be more attractive. When monitoring the overall competitive environment, on the other hand, your purpose and scope are much broader. Your purpose is to identify potential opportunities and threats and avoid mistakes, and your scope is global. When your purpose and scope are broad, consider focusing your efforts on *ten-forces analysis* — collecting and analyzing information that pertains to the ten forces that affect any organization.

In the following sections, I explain ten-forces analysis in greater detail and describe specific factors you may want to consider when formulating the purpose and scope of your CI efforts.

Narrowing your scope

Albert Einstein once said, "If I had one hour to save the world, I would spend 55 minutes defining the problem and only 5 minutes finding the solution." Cliff Kalb, former Senior Director of Strategic Business Analysis for a global pharmaceuticals company, told me an interesting and important story about just how critical it is to narrow your scope or the definition of whatever problem you're trying to solve.

Cliff got a call from a European brand manager who said, "I need all of the statistics on heart attacks annually in the world." Kalb explained that the scope of the study could be massive, so he began asking questions:

"Do you need the statistics for the entire world?"

"Well, maybe just Europe," the brand manager answered.

"What part of Europe are you interested in?"

"Mainly Scandinavia," he replied.

"Is there a part of Scandinavia that you are most concerned with?"

"Mainly Denmark."

"What about age? Is there a certain age you are interested in?"

"Yes, 45 to 55."

Then Cliff asked, "Are you doing research for a print ad that advertises a heart medication for men age 45 to 55 in Denmark?"

"Yes, I am," answered the branch manager.

Notice how much time and money Cliff was able to save by getting the internal customer to tell him what he really needed and for what purpose.

Monitoring the global environment

Executives and managers tend to operate with a very narrow focus, basing their decisions on internal data and perhaps expanding their scope to include information about direct competitors. In today's world, however, organizations are often impacted by entities and events that are clearly external to their own operations and even beyond the markets in which they compete. Furthermore, organizations don't have the power or reach to influence many of the factors that impact their operations. Just look at how the movie-rental industry has changed over the years in response to technologies like streaming video and high-tech vending machines.

As you're formulating the purpose and scope for your CI function, think outside the circle of your own company and even beyond the circle that encompasses your competitive market to consider forces that reside in the global environment, as shown in Figure 2-2. The following section describes these forces.

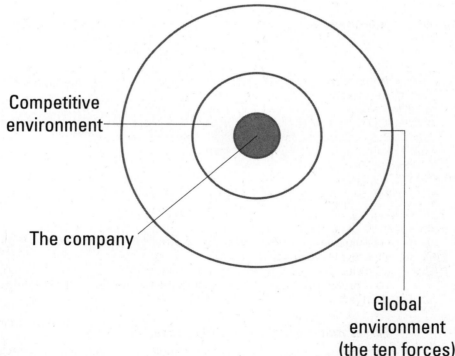

Figure 2-2:
Global
forces
impact all
organiza-
tions.

Competitive
environment

The company

Global
environment
(the ten forces)

Illustration by Wiley, Composition Services Graphics

Engaging in ten-forces analysis

When you're monitoring the global environment for opportunities and threats, you need to consider ten forces that are likely to impact your organization. The ten forces fall into two categories: those that affect the velocity (speed) of change and those that affect the complexity of change (the number of issues that may impact an organization). As these forces increase from low impact to high, the level of chaos increases proportionately, making it increasingly more difficult to stay on top of the changes required to remain competitive (see Figure 2-3).

The Ten Forces

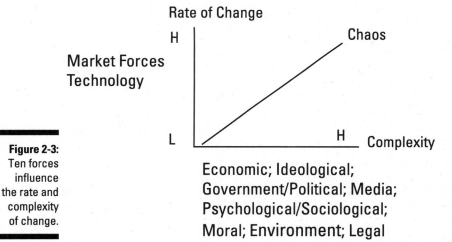

Figure 2-3: Ten forces influence the rate and complexity of change.

In studying global forces, you need a solid systematic approach in order to constantly monitor for potential opportunities and threats. Ten-forces analysis provides a reliable methodology for evaluating the global context. In the following sections, I describe the ten global forces that are likely to impact your organization, dividing them into the two forces related to the velocity of change and the eight forces related to the complexity of change.

Forces that deal with velocity or speed of change

Two forces — market forces and technology — can quickly accelerate the speed at which you must respond to changes to remain competitive:

✔ **Market forces** affect the supply, demand, and price of products. For example, when a market segment reaches over capacity (too many competitors), pricing shifts from differentiated to commodity based, and prices plunge. The velocity of change can become overwhelming and drive the need to significantly shorten new product-development cycles.

✔ **Technological forces** can impact everything from how a product is produced to how it reaches the customer. You need to carefully monitor these forces because they can change the dynamics of global competition and demand adjustments in production, distribution, and marketing.

Forces that deal with level of complexity

Eight forces are related the complexity of change — the number of factors that may affect your organization:

✔ **Economic forces** affect how much money consumers spend, what they choose to purchase, and whom they buy it from. By keeping yourself in the loop on economic forces, you're less likely to be surprised by sudden changes in consumer spending and behaviors.

✔ **Ideological forces** are any beliefs that affect what consumers buy or where they buy. For example, whenever the United States has a recession, the "Buy American" movement gathers steam. Certain retailers have built businesses to cater specifically to consumers who want to purchase products made in the U.S.A.

✔ **Political and governmental changes**, including who gets elected and which political party has the most power and influence, may affect government regulation that opens opportunities or poses a threat to your organization. By monitoring the political landscape, you place your organization in a better position to capitalize on changes.

✔ **Media issues** are related to any publicity that positively or negatively affects your organization or your products, competitors, suppliers, or distributors. Bad news may require you to crank up your public-relations machine for damage control. If the bad news is about a competitor, it may open an opportunity for you to increase market share or at least help you avoid repeating that mistake.

✔ **Psychological and sociological factors** often play a role in consumer behavior. With more people spending more time on social-networking sites, for example, businesses have had to shift some of their marketing resources to social media.

✔ **Moral and ethical factors** come into play as social norms change or when an organization is looking to do business in a foreign country where the rules are different. For example, recent studies have shown that the new 20-something workforce (recent college grads) tend to see right and wrong simply as "getting what I want" instead of doing the right thing for company, customer, or vendors. Depending on the industry your company operates in, this shift in culture may radically change considerations made in the hiring process. The wrong people can (and will) engage in behaviors that severely damage your company or its reputation.

✔ **Environmental issues** relate to weather, natural disasters, climate change, pollution, and anything else that can impact business. Climate change, for example, has significantly increased demand for green energy technology. On a smaller scale, events such as the eruption of a volcano can impact the weather and the economy in your markets.

✔ **Legal and regulatory factors** may impact employment, marketing, manufacturing, and other areas. Constantly monitor regulations and legislation in all relevant markets.

In Chapter 6, I describe several external sources of information that shed light on the ten forces that affect your business.

Starting with a purpose

Ten-forces analysis is a good theoretical framework for CI, but it may leave you wondering about its practical application or your ultimate goal in conducting CI. To approach CI with a more practical mindset, think about it in terms of what you want to accomplish: your purpose. You may want to identify unmet customer needs, predict what a competitor is going to do, or decide whether to invest in a new technology. The following sections describe several practical applications for CI.

Don't spark turf wars with other departments. As you begin to formulate a purpose and scope for your CI program, partner with other departments to formulate your purpose and scope and operate as a service provider for these other departments. Provide them with the information and intelligence they need without taking credit for the work in order to gain the cooperation and support required to improve your impact. To avoid the fallout of office politics, consider drafting a purpose statement that clearly communicates CI's role as a service provider.

Identifying unmet customer needs

You can find out a great deal from customers, especially when they're calling to complain about the poor service they received or posting a complaint in a discussion forum. Every complaint represents a need that's not being met. One purpose of CI is to identify these unmet needs so that your organization can work toward meeting those needs.

Don't limit your scope to the unmet needs of your own customers. Look to the unmet needs of your competitors' customers and monitor any unmet customer needs that your organization is uniquely qualified to address, even if the need is outside your traditional market.

Discovering nontraditional customers

Finding new, nontraditional customers for existing products can be highly profitable. A number of years ago, a university discovered that cornmeal (a byproduct of corn) was a great organic fertilizer and weed control product for grass. As a result, the company processing the corn was able to expand into an entirely new and very profitable market.

Sometimes nontraditional customers discover a new use for an existing product. Get to know the people who use your product and what they use it for. They may open the door to an entirely new market!

Entering a new market

CI can help identify new market opportunities and serve as a valuable tool for assessing the potential upside and downside of entering a new market. The info you gather can help you gauge demand for your product or service, size up potential competitors, and determine whether anyone has already tried entering this particular market and whether and why they succeeded or failed.

In addition to helping identify potential opportunities, CI can also prevent you from wasting valuable resources on unprofitable ventures.

Keeping abreast of changes in your industry

Even standard operating procedures across an industry are subject to change, and when competitors start to change the way they do business, the last organization to take action is usually the loser. Your company should continuously monitor changes in your industry (using CI) and implement those changes when appropriate in order to remain competitive.

Predicting competitor activities

One purpose of CI is to keep an eye on the competition. The intention isn't to mimic what competitors do but to predict what they're going to do so that you can respond in a way that gives your organization a competitive advantage. CI can help you identify a variety of market or industry scenarios and plan several moves ahead to give you the lead and help you maintain it.

Responding to economic change

Most businesses rise and fall based on economic conditions, but the relationship between sales and the economy isn't always so predictable. Yes, the economy affects what consumers buy and how much money they spend, but a downturn in the economy can trigger increased spending in certain markets. After the 9/11 terrorist attack, for example, spending on vacation travel plunged, but sales of big-screen TVs soared.

Economic data is readily available. In the United States, you can thank the federal government for providing a lot of this information about U.S.-based companies. In addition, most investment firms have a chief economist who issues periodic updates about companies those firms invest in; most of these updates are publicly available. By analyzing and comparing different views of the emerging economy, a CI team can effectively synthesize the data and help to proactively prepare for economic shifts.

Capitalizing on consumer trends

A big factor in maintaining a competitive advantage is the ability to predict consumer behavior. By combining weak signals (uncertain or ambiguous data) and using special tools, such as analytics and scenarios, the CI team can pick up on trends and develop predictions that help senior management capitalize on opportunities and avoid threats. Certain trends, such cash-free transactions, affect all markets. Other trends, such as do-it-yourself health-care, apply to specific industries.

To understand the value of weak signals, assume that you stumble across a job listing that a competitor has posted advertising for an engineer who can design specific types of computer chips. (That's a weak signal.) As you dig deeper, you discover that the chips specified in the ad involve an entirely different market than what that competitor has historically been involved in. That's a slightly stronger signal that may suggest that the company is planning to enter a new market. However, you still need to perform additional research to confirm your suspicions or find out what's really going on.

By the time a consumer trend negatively impacts your bottom line, you've probably missed your chance to respond.

Making a substantial investment

Before your organization puts time, money, or other resources into a course of action, decision makers should employ CI to investigate the pros and cons of the investment and look into other options. You can avoid costly mistakes by performing due diligence before moving forward on any decision to invest substantial amounts of money or other resources.

Acquiring or partnering with another organization

Acquiring or partnering with another organization is essentially marriage at the corporate level. To avoid potential pitfalls, CI should perform a background check on the targeted organization and analysis of whether the partnership or acquisition is likely to further your organization's strategic goals.

Developing a Security Classification System

When you begin to engage in CI, you start producing intelligence about your own organization as well as about your competitors. This intelligence is sensitive. If it were to fall into the wrong hands, your competitors could use the intelligence you produce to gain an advantage over you!

The concern isn't that people in your organization will intentionally share sensitive information with your competitors, but if they don't understand how sensitive it is, they may share it inadvertently. To prevent and discourage the sharing of sensitive information, do the following:

✔ **Identify which people in your organization are approved to receive critical information.** You may want to assign different security clearance levels, such as the following (see Chapter 10):

- **Highly classified:** Executives only
- **Classified:** Executives and management only
- **Unclassified:** Everyone in the company

✔ **Classify all CI documents and mark them with their security level prior to any distribution within the company.**

For guidance on how to defend against competitive counterintelligence, see Chapter 18.

Chapter 3

Doing Competitive Intelligence on a Low Budget

*A*lthough CI can generate significant profits and growth, it doesn't require a huge dollar or time commitment to be effective. Your organization is probably gathering data already. You simply need to formalize the process. In addition, certain employees probably have the expertise needed to analyze that data and transform it into actionable intelligence, so you don't need to hire CI consultants. You can perform most tasks in-house.

In this chapter, I explain how to create a CI function without spending a lot of money by using existing personnel and resources. You also discover how to use membership on the intelligence team as a reward for top-performing employees.

Small businesses are often the first to feel the impact of competitive change in the marketplace, so if you're a small-business owner, don't dismiss CI as too costly to implement. Failing to engage in CI is likely to cost you even more and may even put the existence of your business at risk.

Creating a CI Team on the Cheap

Major corporations are likely to have a formal CI department complete with a director, data-entry personnel, and one or more dedicated analysts, but you don't need a separate CI department to achieve success. Instead, you can integrate CI with what management and employees are already doing by adding it as a job responsibility.

On a daily basis, real-time competitive intelligence is pouring into your people. Salespeople hear about competitors, customer-service reps listen to customer needs, and nearly all personnel consume news and information that may shed light on the company or the industry. All you need to do is formalize these activities as part of each person's job description and provide an easy way for them to input data into the system and extract data for analysis. For details about building a storage and retrieval system, see Chapter 5.

CI is a team sport, but you don't have to recruit players and sign them to megadollar contracts to win the CI game. You can create your own pickup team by getting all your existing personnel involved in the CI process. In the following sections, I explain how to harness the power of your people to start collecting and analyzing data.

Designating someone to serve as CI team leader

Regardless of whether your organization chooses to establish a formal CI department or proceed on an informal basis, designating one individual to serve as a team leader is important. You need to make someone ultimately responsible for gathering the relevant information from internal sources, aggregating it, making sure that it's analyzed, and reporting to the corporate decision maker(s), including the CEO. The team leader should also be responsible for establishing the internal management processes and rules of engagement for the rest of the team; for example, ensuring that each department collects and passes information to the CI team and receives actionable intel and feedback from the CI team.

After designating someone to serve as the team leader (even if it's only part time), you can then add members from other parts of the company to the team.

Recruiting readers for the intel team

A great way to gather data is to assemble a team of readers to produce a monthly CI report. *Readers* are simply employees who commit to remaining plugged in to certain sources of information (perhaps trade journals, news media, social media, and so on) and either entering it into the system or passing it along to another CI team member who enters it into the system. Although readers are usually most involved in collecting information, they may also be involved in analysis, especially if your readers have expertise in certain areas of interest.

Adding readers to your CI team offers the following benefits:

- ✔ **Job enrichment:** Readership gives employees the opportunity to contribute something of value to the future success of the organization, making them feel more important in the grand scheme of things.

- ✔ **Spreading the workload:** By divvying up the intel sources (trade journals, social media, websites, white papers, and so on) or assigning topical areas, each reader has a small slice of the intelligence pie so nobody feels overwhelmed.

- ✔ **Specialization:** Over time, each reader can work toward becoming an expert on a specific source or topic area.

- ✔ **Efficiency:** Using a team of readers, CI can pull together a monthly CI report fairly quickly and without adding to CI's operating cost.

Take the following steps to recruit readers and coordinate their efforts:

1. **Find people in different departments who are willing to be a part of an intelligence team.**

    Get the right mix of people by forming your team around the five personalities of change, which I discuss in Chapter 2. Be sure to include at least one pathfinder, because pathfinders are

    - Natural intelligence gatherers.

    - Unbiased — they tend to see data for what it is.

    - Motivated by variations in job responsibilities; pathfinders often get bored when restricted to a single job area, so allowing them to serve on the intel team benefits everyone. (I explain how to identify pathfinders and other personality types in Chapter 15.)

2. **Assign each person an area of responsibility.**

    Try to assign areas of responsibility based on each individual's area of expertise; for example, someone in customer service or sales is probably best qualified to gather information about customer needs, and someone in product development may be best suited to monitor emerging technologies and processes/procedures. You may want to designate the following areas of responsibility:

    - Competitors

    - Customer needs

    - Technologies

- Procedures/processes
- Legislation
- Acquisitions/mergers

Consider organizing your readers around the ten forces discussed in Chapter 2.

3. **Collaborate as a team to compile a list of resources for each area.**

Consider both internal and external resources. Internal resources include information from other personnel (see Chapter 5). External resources may include industry journals, trade shows, social media, patent records, Security and Exchange Commission (SEC) filings, online discussion groups, and so on (see Chapter 6).

4. **Work together to gather and analyze information.**

To find out more about gathering information, see Part II. For more about analyzing information, turn to Part III.

5. **As a team, compile the research and analysis into a monthly state-of-the-industry report (briefing document).**

Your report should include the following:

- A one-page executive overview that can be read in 120 seconds, max
- Supporting analysis in the see-mean-do (SMD) format (see "Engaging in SMD analysis," later in this chapter, for details)

See Chapter 10 for guidance on creating briefing documents.

Inform all team members to communicate urgent information to the CI team leader immediately so the team leader can report it to the designated contact person on the executive team (in most cases, the CEO). Urgent information includes anything that could possibly affect the business positively or negatively in the next two to three months; for example, if a hurricane is threatening to delay shipment of materials needed for production, management needs to know as soon as possible to line up an alternative.

Publicly recognize the people who take on these duties in addition to their regular jobs. From a motivational standpoint, recognition is much more powerful than money. If you make selection for the intel team a big deal and continually recognize the members, serving on the team becomes a sought-after honor in the organization.

Enlisting all personnel as intel agents

Although the intelligence team is responsible for gathering and analyzing data, you should encourage everyone in the organization to contribute. To mine information from the various departments, take the following steps:

1. **Draw team members from each department to ensure connectivity between the CI team and the department heads.**

   Having an inside person operating within each department helps get buy-in from department heads because they know that someone on the CI team is watching out for them. Another option is to assign each intelligence team member to a specific department and encourage them to spend time in their assigned departments once a week or every two weeks.

2. **Coordinate with the department heads and make sure that they're stressing to their staff the importance of passing on information to the intelligence team members.**

3. **Create a process for logging information from each department into the system.**

   The process can be as simple as having the CI rep from each department send an e-mail message to the person on the CI team who's in charge of data entry on a regular basis.

Recognize, recognize, recognize! Recognize contributors and CI team members for a job well done. Recognition is the engine that drives CI success. See the later section "Rewarding and Motivating CI Team Members" for more on how to encourage participation in CI.

Forming a small company board to analyze the information

If your business has enough personnel to form a CI team, the team can work together to collect and analyze data. If you're running a small business, however, you may not have enough different perspectives to properly analyze the data. You may not even have a board of directors in place to offer guidance, challenge your assumptions, and call attention to potential threats. If you're strapped for resources, here are some ways to reap the benefits of outside help without spending a lot of money:

1. **Form a company advisory board of talented friends and business associates.** You could include college professors you've had, business-savvy friends, and CEOs of noncompeting businesses.

Avoid "yes" people. Recruit independent thinkers who aren't afraid to challenge you and who encourage you to think outside the box. You don't want dream killers who shoot down all your ideas, but you do want people who aren't afraid to speak their mind.

2. **Keep the board posted concerning actionable intelligence and any progress you've made in implementing strategies.** The board can help hold you accountable for putting your intelligence into action.

3. **Schedule a quarterly lunch meeting to tap into your advisory board's group wisdom.** One week prior to the scheduled meeting, make sure that the board has all the information you've gathered.

If you're the CEO of your own small business, consider joining or creating a *CEO roundtable,* a small group of local CEOs and business owners that meet regularly to network and share insights and ideas. Your CEO roundtable can be a forum for sharing information and helping each other conduct analysis. Unbiased third-party thinking can force you to think outside the box, where future opportunities exist.

Using MBA teams for target studies

College students enrolled in masters of business administration (MBA) degree programs are eager for real-world experience in CI and problem solving. You can help provide them with that experience while tapping their collective brainpower — and the brain of their professor. Consider contacting grad school professors at nearby university business schools and asking if they're willing to conduct some competitive intelligence for your business as a class project.

Many university professors love to assign special projects to their MBA teams. These projects not only help the students but also promote the value of the university to the community.

Intelligence produced by grad students can vary quite a bit in terms of quality, and you probably have little or no time to waste working with students who lack the skills and motivation to produce good intelligence. Make sure that the students you work with are in an MBA class taught by a professor who's "been there and done that" and knows how to guide and encourage the MBA team to deliver value. Ask to see some examples of prior work or a summary of the success stories that the professor's classes have been involved with in the past.

Avoid MBA teams that don't understand rigor and exceptional quality. Too often, MBA teams are not facilitated by a professor who understands how to deliver a professional-level project. The usual strength-weaknesses-opportunities-threats (SWOT) analysis can lack the required rigor of a more comprehensive analysis.

To find an MBA team to work with, look for nearby colleges and universities that offer MBA programs, especially programs that offer courses in competitive intelligence, which is rare. If nothing local fits the bill, expand your range; an MBA team can serve your needs from a remote location. Ask the MBA program director if any professors do CI consulting for outside firms, and then contact any professors who do.

When you're evaluating your MBA options, get answers to the following questions related to the professor's qualifications:

- ✔ **How experienced is the professor in consulting with organizations outside the university?** Ask the professor to provide a list of organizations that he or she has done CI reports for in the past. You want someone with real-world experience, not necessarily in your specific industry. You don't want a prof whose experience is limited to academia. Keep in mind that some professors may produce CI but call it something else, such as *industry study, strategic information,* or *white papers.*

- ✔ **What's the professor's track record in creating actionable intelligence out of business information?** Obtain the names of other organizations that the professor has worked for and contact them to determine their satisfaction with the results.

- ✔ **Are you convinced that this professor is capable of leading your MBA consulting team to achieve substantive output that can help your company?** Speak directly with the professor to develop a sense of how experienced and knowledgeable he or she is and gain insight on the person's ability to lead a CI team.

- ✔ **How closely will the MBA team's work resemble the work product of a professional consulting firm?** If possible, look at samples of work produced under this professor's tutelage.

When choosing an MBA team to work with, make sure that team members:

- ✔ Understand that your time is valuable and respect that reality.

- ✔ Have a plan that communicates organization, process, and professionalism.

- ✔ Have a mentor/leader who understands real-world consulting and research.

- ✔ Will present a *statement of work* (a detailed description of the project, including timelines and deliverables) prior to starting the project.

- ✔ Will each individually sign a confidentiality agreement with your company.

  Confidentiality agreements often allow the grad students to mention their contributions to a CI project without actually divulging the project's content. If the work is very sensitive, the confidentiality agreement may prohibit the students and their professor from disclosing the company or the area of study. Consider asking your CI client or your organization's legal counsel to approve the exact wording of the project that students may use on their résumés.

- ✔ Will prepare a professional document that summarizes their work.

- ✔ Will make a 30-minute (maximum) executive-quality presentation of their results.

Don't waste your time with an MBA team that lacks the professionalism to produce a quality CI presentation. If you're not confident in the team, continue your search.

Tapping Free and Nearly Free Data Sources and Analysis

If you decide to fly solo and manage CI internally, your costs are measured primarily by the time and effort you invest in it. As I point out in the following sections, you can gather most of the information you need for free, or at a very low cost, and perform the analysis on your own following the see-mean-do (SMD) approach.

Exploring free and low-cost data sources

Here are a few sources of information that are generally free or cost very little:

- ✔ **Relationships:** Although everyone wants to hear about high-tech data mining and analytics, the truth is that low-tech intel sometimes is more valuable. Foster relationships with customers, suppliers, analysts, industry journalists, and even competitors to find out what people are thinking and saying and raving and complaining about.

- ✔ **Corporate annual reports:** Annual reports from your competitors are free, but you definitely get what you pay for here. More often than not, annual reports are marketing tools, so read them with a degree of skepticism.

- ✔ **Corporate SEC filings:** 8-K and 10-K filings can be exceptionally helpful in analyzing publicly traded competitors. The easiest way to access a company's SEC filings is to go to Yahoo! Finance at `http://finance.yahoo.com` and search for the company by name or ticker symbol. The resulting profile page for the company contains links to various SEC filings.

See Chapter 6 for additional details on how to track down annual reports, SEC filings, and other information about public companies.

The 8-K is required when a company is compelled by SEC mandate to disclose events or information that are material to the financial standing of the firm. Although such filings do provide disclosure, most companies are adept at purposely omitting the behind-the-scenes information about those filings. You may need to strike up a conversation with an analyst in the industry to get the back story. Sometimes solid CI analysis can give you that answer.

- ✔ **Press releases:** Most companies publish press releases to announce new products and leadership changes and major events. You can usually find press releases on company websites.

- ✔ **Libraries:** University and public libraries can provide access to numerous financial databases. In some cases, the university subscribes to a service like Hoover's (`www.hoovers.com`), which isn't free, but as a library patron, it's free for you.

- ✔ **Web searches:** For a fairly complete listing of companies, go to `www.info.com` and search for "corporate information." Info.com consolidates search results from Google, Yahoo!, and Bing and delivers a listing of numerous resources that provide corporate information. Google is also a great place to start, simply because of the advanced search analytics the company now utilizes.

Set up Google or Yahoo! News Alerts to keep you posted via e-mail regarding news events related to any business entity, individual, product, competitor, or topic that you want to monitor. For details, visit `www.google.com/alerts` or `http://alerts.yahoo.com`.

Make sure that you don't overlook the *invisible web* — the enormous amount of information on the web that Google and other search engines don't index. Use Google to try to find relevant websites and then use the search tools on those sites to look for specific information. I guarantee that you'll find a lot more pertinent information by taking this approach.

- ✔ **Social media:** Social-media venues, including Facebook, Twitter, LinkedIn, Wikipedia, YouTube, and SlideShare often contain valuable information and insight that may be posted by your competitors, suppliers, or distributors; your own or your competitors' customers; analysts; technology companies and individual innovators; and more. Because social-media outlets are rarely policed, they're more likely to contain information over which organizations have little control in keeping secret. However, you need to be especially careful about validating any information you find in the social media.

✔ **Industry associations and publications:** Trade publications can often be a bit suspect because a lot of companies feed stories to the publications that may be self-serving. Even so, always follow such publications and be sure that you occasionally make contact with the editor of each publication to ask about white papers or other association-sponsored research that may be available.

✔ **CIA's *The World Factbook*:** If you're doing business abroad, *The World Factbook* can be a valuable resource for tracking down information about the geography, people, government, and economy of the country in which you're doing or planning to do business. To access *The World Factbook*, visit www.cia.gov/library/publications/the-world-factbook.

✔ **United States Patent and Trademark Office (USPTO):** The USPTO website (www.uspto.gov) enables you to search for patents by the name of the person or company that filed for the patent. Keep in mind, however, that some companies file patents under the name of lesser-known subsidiaries. When doing a patent search, include the names of all related companies and divisions.

Carefully examine each source for accuracy and reliability. See Chapter 9 for details.

Engaging in SMD analysis

You don't have to pay a professional analyst to transform information into valuable intelligence. Your intel team can tackle the job by following a three-step analysis process that I like to refer to as *see-mean-do* (SMD) analysis, which can also be described as *do-it-yourself* (DIY) analysis.

See: What do you see?

Look at the information you gathered and describe it in your own words without reading anything into it; for example, "ACME is planning to acquire three smaller competitors in the next quarter." Be objective. Let the information speak to you.

Avoid bias. Don't try to interpret the data. Just describe it. In the next step, you start to think about what it means.

Mean: What does it mean?

Ask questions to uncover the relevance and significance of the information. The most common question to ask when trying to find out what something means is "Why?" To continue with the example from the preceding section, you may ask, "Why is ACME planning to acquire these three smaller competitors in the next quarter?"

You may need to collect additional information to answer that question. Perhaps ACME is looking for additional production capabilities or customers or distribution channels that these competitors have to offer. Perhaps ACME has targeted the other companies because of their creative assets. Whatever the reason, you need to interpret the information to reveal the underlying why.

As you interpret what the information means, also assess its significance. Ask yourself the question, "So what?" If your answer to that question seems ho-hum, you're probably looking at something that's relatively insignificant. If your response to the answer is more along the lines of "Eureka!" or "Ah-ha!," then you probably have some pretty powerful intelligence. For example, you may discover that ACME is planning to target a new sector that the three smaller competitors have had some success in serving. That maneuver may pose a threat to your own expansion plans.

Do: What should we do about it?

After you figure out what's going on and what it means, the next step is to decide what you're going to do about it, if anything. You usually have five options:

- ✔ **Do nothing.** Sometimes, doing nothing is the best approach. Your competitors may act impulsively in response to certain changes in the industry, giving you a competitive advantage.

- ✔ **Monitor the issue.** Set up a CI monitoring program for factors that are questionable after they have been initially analyzed. Sometimes later developments clarify the importance of an issue.

- ✔ **Stop what you had planned to do.** Intelligence can often help you avoid pitfalls that result from miscalculations. For example, suppose you're pursuing an acquisition of a company and discover that the creative assets you're planning to acquire have suddenly left the company to form their own consulting business.

- ✔ **Take action.** When intelligence exposes a potential threat or opportunity, you need to decide what to do to avoid that threat or capitalize on the opportunity. Additional CI may be required to determine which course of action would be most effective.

- ✔ **Move more aggressively.** You may use intelligence to confirm what you were already thinking and planning, in which case you may decide to move faster and more aggressively to maximize the impact of a planned change.

Pardon the acronyms

The CI community loves its acronyms, perhaps because the discipline is deeply rooted in the history of the CIA and FBI or maybe because business people, such as CEOs, especially those with MBAs (masters of business administration degrees), love to use TLAs (three-letter acronyms) as a form of shorthand and insider lingo.

To maintain the tradition, I introduce acronyms throughout this book, create my very own TLAs to describe strategies and techniques — including see-mean-do (SMD) — and even repurpose the age-old acronym IRS in reference to the *intelligence rating system*.

Rewarding and Motivating CI Team Members

How do you reward CI team members for their efforts and expertise? Well, increased pay, extra benefits, and bonuses are always effective, but assuming that you're already paying your employees a decent wage, you may want a less expensive way to reward and motivate team members for the extra work they put in by serving on the intel team.

Of course, there's no substitute for monetary compensation, but when employees feel that they're already being paid a respectable wage, recognition and the opportunity to be involved in compelling projects are often all the perks they need to serve enthusiastically on the CI team. In the following sections, I describe a few ways to reward and motivate CI team members without spending a lot of dough.

Managers often mistakenly believe that money is a strong motivator, but research proves otherwise. Studies show that lack of appropriate compensation is a dissatisfier, whereas recognition is a motivator.

Establishing the vital importance of CI

More than ever, people want to feel as though their life has significance and a purpose. By establishing CI as a vital component of your organization's success, you convince members of the intel team that they're contributing to something that's vitally important.

Only the CEO can really make a statement about the value of the CI team. Continually demonstrate the value of CI to the CEO, and make sure that the CEO is aware of CI wins as they occur. Also, remind the CEO, as necessary, of the importance of publicly recognizing CI's contributions to the organization's existence and success.

Never let a member of your CI team labor in obscurity.

Using conventions and trade shows as rewards and recognition

The workaday world gets boring, especially to pathfinders and listeners, who hunger for stimulation. Change things up occasionally by sending CI team members to conventions, conferences, and trade shows. Encourage qualified personnel to get involved in *standards groups* — professional organizations that encourage an industry to adopt a standard, such as a certain cellphone protocol. In addition to rewarding and motivating team members, these venues are a prime source for competitive intel, where team members can gather the following resources:

- Catalogs and information sheets with details of products that are soon to hit the market

- Contact information for industry insiders

- Introductions to potential suppliers and distributors

- Information from conversations with industry insiders

  Review the ethical standards with the intel team members before they attend an event. Make sure they don't obtain information from a competitor by crossing legal or ethical lines. At such events, there's usually a boatload of information available in plain view (out in the open), where no legal or ethical restrictions apply to your acquisition and use of the information for CI purposes. See Chapter 4 for more about legal and ethical guidelines.

- Insights about the future of the industry and which standards are likely to prevail

Personnel who gather information for CI by attending trade shows and conferences and participating in standards groups are often referred to as *stealth team members*. For example, engineers attending a professional gathering may view a presentation that involves technology that may impact the future of your company. Their membership to certain professional groups gives them access to highly specialized information and enables them to work undercover for CI at the same time. They're not breaking any laws or acting unethically, because the information is in plain view.

Plan ahead. Discuss the type of information you want to gather and from whom, and ask CI team members to produce an intelligence report that details what they discovered. Far too often, people attend these events and gather valuable information that remains in a bag when they return home. For more about making the most of trade show intel, see Chapter 6.

Springing for classes and other training

CI classes, seminars, books, and memberships to CI organizations all cost money, so they're not exactly ways to do CI on a shoestring budget, but they are more affordable solutions for developing the requisite expertise internally as compared to hiring outside experts. Consider setting aside a small portion of your budget to cover CI training for top-performing members of your CI team. They can pass on what they learn to other team members. Some extra education is a great way to improve the CI team while maintaining the team's commitment to your organization.

Chapter 4

Addressing Legal and Ethical Issues

Can competitive intelligence be conducted legally and ethically? The short answer is yes. In fact, if what an organization is doing is illegal or unethical, it's not CI. It's something else, such as spying, stealing, or conducting industrial espionage. That's not what CI is all about. CI doesn't involve lying, trespassing, dumpster diving, hacking into networks, or bribing your competitors' employees.

Quality CI starts with information that's already "out there" — information that's publicly accessible *(open source)* and shared freely. CI isn't so much about finding out what a competitor is doing or how they're doing it. It's more about finding out what you and your competitors *aren't* doing and should be doing to meet the ever-changing needs and desires of customers. It's about monitoring the forces that drive business in your industry and adapting as market conditions change. It's about spotting and seizing opportunities and avoiding threats before your competitors are even aware they exist. It's about predicting which technologies are likely to disrupt your industry and the markets in which you do business. It's about using information that isn't the kind you get by spying on the competition.

The information age has given the world unprecedented public access to more data and analysis than ever before, and certainly more than enough quality data to conduct effective CI, so you don't need to engage in illegal or unethical activities to gather the information you need. But you still need to know about the legal and ethical guidelines that are relevant to CI so you don't cross the line.

I begin this chapter by tackling the question of whether CI can be conducted ethically — a question that, unfortunately, discourages many organizations from conducting CI and reaping its benefits. Next, I explain some of the laws in the U.S. that apply to CI. (Legal aspects of CI tend to be more clearly delineated than the ethical standards, so I cover the legal stuff first.) I then explain how to formulate and communicate ethical guidelines in your organization to avoid potential pitfalls. Finally, I present some common gray areas to help you figure out what to do when the line that divides right and wrong gets fuzzy.

The risks of using illegal or unethical methods to gather CI far outweigh any false perceptions of gain from such methods.

Brushing Up on CI-Related Laws

Whether you're conducting business domestically or abroad in the U.S., you need to be aware of a few laws that directly or indirectly apply to CI. I explain these laws in the following sections to help you operate squarely in legal territory.

Although you need to be aware of laws that apply to CI, I encourage you later in this chapter to adopt ethical standards that are even more stringent than the law calls for. If everyone in your organization adheres to strict ethical standards, you don't need to worry about breaking the law.

Steering clear of economic espionage: The Economic Espionage Act of 1996

The Economic Espionage Act (EEA) of 1996 makes the theft of trade secrets (proprietary information) a federal crime. The EEA defines *trade secret* as follows:

> *The term "trade secret" means all forms and types of financial, business, scientific, technical, economic, or engineering information, including patterns, plans, compilations, program devices, formulas, designs, prototypes,*

methods, techniques, processes, procedures, programs, or codes, whether tangible or intangible, and whether or how stored, compiled, or memorialized physically, electronically, graphically, photographically, or in writing if

(A) the owner thereof has taken reasonable measures to keep such information secret; and

(B) the information derives independent economic value, actual or potential, from not being generally known to, and not being readily ascertainable through proper means by, the public.

In other words, you can't take anything from a business that gives it a competitive advantage if the company has taken reasonable measures to protect it.

If an organization releases information, it's fair game. For example, if a CEO talks about the organization's marketing strategy in an interview published in a trade journal, that organization hasn't taken reasonable measures to protect that information, so you can use it. However, if a disgruntled employee of that same organization offers to sell or give you that same information, you are legally bound not to accept it. In fact, you really should inform the organization of the incident. More often than not, behaving in a way that's above reproach protects your organization from unfounded charges of attempting to steal a competitor's trade secret.

Navigating international issues: The Foreign Corrupt Practices Act

According to the Foreign Corrupt Practices Act (FCPA), paying a foreign official for the purpose of retaining or obtaining business is illegal. In the context of CI, that means you're prohibited from paying a foreign official for any information that might give your business a competitive advantage. In short, bribery is illegal.

Most people are well aware that you're not supposed to commit bribery in the United States, but when you're doing business in a foreign culture in which bribery is an acceptable and even expected way of doing business, buying information from foreign officials may seem neither illegal nor unethical. The old adage "When in Rome, do as the Romans do" doesn't apply here. If you're a U.S. firm doing business in a foreign country or a foreign firm doing business in the U.S., bribing government officials is a crime.

An international perspective: Bribery and Walmart

In 2005, information came to the attention of senior Walmart executives in the U.S. that the company's largest foreign subsidiary, Walmart de Mexico, had paid over $24 million to officials in Mexico for the purpose of getting approval to build stores in various parts of the country. That $24 million scratches the surface of what Walmart will ultimately pay in fines, legal fees, and negative public relations.

Although this particular incident isn't related to CI, CI experts often face similar dilemmas: How do you get what you want when the accepted way of getting it is illegal? In other words, what should you do when "everyone is doing it?" And the answer to that question is that you should abide by the law and any ethical standards you've established.

The "everyone is doing it" defense doesn't hold up in the court of law or in the court of public opinion, and it really brings you no benefit if you're the one who gets caught. Besides, in CI, bribery is never necessary. You can always get the information you need through legal, ethical means.

 Don't put profit before ethics. In certain countries, bribery, sexual slavery, discrimination, and other illegal and unethical practices are acceptable in business circles, but your organization and your employees need to answer to a higher set of values. Before doing business or conducting CI in a foreign land, answer the following three questions:

- ✔ Does our organization need to violate its ethical standards in order to do business in this country?
- ✔ Has our organization done everything possible to convince our local hosts that we can't engage in certain practices?
- ✔ Is our organization willing to put ethics above profit?

If you answer no to any one of those questions, don't do business in that particular locale.

Avoiding SEC issues related to public companies

When you're gathering intelligence about publicly traded companies, be careful not to engage in any activities that violate fair-trade laws. Situations you need to be concerned about usually involve cooperative CI between two competing businesses. When collaborating with a competitor, avoid any activities that could possibly be perceived as giving either business an unfair advantage over other competitors, such as exchanging information about pricing or marketing.

Another pitfall is the disclosure requirements related to *material information* — anything that could possibly affect a stock's price after the public finds out about it, such as an acquisition or critical changes in management. Disclosure of material information to an outside party may trigger SEC requirements that require public disclosure of such information. Those disclosures, under certain circumstances, may trigger legal disclosure requirements that can damage a company. Additionally, the disclosure can be expensive to file, depending on its nature.

Gathering intelligence about public companies without crossing the line can be tricky. If you obtain information from an internal source at a publicly traded company, you may open yourself and your organization to substantial penalties, as well as damages. Here are some basic guidelines for avoiding such conflicts:

✔ All information you gather must meet the "plain view" rule. In other words, it must be publicly accessible.

✔ When preparing internal documents, always cite the resource you used to obtain the information, such as an annual report; 8-K filing, or analyst opinion.

Avoiding tortious interference

Tortious interference occurs when a third party damages a contractual relationship between two other parties. In the context of competitive intelligence, you need to be careful about obtaining information from someone or a business entity that has a contractual relationship with another party when sharing information could harm that relationship if the other party were to find out about it. Before accepting or using information from a source, take the following precautions:

✔ Make sure that your source is not providing any information that would put her in breach of any contract with a third party.

✔ Always get approval from your legal department prior to engaging with any third party source if the transaction has any possibility of negatively affecting the relationship between your source and another party.

✔ When in doubt, don't request or use information from the source.

Determining Whether Your Organization Is Ethically Sound

When performing CI, your organization needs to be squeaky clean. Nobody should engage in illegal, unethical, unprofessional, or otherwise questionable activities when collecting data, because doing so places your organization at risk of becoming a target for lawsuits and tainting its reputation in the industry. Questionable practices also make your external CI sources dry up, because analysts and other knowledgeable individuals in your industry or in the markets in which you operate will try to distance themselves from you and protect their own reputations.

The most significant threat to conducting CI legally, ethically, and professionally arises from the notions of ethical relativism and situational ethics — philosophies that define morality in context rather than in absolutes. In a system of absolutes, for example, taking something that's not yours is wrong, whereas situational ethics may allow for hungry people to take food without paying for it or someone to keep $500 that someone else left behind on a bus.

To ensure that your organization is operating legally and ethically, you must establish rigid standards; otherwise, moral decisions become a matter of interpretation, and people can justify any action they choose to take. To determine how effectively your firm's ethical standards guide the actions of its personnel, answer the following five questions:

- ✔ Do we have a written set of ethical standards that are clear, actionable, and not subject to interpretation?
- ✔ Do we continually keep those standards at the forefront of how we operate out business?
- ✔ Do our ethical standards ensure unquestioned accountability?
- ✔ Do we live our ethics as an organization?
- ✔ Are we willing to terminate employees who violate our ethical standards?

If you answered yes to all those questions, your organization is prepared to conduct CI legally, ethically, and professionally. If you answered no to any question, you have some work to do. In the remaining sections of this chapter, I explain how to establish a firm ethical foundation on which to build your CI program.

Creating a Code of Ethics

When developing a code of ethics to govern behavior throughout your organization, the goal must be unmovable standards — clear rules that aren't open to interpretation. In the following sections, I provide guidance on how to define ethical standards for your organization, and I point out a couple common mistakes to avoid.

Establishing an immovable set of ethical standards

Here's an approach to creating ethical standards for your organization that establish clear directives and discourage creative moral thinking:

1. **Begin with the four basic rights that appear to be universal in all cultures and societies. State that all people have these rights and that every employee in the company must respect them:**

   - Right to live (covers assault and life issues)

   - Right to own property (prohibits theft and fraud)

   - Right to freedom (bans discrimination and sexual harassment)

   - Right to be told the truth (prohibits fraud and deception)

2. **Add one more item to complete your ethics statement:**

   - Every person in the company must obey all applicable laws and regulations (international, federal, state, and local).

The absolute and universal nature of the ethical standards leaves little room for individuals to convince themselves that unethical behaviors are okay depending on the situation. When applied to CI, these universal standards may translate into the following rules of engagement:

✔ Don't lie, cheat, or steal.

✔ No looking through another organization's trash (also known as dumpster diving).

✔ Don't take or receive an organization's proprietary information.

✔ Don't hack into an organization's network.

✔ Don't listen in on conversations, spoken or written, that you're not engaged in.

- ✔ Don't pay for confidential information.

- ✔ Always identify yourself — your name, position, and the organization you represent — when requesting information. (Never misrepresent who you are.)

- ✔ Don't mislead anyone or otherwise coerce them into sharing information.

- ✔ Don't request information from someone if the sharing of that information poses a risk to the person's job or reputation.

- ✔ Don't ask new hires to share proprietary information from former employers.

Don't let the board of directors or the senior executive team establish ethical standards for the organization on their own. They may be wise in operating a business, but they're probably amateurs in establishing, encouraging, and enforcing ethical behavior because these positions tend to emphasize growth and profit over ethics. First, brainstorm a list of ethical standards following the guidance provided in this chapter. Then enlist the assistance of an outside party, perhaps an attorney, to draft the proposed ethics to ensure that they're not watered down.

Avoiding common pitfalls

When you're drafting ethical standards for your organization, be careful to avoid two common pitfalls: cultural relativism and legal limits. In the following sections, I describe each of these concepts in detail.

Sidestepping the false floor of cultural relativism

Cultural relativism essentially tells you to behave in whatever manner is acceptable in a particular culture. In some situations, employees may feel that doing business would be much easier if they compromised the organization's unwavering ethical standards. For example, a lot of international managers get caught up in the web of bribery in a country. Sometimes, it's coercive in nature, such as an inspector demanding a bribe before he agrees to grant a business license. The practice can lull the manager to sleep to the point that when a major bribe that violates U.S. law is demanded, the manager unwisely goes along with it. While it may be culturally acceptable in the host country, it's still a violation of the law. However, the reality is that such behavior can threaten the existence of the firm because unless these behaviors are discouraged and perhaps even result in stiff penalties, employees will begin to think of them as acceptable. To prevent the cancer of cultural relativism, your organization's leaders should do the following:

✔ Remind employees that the firm's ethical standards apply regardless of the situation and regardless of which country they happen to be doing business in.

✔ Support people who uphold the ethical standards of behavior.

✔ Correct — or if necessary, terminate — employees who decide to put results ahead of ethics.

Avoid the temptation to subscribe to the "everybody's doing it" school of ethics. Most people who give this excuse are just plain wrong — rarely are the majority engaged in unethical behavior. And even if their assessment is correct, that's not a good enough reason to justify unethical or illegal behavior.

Avoiding the legal-limits approach

According to the *legal-limits approach,* actions are acceptable as long as they're not illegal. It allows and even encourages some people to get as close to the line of illegality as possible without crossing it. This attitude is dangerous in business because it often ultimately leads to crossing the line into illegal behavior. And even if actions don't cross the line, they may create the perception that your organization bends the rules, which violates the rule of remaining above reproach. So to discourage legal-limits thinking throughout the organization, try the following tactics:

✔ Reject legal-limits thinking whenever it arises.

✔ Reinforce the unwavering standard of ethics as defined in the company's ethics statement.

When conducting international business, you may need to work even more diligently to reinforce your ethical standards. Some countries have no limits. Commercial bribery and even human-rights violations may be the norm. Regardless of how liberal the local laws and customs may be, your organization must act in accordance with its own higher principles.

Don't let the pressure to maximize profits drive your organization to test the legal limits or compromise its own ethical standards. Focus on accountability and ethical behavior that's above reproach.

Communicating your standards

Setting standards isn't enough. Everyone in the organization needs to commit to these standards and adhere to them in any and all situations. To ensure adherence, do the following:

- Clearly present your organization's ethical standards to all personnel. Include your standards in your employee handbook and post them in locations where all employees can see them.

- Stress just how important honoring these standards is to the reputation and continued success of your business. Especially educate your organization's leaders so they can help build a culture of ethical behavior.

- Set and enforce consequences for failure to adhere to any of the standards. Consider a system of warnings, penalties, and even termination for repeated or egregious offences.

Tap the power of symbolism to communicate to a large number of people the significance of upholding ethical standards. For example, instead of a supervisor calling in a subordinate to express her appreciation for the subordinate's honesty in handling a certain situation, the executive vice-president of the firm may gather everyone in the department together to recognize the individual. Here are two suggestions for increasing the impact of such symbolic actions:

- Engage higher-ups in symbolic acts. The higher the position of the person making the pronouncement, the deeper the impact of the message.

- Include more people. The larger the audience, the deeper the impact of the message and the wider it spreads.

If you're outsourcing CI, hire only professionals who have a solid reputation, and be sure that you communicate your ethical standards to them. If they break the law or use unethical or unprofessional means to produce intelligence, you may be held legally responsible, and their actions will reflect poorly on your organization.

Applying Ethics to the Three Intelligence Categories

Although you don't want to cloud your ethical standards with situational thinking (that is, letting the circumstances guide what you deem appropriate), you and others in your organization need to know how ethical guidelines apply to various situations. In other words, you need to shift from thinking about ethics in a theoretical framework to thinking about it in a practical way that governs decisions and behaviors. One way to shift your thinking is to look at how ethical standards play out in the three different intelligence categories: human, signal, and image intelligence.

Human intelligence (humint)

Human intelligence, or *humint,* is information or insights you obtain by communicating directly with individuals through face-to-face interviews, phone calls, e-mail messages, and so on. Depending on the source, human intelligence is often the most comprehensive and highest quality intelligence available. At the same time, gathering humint is often the equivalent of digging for gold in an ethical minefield. As you gather humint, answer the following questions to determine whether you're gathering the intelligence and can use it ethically:

- ✔ **Does the acquisition of information pose a conflict of interest?** If your source has ulterior motives for sharing confidential information, such as a desire to harm or get even with a former employer, don't pursue the source or accept or use any information the person shares. In addition, if the person is breaking the law or violating your organization's ethical standards in supplying the information, that information is off limits.

- ✔ **Are your sources expecting any benefit as a result of providing the information?** If your sources are expecting money, a job, proprietary information, or something else of value in exchange for the information, you're essentially bribing the person, which is unethical and may be illegal.

- ✔ **Do any legal issues restrict the provision or use of the information?** For example, you can't dig through a dumpster that's on your competitor's property to gather discarded memos and reports. (If the dumpster is on public property, digging through it to gather competitive intelligence may be legal, but it's still unethical.)

- ✔ **Have you provided full disclosure about yourself, your job, and your objectives?** If you're requesting information, you need to identify yourself, the company you work for, your position, and what you intend to use the information for. Posing as an intern to gather information about a competitor or staging a job interview to extract confidential information from a competitor's current or former employee is unethical.

- ✔ **Are the people communicating the information aware of your presence and that you may be listening to their comments?** Eavesdropping on a conversation at an airport to gather CI may be legal, but it's unethical. If you want to listen in, either introduce yourself and make it clear that you might use what the parties tell you as part of your organization's CI, or walk away so you won't be tempted to listen in.

Confidential information displayed on a computer screen is not fair game. If you're tempted to peek, look away or move to a different seat or another room.

Signals intelligence (sigint)

Signals intelligence (also called *sigint*) is any information that's exchanged electronically; for example, via the Internet, phone lines, or radio transmissions. In the context of sigint, I'm talking about data that's exchanged between parties electronically that could be intercepted by or mistakenly delivered to a third party. I'm not talking about e-mail messages or faxes that are directed to you or digital information that's publicly accessible. Obviously, hacking your competitor's e-mail server, using SMS (text message) spy software to intercept text messages, and tapping the phone of your competitor's CEO are unethical, but what about messages that you receive in error?

If you receive an e-mail, text message, fax, or other form of confidential information that's intended for someone else, advise the sender of his error, inform your legal department of the incident, and destroy and ignore any information you received. Don't use the information or pass it along to anyone else. Using the information is unethical and could ultimately get you into legal trouble.

Image intelligence (imint)

Image intelligence (imint) consists of photographs or video, which may include photos of a competitor's production line, satellite images of building sites, or video footage of competitors loading or unloading trucks. To decide whether you can use certain photos or video footage ethically in CI, answer the following questions:

- ✔ **Does the image show what's in plain view?** If the image shows something that anyone can see, then it's fair game. However, if you have to go out of your way to obtain the image, then it's off limits. For example, a satellite image of a building site is fair game, but surreptitiously taking photos of the inside of a manufacturing facility during a plant tour is unethical.

- ✔ **Are you using any form of deception to obtain the images?** You're not allowed to engage in deception to obtain the images; for example, by posing as a prospective customer to get inside a distribution center and clandestinely snapping photos with a spy-cam or hiring someone on the inside to shoot video for you.

- ✔ **Is this information that could be obtained by anyone?** More often than not, the plain-view test is usually best: Has the owner of the information knowingly and intentionally made the information available in a public manner? If so, it's fair game.

✔ **Are you violating any ethical standards in obtaining the information?**
Information may be off limits even if it passes the plain-view test. Ethics
forbid you, for example, from taking anything from someone just because
that person is careless with it. If someone drops a $50 bill while checking
out at the grocery store, you're not allowed to just pick it up and keep it
for yourself. In the same way, taking a trade secret that's displayed on
a computer screen or overheard in an airport lounge is unethical and
probably may even be illegal.

Conducting CI in the Gray Zone

Assuming that your organization is committed to conducting business above
reproach, you shouldn't have much of a gray zone to worry about. You
shouldn't have to fear landing in court as the target of a lawsuit or on the
front page of *The Wall Street Journal* as a company that cheats. However,
your organization will still find itself facing circumstances in which the law
and your own ethical standards are uncertain as they pertain to CI. In the following sections, I address several situations in which your choices may be
ethically foggy.

Hiring CI firms who worked for competitors

CI consulting firms commonly work for companies in the same industry.
Hiring a firm that has worked for your competitors isn't necessarily a conflict
as long as no proprietary information is shared and the scopes of the two
projects don't overlap. Problems may arise, however, if your outside consultants try to cut corners by simply repurposing the work they did for a different client and selling it to you. Here are a few guidelines to help you steer
clear of potential pitfalls when hiring a CI consulting firm:

1. **Always prepare a written agreement that prohibits the CI firm from
   disclosing proprietary or confidential information from former clients.**

2. **Obtain the firm's agreement that it will not provide you with information that has already been paid for by a competing firm.**

3. **Make sure that the statement of work provided by the expert is not in
   conflict with work performed for any competitors.**

4. **Have the consulting firm sign a nondisclosure agreement that prohibits it from sharing any information about your organization or information obtained for this particular CI project with other clients.**

Caught in the act of double dipping

I once saw a report that a consulting firm had charged a client $250,000 to produce. Unfortunately for the firm, when the consultants prepared the report, they forgot to replace the name of the previous client (a competitor) that had originally ordered the study and had already paid $250,000 for it!

Double dipping like this is obviously unethical, but it's worse than that because it gives both clients identical information and neither of them a competitive advantage.

Hiring employees who worked for competitors

If you're ever in the market to hire a former employee of a competing business, do it for the right reason — that is, because the individual is the best person qualified for the job. Don't hire the person to get inside information. Furthermore, before you offer the person the job, take the following precautions:

- ✔ Make sure that the person doesn't have a contractual relationship with the competitor that contains unacceptably restrictive conditions related to employment with your company. Consult with your organization's legal counsel before offering the person a position.

- ✔ Get any new hires, especially those who've worked for a competitor, to contractually agree that they will not provide any information from a prior employer that was confidential or proprietary. Most important, that agreement must clearly specify that no trade secrets will be shared.

- ✔ Have the employee sign a contract as a condition related to employment, confirming that she had no contractual agreement with her former employer that prohibits her from working for a competitor (such contracts normally provide for a specific period of time).

- ✔ Prohibit the person from bringing any confidential files or other information from the competitor.

Protect your organization's confidential information. Companies have been known to hire former employees of competing firms and keep them on the payroll just long enough to extract valuable information and insight. If a key employee who has had access to critical information is about to leave the company, especially if the employee is disgruntled, take the following precautions to keep sensitive information from being leaked:

✔ Make the individual aware of the legal liability related to disclosing trade secrets.

✔ Make sure that all access to proprietary information is ceased at the moment the employee indicates that she is leaving the company.

✔ Have security or the employee's supervisor pack up the employee's belongings to ensure that the employee doesn't walk out with any confidential documents or other information.

Taking photos or video

When you have the opportunity to take photos or video of a competitor's operation, you may feel as though you're on a reconnaissance mission, sneaking behind enemy lines to steal trade secrets. But snapping photos or shooting video may be perfectly acceptable as long as it passes the plain-view test.

Here are some scenarios that challenge your ability to determine whether the activity crosses the line:

Question: Is it acceptable to hire a private investigator to sit outside a competitor's office and take pictures of all the delivery trucks and shipments that arrive or leave the premises?

Answer: Yes. The competitor is knowingly making this information available in a public setting. It's no different from driving down a road and seeing a truck leaving a competitor's premises.

Question: You have the opportunity to lease an office space that overlooks a competitor's warehouse, which would allow you to photograph and identify customer names and products being shipped. Would this be ethical?

Answer: Yes. Again, the information is in plain view, and the company hasn't taken any precautions to hide it. However, I still have trouble with this practice personally; I sure wouldn't want the local newspaper running an article about me doing this.

Question: You get a call from your human resources director, who tells you that an applicant for a sales position is interested in leaving her position with a competitor. When you contact the applicant, she reveals that she has information about all the products the competitor plans on introducing over the next five years. She has been mistreated by the competitor and says she would have no problem in revealing all that information if your company hires her. Should you accept the information if you hire her?

Answer: No. In this case, your ethics may protect you from bigger issues. A standard of integrity above reproach prohibits you from accepting the information. Additionally, your decision to reject the information will also protect you legally as related to the theft of trade secrets. (See "Steering clear of economic espionage: The Economic Espionage Act of 1996," earlier in this chapter.) I would go even farther and recommend not hiring this applicant; after all, if she's willing to pass along trade secrets, do you really want her working for *you*?

One rule governs how to approach gray area situations: When in doubt, don't do it.

Part II
Gathering, Confirming, and Organizing Relevant Data

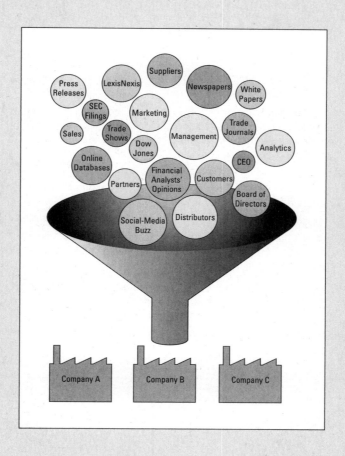

Expert panels are an extremely useful CI tool, but sometimes getting the experts you're interviewing to agree on what's actually going on and why can prove downright challenging. I have a trick for making it easier, though, which I share with you at www. dummies.com/extras/competitiveintelligence.

In this part . . .

- ✔ Pick the brains of your organization's decision makers to evaluate their intel needs and find out what they and other company personnel already know.

- ✔ Dig up valuable information on the web, including SEC filings and analyst opinions, and conduct polls or interviews when you need more information than what your usual sources can provide.

- ✔ Tap the power of analytics to extract insight from *big data feeds* — volumes of data that no mere mortal could possibly process.

- ✔ Solicit valuable third-party perspectives from experts and expert panels (to help understand future trends) and discover how to read a person's body language so you can better tell what she's really getting at.

- ✔ Figure out how determine the true accuracy of the information you've gathered so you can separate fact from fiction and distinguish irrelevant information from valuable data.

- ✔ Create a CI library to organize and store your data for easy access in the future.

Chapter 5

Gathering Intelligence from Internal Resources

In This Chapter

▶ Feeding internal information to the CI team

▶ Synchronizing intelligence duties with different departments

▶ Organizing and storing information to simplify retrieval

*Y*ou're probably sitting on a gold mine of information, and you may not even realize it. Every day, executives in your company soak up relevant information, salespeople and customer service reps talk to customers, IT engages in web analytics, and shipping and receiving personnel encounter problems that beg for solutions. You already have more information than you know what to do with, but unless you gather, organize, and analyze that information, it's likely to go to waste, which is what happens in a huge majority of organizations.

In this chapter, I explain how to begin to mine the information you already have. I encourage you to engage in internal analytics and create a source map for each function of your organization so you have a clear idea of the nature of information that each function needs and can establish a steady flow of information between each function and CI. I also provide guidance on how to organize and store information to make it easily accessible to everyone in the organization who needs it.

Whether your organization is large or small, this chapter helps create the information flow that can provide the foundation for actionable intelligence.

Tapping Internal Intelligence Sources

Extracting the information you need from internal sources requires an approach that may seem a bit like *fracking* — a process that uses hydraulic pressure to crack rocks in order to release natural gas so it can be extracted from the ground. The information is there, but you need to find a way to extract it from the people who have it and move it over to CI where it can be analyzed and processed into actionable intelligence.

In the following sections, I encourage you to implement analytics as a way to gather information internally, and I provide guidance on how to tap other internal sources for potentially valuable information.

Getting up to speed on internal analytics

Business analytics refers to the automated collection and processing of large amounts of data to reveal meaningful patterns. Organizations use analytics to increase process efficiency, improve customer retention, monitor and fine-tune marketing campaigns, build more-effective websites, motivate employees, predict competitor actions, and much more. To make analytics more manageable, you can break it into two categories:

- ✔ **Internal:** Internal analytics essentially crunches the numbers to gauge how well your organization is doing. Sales figures, profit margins, returns, customer complaints, production reports, and other forms of internally accessible data fall in this category.

- ✔ **External:** External analytics sheds light on information outside your organization, such as market trends, customer sentiment (as expressed through social media), consumer confidence, industry regulations, changes in distribution channels, and so on. For more about external analytics, see Chapter 6.

Internal analytics is often insufficient for gaining insight into facts and figures. For example, internal analytics may warn you of a drop in sales, but until you perform external competitive intelligence, you don't have a clear idea of the cause or what you may be able to do to fix the problem.

Following are a few practical applications for internal analytics:

- ✔ Sales figures may indicate trends in what customers are buying more or less of from you.

- ✔ An increase in profit margins may be a good measure of success in telling whether certain initiatives have been effective.

✔ A drop in market share often serves as an early-warning sign that an organization is losing ground to competitors.

If you're not tapping the power of internal analytics to improve at least one area of your organization, you should be. Start by tracking your organization's key performance indicators (KPIs). KPIs are different for each organization. Here are a few examples of how changes in an organization's KPIs can serve as important intel:

✔ Raw materials shipments from Nicaragua drastically decline.

✔ Sales proposals (to customers) drop off significantly.

✔ An airline's load factor on Chicago-Dallas flights declines 2.5 percent.

✔ The inbound call center's hold times increase by 22 percent.

✔ A key product's sales trend down by 11 percent.

✔ Five of eight fulfillment centers are below required inventory levels for a major product.

Internal analytics applies artificial intelligence to big data in order to draw meaning from statistics. For example, suppose your call center's analytics software starts picking up an increased frequency of the word *angry* and the phrase *mad as hell* related to a specific line of products you're carrying. That connection can make you instantly aware of a problem long before anyone in customer service notices it.

Mapping sources and needs

To gain an understanding of where information resides in your organization and the sort of information each decision maker requires, create a source map and a needs map. A *source map* shows you where valuable information in your organization can be found. A *needs map* identifies the decision makers and the intelligence they need to improve their decision making.

Recruit an individual in each department to help you create the two maps. Try to find power players (such as department heads or content experts) who not only supply you with information and use the intelligence you produce but also are likely to promote the CI team's efforts. This person becomes your department insider and does the following:

✔ Helps you identify the department's intelligence needs

✔ Feeds you information that the department gathers

✔ Receives the intel you provide and teams up with the organization's leadership to formulate and execute changes

Meet with your contact from each department to complete a questionnaire, as shown in Figure 5-1.

Competitive Intelligence Sources/Needs Questionnaire

Department: Executive
Key contact: Melody Smith
Title: CEO

Current information sources:

- Gets monthly reports that summarize competitor performance from FFC group

- Receives weekly report from all direct reports on division performance

- Lexis-Nexis to conduct routine information searches about competitors and product

- Dow Jones to conduct routine information searches about competitors and products

- Involved in a number of CEO level organizations

- Serves on the board of advisors for a major university technology group that does industry-related research

-

Current intelligence needs:

- Mash-up of information into one-page snapshots

- Weekly performance statistics

- Wants to know about how customers feel about our company and our service

-

-

-

-

Figure 5-1:
Completed competitive intelligence source/ needs questionnaire.

Illustration by Wiley, Composition Services Graphics

After you obtain questionnaires from the decision makers, condense the information into a sources/needs box for each person, as shown in Figure 5-2. You can do this in any word-processing or desktop-publishing program.

Consider creating a sources/needs card (the size of a business card) for each decision maker with sources on the front and needs on the back. You can use these cards for quick reference.

Melody Smith CEO

Sources: LexisNexis; Dow Jones; competitor performance data; CEO seminars; conventions

Needs: Mash-up of corporate performance data; customer sentiment analytics

---

Susan Jones, Director of Finance

Sources: Internal customer analytics; Hoover's service; annual financial convention

Needs: Projected sales revenues by product segment

Mark Smith, Marketing Sales Analyst

Sources: Internal sales analysis by product; Gartner Group industry segment revenue data; Gartner Group's white papers; attends industry conventions

Needs: Customer sentiment information (focus on dissatisfied clients)

Barney Fife, CFO

Sources: Numerous internal financial break outs by region and product; economic analysis and projections from Accenture

Needs: Need someone to watch different factors as needed on a quarterly basis

---

Samuel Northouse, Chief Legal Officer

Sources: LexisNexis

Needs: Would like a monthly report about any customers who might be having financial or legal problems

Illustration by Wiley, Composition Services Graphics

Figure 5-2:
Sample
sources/
needs
boxes.

To create your source map, strip out the needs and arrange the boxes around a box for CI, as shown in Figure 5-3.

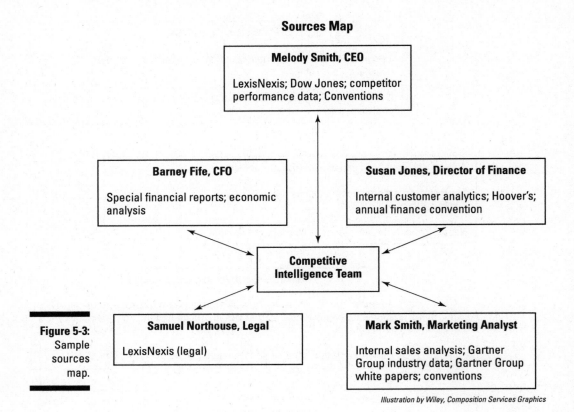

Sources Map

Melody Smith, CEO

LexisNexis; Dow Jones; competitor performance data; Conventions

Barney Fife, CFO

Special financial reports; economic analysis

Susan Jones, Director of Finance

Internal customer analytics; Hoover's; annual finance convention

Competitive Intelligence Team

Samuel Northouse, Legal

LexisNexis (legal)

Mark Smith, Marketing Analyst

Internal sales analysis; Gartner Group industry data; Gartner Group white papers; conventions

Figure 5-3: Sample sources map.

Illustration by Wiley, Composition Services Graphics

To create your needs map, strip out the sources and arrange the boxes around a box for CI, as shown in Figure 5-4.

Needs Map

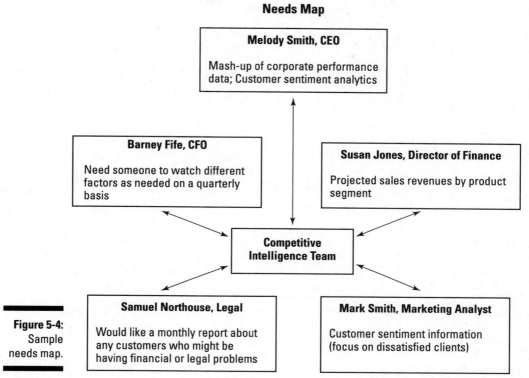

Figure 5-4:
Sample
needs map.

Illustration by Wiley, Composition Services Graphics

Another great way to create a needs map is to set up a bulletin board (a physical board or an online version) and have decision makers or CI reps in each department or area of the organization pin their needs to the board as they arise. See Figure 5-5 for an example.

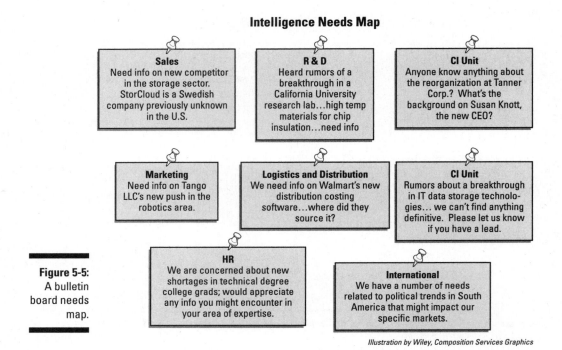

Intelligence Needs Map

Sales
Need info on new competitor in the storage sector. StorCloud is a Swedish company previously unknown in the U.S.

R & D
Heard rumors of a breakthrough in a California University research lab…high temp materials for chip insulation…need info

CI Unit
Anyone know anything about the reorganization at Tanner Corp.? What's the background on Susan Knott, the new CEO?

Marketing
Need info on Tango LLC's new push in the robotics area.

Logistics and Distribution
We need info on Walmart's new distribution costing software…where did they source it?

CI Unit
Rumors about a breakthrough in IT data storage technologies… we can't find anything definitive. Please let us know if you have a lead.

HR
We are concerned about new shortages in technical degree college grads; would appreciate any info you might encounter in your area of expertise.

International
We have a number of needs related to political trends in South America that might impact our specific markets.

Figure 5-5:
A bulletin board needs map.

Illustration by Wiley, Composition Services Graphics

Your source and needs maps provide you not only with an organizational inventory of resources but also with a list of key personnel to serve on your intel team.

Formalizing intelligence gathering by department

Unless intelligence gathering is formalized, it's likely to get crowded out by other job responsibilities that may seem more urgent. To formalize the internal intelligence gathering process, take the following steps:

1. **Ask one person from each department to be in charge of gathering information and passing it along to CI.**

   See Chapter 3 for details about recruiting an individual from each department to serve on the CI team or at least designating one person to serve as a liaison between the department and the CI team.

2. **Establish a convenient means for passing information to CI.**

   This may be via internal e-mail, a central database, or old-school memos.

3. **Establish goals and deadlines.**

    Collaborate with each contact person to determine the quantity and minimum frequency for sending information to you. Also agree on intelligence goals and deadlines that indicate what your contact person can expect to receive back from you, and when, as explained in the next section.

Coordinating Intelligence Gathering by Department

One of each department's job duties should be to gather relevant information and pass it along to CI. After all, intelligence is a team sport, and every department represents a key player on that team. However, the type of information that each of those players collects and passes along to CI is likely to differ. To be sure that CI is getting the information it needs, every department must have a clear understanding of the intelligence activities it must engage in. The following sections break down intelligence activities by department.

The sources and needs maps you created earlier in this chapter can also help break down intelligence duties by department.

Getting the info you need

As you meet with key CI liaisons in each department, take the following steps to establish areas of understanding that will facilitate the effectiveness of the CI effort:

1. **Arrange a monthly appointment with the individual (in person, over the phone, or via Skype) to obtain information and to determine any specific CI needs the department may have.**

2. **Send the following forms to the person a few days prior to the scheduled meeting, along with a request to complete both forms.**

    • A competitive intelligence briefing sheet (see Figure 5-6) enables a department contact to supply you with information the person has gathered and explain the perceived significance of the information.

    • A competitive intelligence request sheet (see Figure 5-7) enables a department contact to request information from CI.

Competitive Intelligence Briefing Sheet

Area of Study: ______________________________

Classification

Highly Sensitive-Confidential _____
Sensitive _____
General Information _____

Priority Recommendation:

Urgent _______
Important _____
Normal _______

Submitted by ______________________________ Date ______________________________

Summary of Information (short summary of information; key issues; who needs this information?):

What sources were used to obtain the information?

In your opinion, how reliable are your sources (explain)?

In your opinion, how important is this information (explain)?

Recommendations:

List of materials in file or attached:

Figure 5-6: Competitive intelligence briefing sheet.

Illustration courtesy of Jim Underwood

Competitive Intelligence Request

Area of proposed study: _____

Classification   **Priority Recommendation**

Highly Sensitive-Confidential _____   Urgent _____
Sensitive: _____   Important _____
General Information _____   Normal _____

Action requested by: _____ Date: _____

General area of information (Company____; Technology ____; Other _____)

Description of proposed project:

Please provide any details that may help in framing the research:

Summary of information resources that might be accessible by the CI team that might facilitate the gathering of information:

Names of any internal content experts that might be able to help in designing the study:

Other comments:

Figure 5-7:
Competitive
intelligence
request
sheet.

Illustration courtesy of Jim Underwood

When coordinating intelligence gathering by department, act as though you're creating your own social network, such as Facebook. Often, some of the best information comes to light during discussion when participants think of sharing information that they hadn't considered important or just didn't think of bringing up in the past. In other words, don't stop with the form; engage in a conversation.

Enlisting the CEO as chief intelligence officer

Some organizations actually have their own chief intelligence officer, who's in charge of CI and works directly with the CEO to formulate strategy. If your organization has no such position, then your CEO may need to do double duty as the chief intelligence officer and perform the following job duties:

- ✔ **Serve as the top-level sponsor for CI, communicating its value to the rest of the organization.** The CEO is a figurehead with the power and visibility needed to promote CI's efforts and hold others accountable for implementing recommended changes.

- ✔ **Assist in identifying strategic areas that are most likely to benefit from CI.** The CEO is in the best position to formulate the big-picture view of what the organization must do to remain competitive, so he probably has a pretty clear idea of the types of information required to identify opportunities and threats and forecast where the industry and different markets are headed.

- ✔ **Collaborate with CI and department heads to formulate and execute strategic initiatives and other changes.** The CEO really holds the power of the bully pulpit to implement changes in the organization and how it operates. When the CEO plays an active role in spearheading change initiatives, the organization is much more successful in putting intelligence into action.

Here are a couple tips for how to enlist your organization's CEO to serve as its chief intelligence officer and how to harness her power:

- ✔ Suggest that the CEO demonstrate the value that she places on competitive intelligence, such as by commenting on it in corporate newsletters and other organization-wide communications.

- ✔ Meet with your CEO for five minutes each month to pass along the monthly intelligence briefing and gather any intel that she has collected during the past month at industry meetings or other gatherings. (See Chapter 10 for guidance on how to create intelligence briefings.)

If you take the initiative to meet and also limit your time to five minutes, the CEO will always welcome your visit. Senior-level executives usually work 70+ hours per week, and their calendars are overbooked. If you can work with the CEO's administrative assistant to get your five minutes per month, it will benefit the entire CI gathering process.

Identifying executive intelligence activities

All executives in your organization have a role to play in CI. If nothing else, each executive should be happy to provide you with a five-minute debriefing on a monthly or quarterly basis. Here are just a few ways the executives of the company can help with the CI effort:

- The CEO often has the only access to special briefings, reports, or conferences where industry or technology trends are discussed, so a briefing from the CEO to the CI group can be invaluable.

- The CFO can be a resource when it comes to economic, competitor, or industry trends that often include CI.

- The CTO (chief technology officer) often receives information from technology providers that deal with emerging or future technologies.

- Every C-level executive, such as the chief marketing officer (CMO), has access to associations that focus on competitive issues that may be emerging in the industry.

What all these people have is a wealth of information, and it's the CI unit's goal to mine that data.

During your debriefings, listen closely and try to identify questions or problems that the executive is struggling with and that CI may be able to answer or solve. By helping to answer those questions or solve those problems, you demonstrate CI's value and earn future cooperation and support.

Getting marketing to pitch in

People in marketing are often excellent sources for intel because they're probably gathering data and analyzing it for their own purposes on a daily basis. They're tracking website traffic and activity and fine-tuning their web-based efforts accordingly, listening in to what customers are saying about the company and its products in social-media venues, and collaborating with sales to improve marketing, sales, and customer satisfaction.

As you approach marketing, keep the following info in mind:

- ✔ Marketing is often privy to custom market research. Getting marketing personnel to share their information can really give weight and importance to the CI's body of information.

- ✔ Sales is often a part of the marketing department and can provide valuable insight into customer needs and the problems they're dealing with. In addition, salespeople often hear about competitors through customers.

- ✔ Marketing and sales teams often get analytics-based reporting that can provide early input related to product sales trends and opportunities. More often than not, that information has value to CI projects as well.

Never forget the exchange opportunities you can facilitate with marketing. For example, you may get intelligence about a specific client from the finance department that ends up being something that helps an account manager in the marketing area.

- ✔ Marketing and sales folks are pretty busy at conventions and trade shows, so try to help them by gathering information at these events.

Bottom line: Marketing and salespeople can provide extensive intelligence that you may not be able to get from any other resource. Discover how to use them effectively!

Unfortunately, because the marketing department is often already involved in its own intelligence work, CI is most likely to get into a turf war with this group over sharing information and competing over approaches to grow market share. So approach marketing very carefully, with an attitude of gratitude and a commitment to give more than you get. Avoiding political sensitivities can be challenging at times, but if you can convince departments that have extensive market interface of your desire to help them, you can also establish key resource relationships for CI information gathering.

Your challenge often involves power or money. Sometimes a manager's compensation is tied to the number of people he supervises. He may want to try to justify his headcount by trying to bring all the CI work into his department. Conversely, CI provides service for multiple users, so CI can be caught in the middle because CI also needs personnel to do its work.

Treating a salesperson to lunch

Because they like to talk, salespeople often gather gobs of information from customers and are easy to extract information from, so take a salesperson to lunch every so often and talk shop. Ask if you can go on a few sales calls so you can hear for yourself what customers have to say about your company, its products, issues that customers often struggle with, questions they ask, what they have to say about competitors, and so on. You may pick up on something important that someone in sales dismisses as too insignificant to mention to you.

Having customer service lend an ear

Like salespeople, customer-service personnel deal directly with customers, especially dissatisfied customers, so they're likely to hear about problems and unmet needs that often lead to future opportunities. Tap customer-service personnel for information in the following ways:

✔ Ask customer service to log all customer complaints, concerns, and comments and send them to the CI team.

✔ Request that customer service listen for unmet needs — products or services that customers are looking for but not finding.

✔ Ask customer service to listen for any comments that customers make about using products for nontraditional uses; for example, using a tool-box for organizing art supplies.

✔ Request that customer service reps tune their ears to pick up any other potentially valuable information from customers, including comments about specific products, technologies, or offerings.

Inviting manufacturing to the intel party

Your organization's manufacturing department may be a valuable source of information related to suppliers, technology, processes, and even the competition:

✔ **Suppliers:** Manufacturing should be constantly searching for new suppliers to lower costs and improve efficiency and reliability. They should also be constantly monitoring current suppliers for signs of any problems, such as financial troubles that could force a key supplier out of business or a supplier becoming an acquisition target for a competing company.

✔ **Technology:** Marketing personnel need to monitor emerging technologies for innovations that may lower costs or improve quality and efficiency.

Vendor or supplier sales reps are often valuable resources for the latest information on emerging technologies. In an effort to sell the latest equipment, sales reps are often eager to tell customers about what competitors are buying or doing; it's a sort of "keeping up with the Joneses" approach to selling products.

✔ **Processes:** Changes in processes may improve efficiency, lower costs, reduce waste, and perhaps even help your company save money by adhering to certain regulations. Decision makers in manufacturing need to stay abreast of any changes in the industry that could improve processes.

✔ **Competitors:** Vendor or supplier sales reps often know a lot about what the competition is up to regarding future products, credit problems, and other issues.

People in manufacturing may not realize how strategically significant the information they have really is. Encourage them to pass their information and insights along to the CI team.

If vendors talk freely about your competitors to you, they'll talk about you to your competitors, as well. Remind the manufacturing department not to share sensitive information with suppliers or vendors who may pass the information along to competitors.

Developing an Intelligence Information Repository

Before you start gathering information, you need somewhere to put it — ideally, a secure, centralized database that enables anyone within the organization to input and extract information. What this somewhere looks like and where it resides varies according to your needs and budget, but it should meet the following requirements:

✔ Ability to store and index different types of digital content, including text, images, audio, and video

✔ Easily accessible for anyone in the organization to input or extract data

✔ Ability to search and filter results depending on your intelligence needs

✔ Secure against external threats from malware and malicious hackers

✔ Ability to set user privileges, restrict access to certain information, and monitor users

What your information repository looks like varies according to the technologies you choose or have at your disposal. Here are a few options:

✓ **A searchable database:** You can create a custom database by using any database program, such as Microsoft Access. In Access, you can input text documents, images, audio and video clips, PDFs, and more; and create retrieval tags to help find entries later. This is a great, cheap way for smaller organizations to create an information repository.

✓ **Data warehousing solutions:** If your organization is large and comprised of many departments, each of which has a different system for entering and storing information, consider a more robust data warehousing solution. A data warehouse (DW or DWH) is a large central database that stores data from various sources and enables authorized personnel from anywhere in the organization to access the data, produce reports, and perform analysis. An added advantage of a data warehouse is that it increases security, enabling you to assign different levels of access to different people.

Consider cloud-based (cloud computing) solutions, which provide easier access to data from anywhere in the world and are much less likely than any internal database solution to encounter storage limitations.

✓ **A filing system on a centralized computer or a folder on the organization's network:** Subfolders can be used to organize information by category.

✓ **An internal website with search capabilities:** An internal website can provide the same search and retrieval functions as a standard website, while providing access only to authorized personnel.

The ideal solution for you will likely be born through a collaboration between CI and IT. Explain to IT what you need and work with them to evaluate the various options.

Plan ahead. Consider how the people in your organization are likely to access the information in the repository. In most cases, personnel are going to look for information on specific competitors, product segments, or competitive segments (such as country, region, or customer base). In the following sections, I explain how to organize information to facilitate retrieval.

Entering information into the system

When you receive information (content), you need to enter it into the system. The steps vary depending on the system you're using. In some cases, you may enter everything into a database. In other cases, you may create a separate folder and save all related documents and information to that folder. (See the next section on categorizing information for details.)

If your internal source hasn't supplied you with a competitive intelligence briefing sheet (see Figure 5-6), create one before you enter information into the system. This sheet contains the area of study, a summary of the information, a list of sources, any recommendations for action, and so forth. Your briefing sheet provides guidance on what you need to enter into the system.

Categorizing information

One way to organize information to facilitate retrieval is to categorize it according to CI or department needs. For example, certain information may be more relevant to marketing or sales, whereas other information deals more with distribution or manufacturing. If you're using a database or website to organize your information repository, you can use field entries to categorize each entry. If you're using a file system, you can create a separate folder for each category.

Another way to categorize entries is by which of the ten forces they pertain to, as explained in Chapter 2. The ten forces are market, technology, economy, ideology, politics/government, media, psycho/social, moral/ethical, environment, and law/regulations.

When organizing data, consider how your clients (your internal CI customers) will retrieve and use it. In most cases, they'll access the information repository to extract information related to the following:

- Competitors
- Product segments
- Competitive segments (country, region, or customer base, for example)

Tagging CI entries

In many systems, including databases and internal websites, you can tag entries with keywords to facilitate searches. In Microsoft Windows, for example, you can tag content that doesn't contain text, such as images, audio, and video files, in such a way that Windows can index them. When you search Windows for a file, tagged entries appear along with indexed entries. Likewise, in most content management systems (CMSs) that are used to manage web content, you can tag pages so they appear in the results when you search the site for specific content.

Chapter 6

Exploring External Sources for Valuable CI Information

Although internal information is important for spotting issues you need to address, external information is essential for providing insight into those issues and for monitoring the ever-changing competitive landscape. Far too many companies are overly focused on what's happening inside their organization and suffer for it with missed opportunities, costly mistakes, and overlooked threats. To maximize the impact of intelligence, CI needs to shift its gaze to external sources. In this chapter, I tell you where to look and how to find the most valuable information.

Although CI's job is to ensure that information is gathered from external sources, everyone in the organization should be encouraged to explore the resources described in this chapter and pass along valuable discoveries to the CI team. For more about delegating research by department or assigning topic areas to individuals, see Chapter 3.

Relating the Ten Forces to Your External CI Sources

As you read through this chapter (or skip around at your leisure), keep in mind the relationship between ten-forces analysis and external sources. As I explain in Chapter 2, ten forces influence an organization's ability to compete in any given market. These forces include the market, technology, the economy, legislation, industry regulations, and more. The sources I describe in this chapter can help you gain insight into how the ten forces impact your organization. The relationship between ten-forces analysis and external sources ends up looking like what's shown in Figure 6-1.

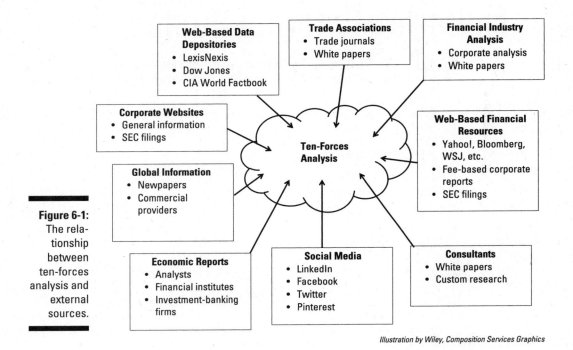

Figure 6-1: The relationship between ten-forces analysis and external sources.

Illustration by Wiley, Composition Services Graphics

Gathering Basic Info on the Web

You can get plenty of information for free on the web, but this high-tech resource is likely to produce a lot of low-value intel for several reasons:

✔ Search engines, such as Bing, Google, and Yahoo!, often fail to reveal the most relevant content. The majority of the best information on the web is part of the *deep web* — content that doesn't appear in typical search results.

✔ Organizations are likely to filter and spin the information they post to present themselves in a more positive light. You may be misled by biased or intentionally omitted information.

✔ Information is often too old to be of value for producing useful intel. Remember, good intel is future focused.

Even with these potential drawbacks, the web is a good place to begin your search, and if you know where to look, you can find some enlightening, accurate, and current information along with leads to more valuable sources. In the following sections, I point out several web-based resources to explore.

Scouring the web

Start with a basic web search, using any of the three leading search engines — Bing, Google, or Yahoo! — but don't stop there. Figure out how to use the search engine's advanced tools. If you're using Google, you can narrow the search results to web content, images, maps, videos, or news; a specific location; a time frame, such as past week or month (to filter out old content); and so on. Look for a Search Tools link or button, which may appear above or to the left of the search results for additional options. You can also scroll to the bottom of any page search results page to find the advanced search option.

For consolidated search results from all three leading search engines, perform your search at www.info.com. Try searching for "corporate information" to get a wide-angle view of corporate information from a variety of sources.

To tap into the deep web for information, don't restrict yourself to the leading search engines. Instead, visit specific websites and use their internal search engines to find what you're looking for. Here are a few websites to get you started:

- ✔ Bloomberg: www.bloomberg.com
- ✔ BusinessWeek: www.businessweek.com
- ✔ Financial Times: www.ft.com
- ✔ Forbes: www.forbes.com
- ✔ The Wall Street Journal: online.wsj.com
- ✔ Yahoo! Finance: finance.yahoo.com

Monitoring social media

Social media consist of discussions on blogs, Facebook, Twitter, LinkedIn, Pinterest, and other such venues. These conversations often center on products and services that customers like or dislike, companies that went above and beyond to serve a customer or failed miserably to do so, friends asking friends for recommendations on what to buy or where to eat, and nearly every other topic imaginable.

Imagine if you could listen in on these conversations and extract insights to help you improve your business, more effectively meet your customers' needs, or even develop new product offerings. Well, you can with the help of analytics, as discussed later in this chapter in the section "Extracting Meaning from 'Big Data' through External Analytics."

Mining corporate websites

Corporate websites, including your competitors' websites, may not be the most valuable resources for gaining insight into an organization's inner workings or strategic plans, but you can use such sites to dig up a few valuable pieces of information, including the following:

- ✔ Names, bios, and contact information for the organization's key personnel
- ✔ Mission statements that may provide insight into the organization's identity and overall competitive strategy (a change in mission statement can be particularly revealing)
- ✔ Job openings that may provide insight into what an organization is gearing up for in the future
- ✔ Information about *your* organization that may reveal areas that require change; for example, a feature list comparison that reveals weaknesses in your product
- ✔ Financial reports, such as SEC filings, provided for investors
- ✔ Executive presentations (webinars) delivered to Wall Street analysts, which are often a good source of information on top-level strategic directions and new initiatives for publicly traded companies in the U.S.
- ✔ New product announcements that may provide insight into the organization's future direction
- ✔ Links for downloading white papers or subscribing to newsletters and other publications (see "Researching Industry White Papers and Reports," later in this chapter)
- ✔ Discussion forums, where you may be able to gauge customer sentiment or identify unmet customer needs
- ✔ Insight into what the organization is doing to improve customer service and communication

Approach corporate websites with skepticism. A corporate website is primarily a marketing tool, but some organizations are more transparent than others.

Pulling up SEC filings

You can find 8-K, 10Q, and 10K filings on corporate websites for publicly traded companies and also on numerous financial websites. To examine a company's filings with the Securities and Exchange Commission (SEC), head to Yahoo! Finance (`http://finance.yahoo.com`), click in the box next to Get Quotes, type the company's name or ticker symbol, and press Enter. This should display a page with all sorts of financial information about the company. In the navigation bar (on the left), click SEC Filings.

I prefer Yahoo! Finance over the SEC's EDGAR search tool at `www.sec.gov/edgar/searchedgar/companysearch.html` because Yahoo! Finance makes it easier to find the information you need. You can usually find a company's SEC filings on its corporate website, as well.

In the following sections, I tell you which SEC filings to look at and offer guidance on what to look for in each one.

10K filing

The 10K is an audited financial report that all publicly traded companies in the United States are required to file with the SEC annually. The financial information contained in the report may be useful depending on your intelligence needs, but the SEC requires some additional information that may be of value, including the following:

- Risk factors
- Legal proceedings
- Consolidated financial data
- Management's discussion and analysis
- Ownership changes of 5 percent or more
- Numerous other corporate-related reports

Always check to see if the auditors have filed a "Going Concern Letter" on the company. That usually means that they have serious concerns about the future viability of the company. Such filings can often provide your senior management with acquisition opportunities.

10Q filing

Public companies in the United States are required to file quarterly financial reports with the SEC. While unaudited, these reports along with the related information can also provide solid intelligence about a company.

8K filing

The SEC 8K requirement is a way of making sure that material changes at a company are reported within four business days of the occurrence of an event. A *material change* is anything that could significantly affect the market value of a company, such as the resignation of a CEO, loss of a major client, or a change in the board of directors.

Checking out analysts' opinions

The major investment-banking firms all have analysts who cover specific business sectors, and many analysts have incredible "back channel" feeds from former employees of the organizations they cover. As always, be skeptical of the validity of information, but remember that these analysts can provide incredible insight into companies, both present and future.

The resources available from investment-banking companies and other corporate information resources and their analysts can be very valuable to the CI analyst. You typically have to pay for an analyst's report, but the report is usually well worth the price.

When it comes to naming specific resources for obtaining analyst reports, the sources are too numerous to list in this chapter. Here are a few to get you started (on most of these websites, you pull up the company profile, which provides a link to the analysts' opinions):

- ✓ **Bloomberg Businessweek** (www.businessweek.com) lets you search for corporate information.

- ✓ **footnoted*** (www.footnoted.com) analysts study the fine print of the SEC documents, looking for "hidden" information — facts the corporation buried, legally, in the fine print. Emerging out of the Enron debacle, footnoted* is a great source for information on publicly traded companies in the U.S.

- ✓ **iStockAnalyst** (www.istockanalyst.com) is another great place to look for analysts' opinions and research. As with almost all such sites, the good stuff costs money to access.

- ✓ **Morningstar** (www.morningstar.com) started as a service that ranked mutual funds, but now it's a great research tool for finding information about specific companies. As on Yahoo! Finance, you can search for a company by name or ticker symbol, and Morningstar displays the company's profile page. From there, you can choose Morningstar Premium and subscribe to the service for access to additional information.

✔ **Yahoo! Finance** (`http://finance.yahoo.com`) allows you to go in-depth when looking for analysts and reports. Click in the box next to Get Quotes, search for the company you want information about, and click its link, if necessary. When the company's profile page appears, you can click the Analyst Coverage links to obtain more information. If you click Research Reports or Star Analysts, you get links to key analysts who follow the company, along with links to obtain research reports (usually for a fee).

Strategic and Competitive Intelligence Professionals (SCIP) has a list of Internet resources that it maintains and provides access to for its members. (You have to log in to the site.) To gain access to this list, head to `www.scip.org`, click Resources in the navigation bar on the left, click Internet Resources, click the link to access the list, and follow the on-screen instructions to log in.

The major investment-banking resources, including Cantor Fitzgerald, Goldman Sachs, JP Morgan Chase, UBS, and Bank of America/Merrill Lynch, all have analysts who specialize in certain industries and follow specific companies. In some cases you can find free information, but more often than not, their analysts' reports and white papers are available only to clients.

Consider subscribing to a subscription service, such as `www.morningstar.com`, to get access to analyst insights.

Reading international newspapers and media feeds

Newspapers can be a great source for leads, and `www.refdesk.com` is a great place to find links to hundreds of newspapers in the U.S. and around the world. Just head to `www.refdesk.com/paper.html` to skim the directory of newspapers grouped by country and state. The site provides mostly English versions of many of the major news outlets in the world. Choose one of the English translations of a newspaper published anywhere in the world and enter the name of your target company in the search box. You're likely to come up with at least something that's relevant and perhaps a news story of real value. Google News (`news.google.com`) is another great source that has the added advantage of being able to translate foreign newspapers into English.

Consider subscribing to a fee-based news feed service, such as the one at www.reuters.com, that can filter out the noise and provide you with only the most relevant data. LinkedIn also provides a feature, called LinkedIn Today (www.linkedin.com/today), that's designed to deliver to you the day's top news stories tailored for you based on your professional relationships and what you've shown an interest in on LinkedIn.

Also consider targeting your searches to specific local newspapers for certain CI projects. For example, if you're thinking about expanding operations to certain geographical areas and have your choices narrowed down to three cities, you may want to search newspapers in those cities for recent news or editorials that provide insight into how accommodating they may be.

Digging Deeper with Fee-Based Services

When you're gathering information for CI, it's not always a case of getting what you pay for. Sometimes the most valuable information drops in your lap. However, several fee-based services can be very useful in collecting information from sources around the world and consolidating it in a single database that you can search, sort, and filter according to your CI needs. If you're willing to pay for information, you generally have two options:

- **Self-serve:** With the self-serve option, you subscribe to a database equipped with tools to search, sort, and filter information. The benefits are that your searches are self-directed and on-demand, and you can perform unlimited research as long as your subscription remains active. The drawback is that any self-serve option has a learning curve; you need to get up to speed on how to unleash the power of the database.

  When considering self-serve options, you need to distinguish between general-purpose options (for publicly traded companies) and sources for information on privately held companies.

- **Hire a data-mining consultant:** If you're doing an ad hoc CI project to answer a specific question or deal with a particular issue, then hiring a data-mining consultant may be a wise choice. You simply describe the insight you're trying to gain, and the data-mining consultant does the heavy lifting.

In the following sections, I describe these options in greater detail and offer some guidance on how to pursue each one.

General-purpose fee-based data services

General-purpose fee-based data services are useful for any organization, regardless of the industry. The heavy hitters in this group include the following:

- ✔ **Bureau Van Dijk** (www.bvdinfo.com) specializes in company information and intelligence.

- ✔ **Corporate Information** (www.corporateinformation.com) has information on over 35,000 public companies. The company sells reports about specific companies.

- ✔ **Dow Jones** (dowjones.com) offers several products broken down into the following categories: Print and Digital Media, Financial News and Information, Risk and Compliance, Research and Intelligence, and Corporate Communications and PR.

- ✔ **Hoovers** (www.hoovers.com) offers numerous tools, reports, and database subscriptions to help you research millions of companies that span more than 900 industry segments.

- ✔ **LexisNexis** (www.lexisnexis.com) features a range of products, including online business news research, global company profiler, corporate investigative database tool, online public records tool, corporate legal resource management tool, and contact development analysis software.

- ✔ **Stratfor** (www.stratfor.com) is one of the most broadly used intelligence information services. Stratfor has resources around the world that are adept at getting time-critical information to their clients at the speed of light. Stratfor offers daily briefings plus frequent in-depth analysis about key global or political issues.

- ✔ **The Economist Intelligence Unit** (www.eiu.com) provides global intelligence services that can be customized to the your intelligence needs. This organization has a rich background in CI.

Many fee-based databases have access to executives' speeches (video or audio), which may offer some valuable insight into the character and mindset of competitors and other key players in your industry. See Chapter 8 for details on how to listen to speeches in order to interpret both verbal and non-verbal meaning.

Sources for financial info on privately held companies

Thanks to SEC filing requirements, you can find plenty of financial information about publicly traded companies, but what about smaller, privately held companies? Fortunately, several sources provide financial info about nonpublicly traded corporations, including family-owned, equity-owned, venture-backed, and international companies that aren't listed on the stock exchanges. Check out the following services, some of which may be quite expensive:

- ✔ D&B Million Dollar Database (www.mergentmddi.com)
- ✔ Hoovers (www.hoovers.com)
- ✔ MarketLine (www.marketline.com)
- ✔ PrivCo (www.privco.com)

Industry-specific consultants

If you decide to hire a data-mining consultant, you can usually find a few options by flipping through the advertisements in your industry's trade publications. Another option is to contact one of the major consulting firms. They usually have industry-specific consulting teams that bring a significant depth and breadth of knowledge to the assignment. Here are a few of the larger consulting firms to get you started:

- ✔ Firms that specialize in CI:
  - Clew (clewllc.com)
  - Competia (www.competia.com)
  - DC Analytics (www.dcanalytics.net)
  - Frost and Sullivan (www.frost.com)
  - Fuld & Co. (www.fuld.com)
  - Infiniti Research (www.infiniti-research.com)
- ✔ General consulting firms that also do CI:
  - Accenture (www.accenture.com)
  - Bain & Co. (www.bain.com)
  - Booz and Co. (www.booz.com)
  - Boston Consulting Group (www.bcg.com)
  - Deloitte Consulting (www.deloitte.com)

- Ernst & Young Consulting (www.ey.com)
- Mercer LLC (www.mercer.com)
- Monitor Group (www.monitor.com)

SCIP has directory of service providers that you can access even if you're not a member. Visit www.scip.org, click Resources in the navigation bar on the left, and click Directory of Service Providers.

Be sure that you evaluate and compare the consultants from each firm. Finding the right expert for an industry-specific project can save money and time, as well as provide much higher quality research.

When drawing up a contract to hire a consulting firm, always include a no-repackaging clause to send a clear signal that you expect the firm to do fresh research specifically for your organization. If the consulting firm refuses to sign the document, that probably means you were going to be sold repackaged research that has already been delivered to your competitor. Another good practice is to give any new consulting firm a small project as a trial run before engaging it in a major project.

Conducting Polls and Interviews

Sometimes existing information isn't enough to evaluate customer needs and expectations or answer the question of why a competitor has changed course. When neither internal analytics nor external information provides the depth of information you need, it's time to go directly to the source and start asking questions through polls or interviews.

In the following sections, I describe the three levels of polls or interviews you may want to conduct:

- ✔ **Polling or opinion research:** When you're pretty sure that the people you're asking will give honest answers, a simple poll can provide valuable information.

- ✔ **Face-to-face interviews:** Face-to-face interviews enable you to pick up on nonverbal messages, which give you a better indication of whether a person is being open and honest. Interviews also give you a chance to ask follow-up questions.

- ✔ **Interviews involving projective techniques:** *Projective techniques* are ways of asking questions that neutralize a person's rational thinking to elicit more honest answers. Instead of asking what a person thinks, the interviewer encourages the person to imagine scenarios or express how he feels about something so he doesn't feel a need to defend his answers.

Consider hiring an individual or a firm that specializes in analyzing human behavior and opinions to conduct polls or interviews. Why outsource this important task? Three reasons:

- ✔ You probably don't have the expertise internally.
- ✔ You won't get honest answers if people being polled know the identity of the consumer of the information.
- ✔ You probably don't have the resources to perform a poll or conduct interviews in a timely manner.

Exploring polling services

Polling or *opinion research* often provides valuable insight into understanding unmet customer needs and predicting when changes are likely to become industry standard. For example, a number of years ago, a client needed to know when a specific technology would be utilized in a large industry. The client thought it might be within five years. But a questionnaire sent to key industry sources determined that it would be deployed by the entire industry within 12 months!

Use polls and opinion research for sampling a large group of people when you're fairly certain they'll answer honestly; for example, when you're asking people about their opinions related to industry trends, consumer preferences, technological concepts, and so on. Don't use polling or opinion research for gathering opinions on highly sensitive issues, such as lifestyle choices and political leanings, because people may bend the truth. Instead, use paid interviewers, as discussed in the next section.

Numerous companies provide polling and opinion research services regionally, nationally, and internationally. Here are a few service providers to get you started:

- ✔ First Research (a research arm of Hoover's) (www.firstresearch.com)
- ✔ Gallup (www.gallup.com)
- ✔ Global Marketing Research Services (www.polling.net)
- ✔ Kelton (www.keltonglobal.com)
- ✔ QuestionPro (questionpro.com)
- ✔ Research America (www.researchamerica.com)
- ✔ SurveyMonkey (www.surveymonkey.com)
- ✔ The Light Point Group (www.lightpointgroup.com)

University marketing professors are often good candidates for the job as well.

Employing professional interviewers

A number of the research firms presented in the previous section employ professionals who are qualified to do in-depth interviews. They have special skills and training to look beneath the obvious and interpret nonverbal messages. They see much more than the average person does, because they go beyond what the interviewee is saying to detect what the person truly feels. A good example of someone who does this well is a law-enforcement professional. Detectives are quick to recognize false statements, disinterest, and anxiety.

Finding the right person can often be difficult. Here are three sources and tips on how you might use each of them to find the right intelligence professional for your project:

- ✔ **Langley Intelligence Group Network** (www.lignet.com): This membership-based site produces global intelligence reports for subscribers. The group doesn't provide you with referrals to members who may have an appropriate intelligence background, but a scan of the board of directors listing may provide the names of some firms with which they're associated.

- ✔ **Strategic and Competitive Intelligence Professionals** (www.scip.org): SCIP is an organization that has a varied membership. Members have access to numerous resources, and you can generally find the type of intelligence professional you're looking for among members.

- ✔ **Association of Former Intelligence Officers** (www.afio.org): AFIO produces some very nice intelligence analysis for its members. Membership is fairly restrictive, but the organization does have an employment service where intelligence projects or positions may be listed. The organization has more than 5,000 ex-intelligence professionals (as well as current). As with most of these types of organizations, finding resources may involve a lot of digging. The organization does show its board of directors on its website, and you can sometimes find the names of associated intelligence organizations there that provide services to corporate clients.

 Retired intelligence professionals (such as ex-CIA analysts) are excellent candidates for conducting interviews. Most of them have decades of experience and numerous global contacts that can help them dig up information. Many of these professionals have gone on to start highly sophisticated intelligence services of their own. Langley Intelligence group is probably the best place to start your search for former CIA analysts.

Hiring specialists in projective techniques

An obvious way to find out what someone knows or thinks is to ask the person. The problem, though, is that the person you're asking may not give open and honest answers. One way around that problem is to hire specialists to conduct the interviews for you by using projective techniques.

Projective techniques are designed to elicit subjective responses that reveal both thoughts and feelings. They're less structured than multiple-choice and true/false questions, giving the interviewee much more freedom in answering questions. In psychology, the best-known projective technique is the Rorschach test. In CI circles, projective techniques may involve asking the interviewee to complete a sentence or associate feelings with certain brand names. Qualified interrogators know how to phrase questions to elicit more honest answers. For example, if you ask someone who they voted for in the last election, she usually tells you what she thinks you want to hear. But if you ask her who most of her neighbors voted for, the person will probably tell you whom she voted for.

When you're in the market for someone to conduct interviews at this level, you're usually looking for a psychotherapist who specializes in human behavior and communication. You may find psychotherapists who advertise these services. In addition, market research and consumer-research companies often employ people who have special training in projective techniques.

If your research involves sensitive issues pertaining to politics, morals, racial attitudes, and so on, the chances of getting politically correct (and inaccurate) answers are very high. Projective techniques improve the accuracy of the information contained in the responses.

Sizing up candidates for the job

Finding someone who's qualified to conduct a poll or interview can be quite a challenge, but the following steps help you choose the right candidate:

1. **Draft a clear, concise list of the questions that you want customers to answer or a list of insights you hope to gain through customer interviews.**

   I say *draft* the questions because the interviewer you hire will most likely revise the questions to improve their effectiveness.

2. **Contact two or three firms that conduct consumer or industry research and ask the following four questions:**

   - **What are your company's qualifications to do this type of work?** If you're looking for an in-depth interviewer, for example, ask candidates to describe their background in conducting in-depth interviews. Get some success stories that indicate their ability to do the kind of research that fits best with what you need.

   - **What are the qualifications of the person who would do the work?** Obtain a detailed résumé that includes education, training, and references. Consider contacting schools that the person claims to have attended for validation; people have been known to lie and even use phony diplomas and transcripts.

- **What references do you have from former clients that you have done this type of work for in the past?** Ask candidates for two or three references from projects that closely resemble yours. Call the references to check on the quality of the services they obtained.

- **What experience does your firm have in using the techniques required for this type of inquiry?** In other words, if you're hiring someone to conduct a poll, ask about their experience in conducting polls. If you're looking for someone who has skills in projective techniques, ask about their experience in that area.

Extracting Meaning from "Big Data" through External Analytics

The term *analytics* often conjures up images of the CIA tracking key words on millions of cellphone conversations in order to detect brewing terrorist plots, but that definition doesn't really apply to business. In the context of business, analytics is the process of taking big data and transforming it into actionable intelligence that leads to positive change. It's characterized by the following:

- **Big data:** Analytics draws inferences from *big data,* a collection of data that's too massive for mere mortals to manage.

- **Meaning-based computing:** Analytics uses computer technology to draw meaning from data. If you want to know how consumers feel about your products or your organization, for example, you can apply analytics to customer-service e-mails and social media.

- **Dashboards:** Analytics software typically displays one or more dashboards that present data in more meaningful formats: charts. For example, a single dashboard may display the daily number of visitors to your website, the number of new and returning visitors, where visitors arrived from (for example, Bing or Yahoo!), and the bounce rate (the percentage of visitors who arrive at the site and leave without doing anything).

- **Efficient, real-time insight:** Analytics performs the work of hundreds of people to present insights immediately as data become available.

Business analytics actually has two applications:

✔ **Data summaries:** Analytics can comprise a simple summary of data organized around a specific area, such as number of visitors to a website and click-through rates (which measure the success of online advertising campaigns).

✔ **Text analytics:** Sometimes referred to as *meaning-based computing* or *statistical-pattern learning,* text analytics goes much deeper into a body of structured or unstructured data and can pick up on sentiment, meaning, or other important aspects of the data. Generally, when people use the term analytics today, they're talking about text analytics.

To wrap your brain around the concepts of big data and text analytics, check out the word cloud I created at Tagxedo (www.tagxedo.com) for "competitive intelligence" (see Figure 6-2). You can tell with a quick glance at this word cloud which words are most commonly associated with the phrase "competitive intelligence" on the web. Analytics is a way of mining and mashing up the meaning of key ideas in a large body of information.

Investors have used analytics to analyze tweets about the stock market and subsequently predict where it was going. Google uses analytics to determine ranking of search-engine results and which ads to display.

Figure 6-2:
A word cloud helps identify the focus of conversations.

Illustration courtesy of Tagxedo (www.tagxedo.com)

Here are a few of the ways that organizations are using big data and external analytics to improve operations:

- Analyzing millions of social-media messages to gauge customer sentiment about a product in order to develop future improvements

- Monitoring millions of credit-card transactions to recognize patterns that may indicate fraudulent use of a credit card

- Narrowing customer segmentation to more precisely tailor products and services to customers

- Combining analytics with word clouds to provide executives and analysts with an immediate understanding of major themes (such as product problems or complaints) so that immediate action can be taken

- Monitoring customer-service call centers to understand the real nature of conversations and improve customer satisfaction

In Europe, an insurance company uses a voice-analytics program to detect fraudulent claims as they're phoned in to the call center. Analytics output helps identify claims that call for further investigation. The results have been very encouraging.

In the following sections, I explain how to start using analytics to process big data and transform it into actionable intelligence in your organization.

How not to use analytics

Analytics pervades almost everything you do. Want to know just how incredible (and controversial) analytics can be? Consider this:

Suzie, a 16-year-old, had a credit card from a major retailer, and the bills came to her father. Over the period of a month or so, Suzie made a number of purchases, none of which would have triggered her father's suspicions.

Nothing seemed out of the ordinary until dad got a personalized letter in the mail one day saying, "Congratulations on your new baby!" The retailer's analytics program had analyzed all the daughter's purchases, and had correctly deduced that Suzie had been shopping for a yet-to-be-born baby. (A lawsuit has apparently been filed, by the way.)

Privacy laws prohibit such use of analytics, but you can see from this example just how powerful analytics can be in making sense of information and producing actionable intelligence.

Shopping for an analytics solution

Analytics has a wide range of applications that can benefit most areas in an organization. To find out which areas are likely to benefit the most and find solution providers that can meet your needs and budget, take the following steps:

1. **Educate yourself by visiting websites of several of the key players in analytics technology, including the following:**

   - Oracle at www.oracle.com
   - IBM at www.ibm.com
   - HP Labs at www.hpl.hp.com
   - SAS at www.sas.com

   Many of these sites have white papers that explain analytics in greater detail.

   Visit www.kdnuggets.com/companies/consulting.html for a longer list of analytics providers.

2. **Ask sales representatives from different analytics companies to help you understand how analytics can benefit your organization specifically.**

3. **Ask managers in your organization if they're already using analytics and what they're using it for.**

   Your organization may already be using analytics to track product trends, website efficiency, or a number of other marketing-related issues.

   If your organization is already using analytics, arrange to have access to information that already exists.

4. **Consult managers and other decision makers to identify areas where external analytics may be beneficial.**

   Consider asking managers and other decision makers the following questions:

   - Which competitors do you need more information about?
   - Which technologies do we need to follow?
   - Which future issues that the company is likely to face are the biggest unknowns?
   - What keeps you up at night?
   - Are there any external areas where we currently lack enough intelligence to help us make good decisions?

5. **Develop a comprehensive list of analytics needs for everyone who's likely to put analytics to good use.**

   You need this list when you start shopping for a solution in the next section. You want a solution that meets everyone's needs so all information can be stored, accessed, and managed centrally. For details about creating needs maps, see Chapter 5.

6. **Start shopping for analytics solutions that meet your needs and budget.**

   Many of the key players mentioned in Step 1 are also the biggest solution providers.

The best solution isn't necessarily the one that has the most bells and whistles or the most check marks in its features list. The ideal solution should meet the following criteria:

✔ **Quick to deploy:** Some solutions may take six months to over a year to develop and deploy. Look for a vendor that has a track record of deploying its solution, or at least the most critical modules, in 30 to 60 days.

✔ **Affordable:** You don't want the cheapest product, but you do need to make sure that the product you choose meets your budget needs.

✔ **Easy to use:** Ease of use is crucial in actually getting people to use the system and getting buy-in from executives and managers. Find out how long it takes the average user to get up to speed on the software.

✔ **Flexible:** Look for a solution that meets your current analytics needs but is flexible enough to accommodate changes down the road. Find out how long it takes to add a new data source and new analytics tools to an existing package.

Identifying pockets of big data

To start using analytics to make sense of big data, identify pockets of big data that you may be able to access and that hold the promise of producing valuable insights. To start locating pockets of data that are ripe for harvesting analytics, consider the following sources:

✔ **Your organization's website and other online properties:** You can use analytics on your website to track customer visits and overall traffic, determine where traffic is coming from, measure the effectiveness of pay-per-click advertising campaigns, and study user behavior on your site in order to improve navigation and calls to action.

✔ **Pockets of large data within your organization:** You should already have pockets of large data within your organization, including sales, product, SKU, customer orders, and numbers related to other revenue and expense activities.

✔ **Pockets of large data outside your organization:** External data include Twitter feeds, blogs, and other web-based media and data about companies, technologies, geographical locations, and other important information that may be emerging on a daily basis or may be stored in public databases.

After you identify pockets of large data, ask yourself if you're getting all the information out of the data that's obtainable. In other words, if you could hire 1,000 people to analyze the data, would you be able to derive a significant benefit from the output? If your answer is yes, then your organization could certainly benefit from the use of analytics. Instead of hiring 1,000 people, however, you can use technology, which is significantly more efficient and effective and costs a whole lot less. If the answer is no, then the data probably won't benefit from analytics because no amount of effort would be able to convert it into valuable intel.

Reading the Competition

Part of CI's role is to keep an eye on the competition. Fortunately, your competitors are likely to cooperate by providing information in newsletters, speeches, press releases, trade journals, interviews with industry journalists and analysts, presentations at trade shows, and industry white papers. You can literally read the competition by researching these sources, as I explain in the following sections.

Exploring external sources is often like following rabbit holes; one source leads to others that lead to others and so on until you ultimately find something of value or reach a dead end. As you explore sources, remain sensitive to the fact that the sources you're looking at may reveal other, more valuable sources. Conduct your own interrogation of the sources you encounter to dig deeper and develop a fuller understanding. When you encounter a source, ask the following questions:

✔ Who wrote this? Why did he or she write it? What's the objective for writing it? Do I trust the motives and knowledge?

✔ Does the author agree with other research? If so, why? Some information conflict? What is the author trying to convince you of . . . or sell you?

✔ What new search areas or terms can I mine from this writing? Are any inadvertent disclosures contained in the writing? If so, what's their significance?

✔ Is this author/expert someone our organization could use as a resource?

As you gather information about the competition, remain skeptical and look for information that contradicts whatever you happen to discover. In your search, you're likely to discover evidence that supports or contradicts information previously gathered, and either way, that's valuable information.

Decades ago, the "expert opinion" was that Japan would not have a specific steel-producing technology for 25 years. An investigator went to Japan and discovered entire production facilities that were already using the technology, right there in plain view! The morals of this story are that expert opinions aren't always right and that you should always investigate for yourself before accepting a commonly held belief.

Picking apart newsletters, speeches, and press releases

You can often find competitor newsletters, speeches, and press releases on their corporate websites and other online sources, but these public releases are always suspect — organizations tend to release only the information they want the public to have. But who knows, you may get lucky. One of the best ways to convert public communication into meaningful intelligence is through comparisons:

1. **Gather information about a competitor from multiple sources (newsletters, press releases, speeches, trade publications, company website, and so on).**

2. **Compare the information to determine whether the message is consistent.**

   If the message from several sources is consistent, you can probably trust that it's accurate. If the message is inconsistent and hints at something that may be of value, additional research can help reveal what's really going on. Perhaps a competitor is engaging in a head fake to conceal its real plans and motives.

3. **Develop themes or patterns from the different sources. They may provide a better understanding of what a competitor really plans on doing.**

Be very skeptical when reading any company's materials. Companies have been known to release false information to throw competitors off track. Always verify information with at least one other reliable source (preferably two or more) before accepting it as fact.

Using trade journals as resources

Trade journals are an excellent resource for developing a feel for the direction your industry is going, keeping tabs on what your competitors are doing or planning to do, and staying informed about new technologies and processes that are being adopted.

A slip of the lip

You may not think that a public speech can contain any useful information, but sometimes people get caught up in the moment and forget what they're *not* supposed to say.

In one case, a U.S. company was trying to determine which of two different technologies a competitor (also in the U.S.) was going to use when entering a new market. The competitor was careful to avoid disclosing information about its plans.

CI uncovered relevant intel, but the sources provided no clear indication of which direction the competitor was leaning. That is, until CI stumbled upon a speech that the competitor's CEO had delivered halfway around the world, in New Zealand of all places! In that speech, the CEO disclosed his true feelings about the two technologies and which one was superior. Obviously, this outlier was the truth, while the other sources were a smoke screen.

To track down trade journals that may be relevant to your organization, check out *The Standard Periodical Directory* (SPD), which lists more than 60,000 magazines, journals, newsletters, newspaper, and directories. The SPD is a standard fixture at most libraries, so head over to your local library and copy the pages that list periodicals for the topic areas relevant to your industry and any related industries.

When you have a list of three or four trade journals, ask the librarian if the library carries them. If not, you can ask the library to consider subscribing or you can subscribe to them yourself. Another option is to track down the trade association's website and see what it has to offer. Many trade associations have online libraries of past issues, white papers, and industry research they've published. In some cases, you don't even have to be a member of the association to access the data.

Get a library card for your community or county library and any other nearby libraries and ask about resources they have available for business research. Many libraries have access to online databases that you can use 24/7 from the comfort of your home to search for newspaper and magazine articles and more.

Joining trade associations for additional data access

You really should join at least one of the main trade associations for your industry to stay in the loop about what's going on. Trade associations often publish their own magazine and newsletter, white papers that focus on industry-specific issues, and reports that provide insights on economic trends. In addition, the association may sponsor events, where you can gather some valuable human intelligence from other association members.

To find associations that are relevant to your industry, flip through the _Encyclopedia of Associations_ (www.gale.com), which comes in a National (U.S.) and International edition, or the _National Trade and Professional Associations Directory_ (www.columbiabooks.com). You may be able to obtain either of these directories through your local library. The American Society of Association Executives also has an online directory that you can search at www.asaecenter.org/Community/Directories/associationsearch.cfm.

Consider expanding your search beyond trade associations that are directly related to your industry. For example, if your business produces rubber tires, you may want to consider joining trade associations for the auto, motorcycle, and bicycle industries. I've recently noticed tire manufacturers breaking into the shoe industry!

Always try to establish a key relationship at a trade association or trade journal — someone who's able and likely to be willing to help you track down the information you need. Spend time cultivating that relationship; it may turn into a key resource for locating experts or white papers.

Rubbing elbows at trade shows

Trade shows can provide interesting opportunities. To begin with, most companies send a senior executive or product expert to meet and greet clients or prospects at such gatherings. Additionally, participating organizations make a lot of information available to everyone who visits their booths. Before attending a trade show or sending other personnel to a trade show, plan ahead:

- ✔ Obtain a map of the exhibitors and target the ones you want to visit. You may even jot down a list of information you want to obtain from each exhibitor.

- ✔ If other people from your company are attending the trade show as well, remind them to gather intel in addition to their other duties.

- ✔ Establish a procedure for gathering all printed materials that are collected by your team.

You can use cameras and cellphones to take pictures or record presentations. If a competitor makes a presentation at a trade show, it's fair game from an intelligence standpoint.

Using trade association connections to get what you need

In conducting research for a global technology firm about the resources of a specific country, I discovered that all the data about the country (amount and location of resources and levels of production) were routinely switched from year to year to hide the facts. Through a trade group, I finally found an expert who had been hired by the country to calculate all the information about this resource. The only problem was, his information was classified, and I didn't have the security clearance that was required.

Thankfully, my client was deeply involved in similar work and was able to gain access to the information through the government.

Although the trade association didn't give me exactly what I needed, it did provide me with the identity of the expert — the source of the information I needed — which was enough, with the help of my client, to track down and eventually obtain the information I needed.

When you return to your home base, take the following steps to convert the information you gathered into something useful:

1. **Have each attendee complete an intelligence summary sheet, as shown in Figure 6-3.**

2. **Organize the intelligence summaries into a single document with a cover page containing the following information:**

   - Names of companies mentioned in the report

   - Key issues or information revealed in the data

   - Analysis of information

   - Summary of intelligence

   - Recommendations for further investigation or action

3. **Input all relevant data into your CI database to inform future analysis.**

Competitive Intelligence Summary Sheet

Area of Study: _____

Classification: Priority recommendation:

Highly sensitive-confidential _____   Urgent _____
Sensitive _____   Important _____
General Information _____   Normal _____

Submitted by: _____ Date:_____

Summary of Information (short summary of information; importance; key issues; and who needs this information):

Analysis and recommendations from CI team:

Summary of attachments/inclusions:

_____ Obtained by: _____

_____ Obtained by: _____

_____ Obtained by: _____

_____ Obtained by: _____

_____ Obtained by: _____

_____ Obtained by: _____

_____ Obtained by: _____

_____ Obtained by: _____

_____ Obtained by: _____

Final report analyzed and compiled by:_____

E -mail:_____   Phone:_____

Figure 6-3:
Intelligence
summary
sheet.

Illustration courtesy of Jim Underwood

Researching Industry White Papers and Reports

White papers provide in-depth information and insight on a wide range of topics and are typically prepared by well-known experts in a given field. Consulting firms, academics, and consultants are just a few examples of people who prepare such documents. You can use white papers to add value to CI in the following ways:

- Obtain depth and breadth of knowledge about a topic you're working on.
- Capture statistics that may be relevant to the intelligence project you're conducting.
- Identify experts who may serve as future resources for your information gathering.
- Develop an understanding of future trends in a specific area.
- Gather information about competitors, emerging technologies, or market shifts.

You're likely to stumble upon white papers as you engage in a basic search around your topic and as you *interrogate the data* — ask questions about the information you have and follow up on references to additional sources. For example, you may find an article on the web that references a certain white paper as one of its sources.

Digging up intel in a white paper

I was once hired by a global technology client in the telecommunications segment to find out whether the existing network structure would be the structure of the future. My client was interested in finding out about any *disruptive technologies* — innovations that would disrupt the entire market.

During my research, I ran across a white paper on the topic of the "evolution of infrastructure networks," which I was fairly certain would contain the answer my client was looking for. The only problem was that the research cost $60,000!

Thankfully, my client had access to the paper; he just didn't realize how comprehensive it was or how accurately it predicted the future of the technology. It involved a topic that had massive implications across the industry. The white paper not only answered the question, but later also helped my client make a critical decision to pursue the disruptive technology discussed in the paper. (The prediction turned out to be accurate.)

Chapter 7

Tapping the Power of Experts and Expert Panels

When you want a job done right, hire an expert. This statement is just as true for CI as it is for anything else. When you need high-quality information and insight, hire an expert (or several experts, to create a panel) to answer questions and provide guidance on the specific issue you're currently researching. Experts in any given field have the breadth and depth of knowledge required to tackle complex issues and provide foresight into where your industry or customers in a certain market segment are headed.

In this chapter, I introduce the concept of pulling experts into your CI circle and interviewing them to extract relevant information and revealing insights. I begin by leading you through the pros and cons of interviewing experts and then explain how to do it effectively — how to choose experts and pick their brains by using questionnaires and through interviews. Finally, I explain how to facilitate expert panels to work toward arriving at an expert consensus on predictions about the future.

The value of third-party opinions can't be overstated. Voluminous amounts of research indicate that most people inside organizations tend to have difficulty accurately perceiving issues that are likely to impact the organization in the future. Third-party opinions can be incredibly helpful in negating that bias.

Reaping the benefits of process-based intel

Regarding the ability to effectively gather and analyze intelligence, many intel professionals have the attitude that "some people have it, and some people don't." My point in this book runs counter to that view: By using specific processes and by studying external views, you can achieve fairly high levels of accuracy about emerging or future events.

In this chapter, I introduce the concepts of interrogating the data and Modified Delphi Panels, which are both processes that anyone can follow to extract information and intelligence from external sources. See-mean-do (SMD) analysis, which I introduce in Chapter 3, is another process that anyone can use to transform information into intelligence. All these processes can go a long way in helping you work with external sources to obtain and effectively analyze CI.

Weighing the Pros and Cons of Expert Interviews

A pilot I know compared flying in fog to flying in a glass of milk, relying solely on his instrument panel for guidance. In some ways, leading an organization into the future with the help of competitive intelligence is just like that. Sometimes the only way to see into the future is through the use of CI. When you add experts and expert panels into the mix, you gain not only insight into the future but also skilled copilots to provide additional information and insight. Your vision is clearer, which helps you make better decisions.

You really don't need to weigh the pros and cons of expert interviews in order to gauge their value and decide whether to conduct such interviews. The value is obvious. However, in the following sections, I point out a few of the primary benefits just in case you need some further convincing . . . or you need to convince a supervisor to free up some money to cover the cost. I also point out a few potential drawbacks so you'll know what you're getting yourself into and can steer clear of the most common pitfalls.

Recognizing the potential benefits

When combined with CI, experts and expert panels offer the following benefits:

- Insight into and understanding of future events, such as consumer trends or adoption of developing technologies
- Corroboration of internal intel — a way to double-check the CI team's conclusions

✔ Additional, unexpected intelligence that often bubbles to the surface during interviews (for example, in the process of polling expert panels, I've found that they're often willing to go far beyond the scope of the information requested and provide rich additional competitor data)

✔ Valuable contact for future intel

The potential benefits of conducting expert interviews (almost) always outweigh the potential drawbacks. You'll walk away from these interviews knowing more than you did prior to conducting them.

Acknowledging possible drawbacks

As with any endeavor, conducting expert interviews carries a few potential drawbacks, including the following:

✔ If you're not careful, you may ask biased questions, essentially destroying the value of any information you collect.

✔ You may tip your hand to one of the experts. In the course of an interview, your questions may reveal too much about your area of interest; for example, if you're considering expansion into a new market, one of the experts you're interviewing may figure out your company's strategy.

✔ Some experts may be stuck in the past or have some other type of bias that influences how they respond. If you're conducting a group interview, a stubborn expert may doom your efforts to bring the group to consensus.

Almost all the potential drawbacks of conducting expert interviews are attributed to the process of preparing for and conducting interviews, which means you can avoid many of these possible downsides through careful planning and preparation, as discussed throughout this chapter.

Predicting technology winners

In the mid-1990s, numerous technologies were vying to become the technology of choice for broadband service, including DSL, ISDN, cable, and broadband over power lines (BPL). Telecommunications companies were investing hundreds of millions of dollars in each technology to hedge their bets on which one would eventually win out.

At the time, one global technology leader was smart enough to spend some money upfront on expert interviews. The result was overwhelming: the technology known as DSL (digital subscriber line) was the predicted winner.

Since then, other technologies have entered the market, including satellite, Wi-Fi, and wireless ISP. The market is still fairly fragmented, but DSL remains a major player.

Conducting the Necessary Prep Work

When working with experts or expert panels, preparation is key to obtaining the information you need. In the following sections, I explain how to gear up for expert interviews by defining your objective, drafting a questionnaire, and lining up experts in your field of interest. I also explain how to lay the groundwork with your chosen experts to avoid any nasty surprises and extract the most relevant and honest responses.

Don't ad lib. You may need to improvise during an interview, but start with a set of questions that follow a plan of attack. Otherwise, you're unlikely to obtain the information you need.

Identifying your objective

The first step in preparing for interviews is to define your objective. What do you seek to learn from the interviews? Do you have a specific question to answer? Are you wondering about the fate of a certain technology? Do you need to know how different organizations are responding to changes in legislation or regulations?

Although identifying your objective certainly sounds easy enough, it's really not. For example, suppose you want to find out about the future of a technology called WiMax, which is short for Worldwide Interoperability for Microwave Access. A quick bit of research reveals that WiMax was originally hyped as Wi-Fi on steroids and has been adopted by some municipalities for its broadband Internet capabilities. But if you dig deeper, you're likely to discover that WiMax is actually an alternative to the traditional cellphone protocol Long Term Evolution (LTE) and that WiMax requires fewer cell towers than LTE.

Now your objective may not seem as clear as simply finding out more about WiMax. Your objective is likely to take on a more narrow focus, prompting the following core questions:

- Which protocol is superior in terms of performance and cost?
- Is the cellphone industry likely to transition to WiMax in the future, and if so, when?
- How likely is the emergence of more mobile Internet devices to affect which protocol becomes the future standard?
- Should my company work toward producing devices that support both technologies?

Doing your homework

After you define your objective, you need to immerse yourself in the topic of interest. Skilled interviewers always know something about the topic of discussion so they can ask intelligent questions and respond competently to the answers they receive. Study your target objective carefully, as follows:

- ✔ Do some general research to get up to speed on the topic.

- ✔ Note the best data resources for information in this particular area of interest. As you do your research, pay attention to which source is referred to most frequently as authoritative.

- ✔ As you conduct your initial research, jot down the names of people who seem to be recognized as experts in the field so you have some leads on people to interview.

- ✔ Gather as many articles and other information about the topic as possible and read the articles carefully, highlighting key points and taking notes to improve retention.

- ✔ Try to spot current trends according to the available resources.

- ✔ Create a number of hypotheses about the future of any technologies or other topics you're researching. Your predictions don't need to be accurate, but creating them gives you something to challenge as you formulate questions and conduct interviews. Note any competing theories, which can be used in questioning experts to draw out more information.

With a solid base level of knowledge, you're much more capable of selecting the right experts and much more adept at developing questions to elicit the information you need and engaging in intelligent discussions with the experts.

Building an effective questionnaire

A questionnaire to generate feedback is crucial to obtaining the information you need. Ask the right questions in the right way, and you're likely to receive high-quality information from experts you send it to. Ask the wrong questions or use ambiguous wording, and the results are likely to fall short of the goal.

In the following sections, I describe the different question-and-answer formats, explain how to choose the right one, and provide some guidance on composing questions.

Choosing the right Q&A format

When developing a questionnaire, you have several Q&A formats from which to choose:

✔ **Likert scale questions:** A Likert scale involves using an odd number of responses (5, 7, and 9 are most typical); for example:

In your opinion, how successful would you expect a chocoholic to be if promoted to management?

> A. *Highly successful*
>
> B. *Very successful*
>
> C. *Could go either way*
>
> D. *Probably not successful*
>
> E. *Definitely not successful*

Use the Likert scale whenever possible. If properly designed, it covers the entire range of possible responses and is very useful when employing some form of the Delphi Method. (I introduce you to the Delphi Method in the later section "Improving Predictive Accuracy with Delphi Panels.")

✔ **Forced response questions:** A forced response question uses a scale that makes the interviewee indicate a preference or decision. Here's an example:

What is your view of hiring people who are chocoholics (meaning they're addicted to chocolate)?

> A. *I strongly recommend hiring them.*
>
> B. *I moderately recommend hiring them.*
>
> C. *I somewhat oppose hiring them.*
>
> D. *I strongly oppose hiring them.*

When composing forced-response questions, always include an even number of answer choices to discourage people from playing it safe and choosing the middle answer or the "no opinion" response. Many people opt for the least definitive, most noncommittal response — typically 3 or C when given five choices. If you want more honest answers to a question, providing an even number of choices forces them to commit to one side or the other of an issue.

Obtaining honest feedback on emotional or sensitive issues is often difficult because people want to avoid expressing their true opinion on a topic. I advise using forced-response questions whenever the potential for respondent bias is high.

✔ **Open-ended questions:** If you're working with one expert or a small panel of experts, consider using open-ended questions, such as, "In your opinion, what is the future of WiMax?" Open-ended questions are often the easiest to compose, so if you're facing a time crunch, these questions can really come in handy.

Open-ended questions are most suitable when you want the respondent to express an expert opinion and lead you to new areas of knowledge. Just be prepared to ask follow-up questions. Think of your questionnaire as a conversation starter. After you've had time to review each expert's answers, the next step is to discuss their answers with them in person (or via videoconferencing) so you can really go in-depth with them. Your follow-up, face-to-face discussions are often the most valuable part of the information gathering process. See "Interviewing the Experts," later in this chapter, for details.

✔ **Closed questions:** As opposed to open-ended questions, closed questions provide a limited number of choices — usually yes or no or true or false. You may include a third option, such as "Don't know," to let the interviewee opt out.

Closed questions are useful if you want to know someone's opinion within the constraints of two or three choices.

✔ **Multiple-choice questions:** This type of question enables you to give an interviewee several answer options within a given range. Most pollsters use multiple-choice questions that allow for answers from one extreme to the other. However, they can also be used to compare, say, different brands. Here's an example:

Which of the following best describes your view of the future of WiMax?

   A. It will be the technology of the future.

   B. It will continue to have moderate success.

   C. Its future looks marginal.

   D. It will continue to decline.

   E. It's a long-term loser; no future.

Use multiple-choice questions to poll larger groups of experts.

Composing questions

Writing questions that elicit the most accurate information and insight is more art than science, but I can offer you some guidelines to get you started:

✔ **Be clear and concise.** Write your questions as terse statements and then convert the statements to questions. Wordy questions are likely to either bore or confuse respondents, neither of which is good.

✔ **Use concrete language and answer choices.** For example, asking someone if she would recommend a certain technology is more likely to elicit an honest response than if you ask whether the person likes the technology.

Avoid using vague words, such as *effective, efficient,* or *state of the art,* or introducing ambiguous concepts.

✔ **Cover all choices.** When presenting a list of choices, make sure you cover all options; otherwise, you're likely to either receive some unanswered questions or have people choose what they think is the closest match.

✔ **Avoid any biased words or phrases.** You don't want to disclose any information that may reveal your opinion about an issue in question. For example, instead of asking if the respondent supports increased government regulation in the industry (a question that's likely to elicit a negative response), ask what the person thinks would be the likely result if a certain regulation were implemented. Always try your best to eliminate bias from questions and the way you ask them.

✔ **Mix broader questions with those that are more specific.** This helps to obfuscate (to the respondent) the true nature of your line of inquiry. Here's an example of two questions that would work well together because they prevent the expert from guessing why you're asking these questions:

- What are the pros and cons of XYZ technology?
- Which company is leading the pack in XYZ technology?

Try to hide the most significant questions in the midst of a more mundane series of questions so the person completing the questionnaire is more relaxed and open when encountering the big questions.

✔ **Arrange questions logically.** You can arrange questions chronologically, from least to most complex (or vice versa), from less to more sensitive, from general to specific, and so on. Consider grouping related questions to prevent respondents from having to shift from one topic to another.

Contacting the Experts on Your List

Assuming you did your homework, as explained previously in this chapter (see "Doing your homework"), you should have a fairly comprehensive list of experts who have written articles or been quoted related to your target area of investigation. Based on that list, you're nearly ready to begin creating your panel of experts.

Before you contact any candidates on your list, though, be prepared to do the following:

- ✔ Pay leading experts at least their hourly rate. Paying double their hourly rate is good practice to ensure that you get the right people and they feel motivated to provide quality input.

- ✔ Inform the experts of how much time you estimate will be involved in this particular project and the logistics of how the interview(s) will be conducted. Coordinate with their schedules.

- ✔ Sign a mutual confidentiality agreement with each expert stating that you won't reveal the expert by name as a resource and the expert won't disclose anything about your organization or the nature of the questionnaire. Most experts won't open up if they think they'll be identified publicly as the source of whatever they choose to share.

When you have a list of experts in hand, call each expert on your list to find out whether the person is willing and able to participate. This initial conversation shouldn't take longer than ten minutes. Be sure to get answers to the following questions:

- ✔ Are you willing to be considered as a member of an expert panel in [your field of expertise]? Explain the target area of research and ask the expert to explain whether he believes he's qualified to participate in this study.

- ✔ Do you believe that your knowledge enables you to provide insight into both present and future issues in [your field of expertise]?

- ✔ Are you willing to be interviewed over the phone or via Skype as part of this project?

- ✔ Does your schedule permit you to be able to spend the time (always by appointment) to complete this project? (Be prepared to delineate the time commitment you're expecting.)

- ✔ What's your hourly rate?

Before hanging up, address a few other necessities, including the following:

- ✔ Request the person's résumé.

- ✔ Get the person's e-mail address or other contact information.

- ✔ Explain that you'll send a questionnaire but that you want to follow up with an interview to find out more about the response to each question.

- ✔ Schedule a time for a follow-up call. Set a date far enough in advance for the person to complete the questionnaire and for you to review the responses along with the person's résumé and other information you have.

✔ Finalize your agreement so you at least have a verbal commitment regarding expectations, payment, and terms.

Immediately after you hang up, e-mail the person a summary of the key points you discussed along with your contact information.

As you contact experts, don't let them in on the names of the other experts you contacted. You usually want to keep everyone's identity confidential and speak with one person at a time.

Then again, sometimes you may want to engage with several experts at the same time (a panel, which is similar to a focus group). On Skype, for example, you can conduct a group call with up to 24 other people. Videoconferencing works well, because participants don't feel threatened by the presence of others. Videoconferencing can lead to the discovery of some really good stuff as participants try to demonstrate their knowledge and expertise to one another.

Interviewing the Experts

After you lay the groundwork for your interviews, you're ready to get started. How you conduct your interviews is up to you. You may simply send each expert a questionnaire, or you may choose to do live interviews with each expert over the phone or by using some sort of videoconferencing technology, such as Skype. The process I usually follow goes like this:

1. Send the questionnaire to each expert with instructions to complete the questionnaire and return it by such and such a date.

2. Collect the questionnaires by the designated due date.

3. Review the responses and conduct a Skype interview to follow up with each expert and flesh out their responses to the questions.

Note: If you feel like trying your hand at a different interview approach, check out the later section "Improving Predictive Accuracy with Delphi Panels."

As you conduct your follow-up interviews, take the opportunity to triangulate prior findings, discover new information, and dig up hidden treasure, as explained in the following sections.

Easing into your follow-up interview in order to discover hidden treasure

Whenever you're conducting an interview in person, over the phone, or via videoconferencing, you don't exactly want to grill the expert as though you're conducting an interrogation. Just the opposite. Ease into the conversation. Spend the first part of the interview getting the expert to relax. (I generally spend about 20 percent of the interview getting the expert to relax, but I've spent as much as 80 percent of an interview for this purpose.) Don't start your interview until the person's demeanor noticeably shifts to calm and comfortable. In this state of relative relaxation, the expert is much more likely to disclose hidden treasures. Here's how it works:

1. **Begin your interview with a focus on the person you're interviewing by recognizing his accomplishments, or in some other way communicating that you value him as a person.**

   A great way to start an interview is to remember a concept I call _significance_. Everybody has the desire to be recognized, appreciated, and valued. The significance step is the most important step in any sales call, and it's equally important when interviewing an expert. Here are some sample questions you might ask:

   • Do you mind summarizing your experience for me?

   • How did you manage to develop expertise in this particular area?

   • What's your major area of interest (or research) in this area?

2. **As the conversation progresses, occasionally take a moment to be personal in a positive way.**

   For example, if the expert's insight revealed something you didn't know, tell him how important that was to you. You may say something like, "That's admirable. It's clear that you really do have leading edge knowledge in this field."

   Be genuine in your praise and appreciation. People can usually tell when you're just trying to butter them up.

3. **Keep the conversation light until you notice it becoming more conversational and relaxed.**

   You often find that the person has transitioned from being an expert into someone who has a real desire to help you because he senses that you value what he has to offer.

4. **Crank up the intensity of your questions by asking more follow-up questions and perhaps even shifting the direction of your discussion if something of value unexpectedly arises.**

   Generally, the respondent starts opening up and telling you additional things about your research area. In some cases, the topics may be related to areas you hadn't considered. That's how you discover hidden treasure.

Comparing different assessments of the future

During the course of your research and interviews, you develop three different assessments of what's likely to happen in the future:

- ✔ Internal management's view of the future issues, which is usually the least accurate. (For more about investigating internal sources of intel, see Chapter 5.)

- ✔ The data-mined view of the future based on the research you performed prior to interviewing the experts, which is usually more accurate.

- ✔ The experts' view of the future, which is usually the most accurate.

If the three views align, you can be fairly confident that whatever conclusion you arrive at is probably correct. When the different views don't align, the disagreement may reveal a golden opportunity — an opportunity that even the experts may not recognize. Such disagreements are strong signals that you need to dig deeper, perhaps with additional research or by returning to the experts to ask follow-up questions. In trying to resolve different views, you often discover the most important information.

How well you deal with any differences between the three views can determine the future of your company. This is especially true if the opinion of internal management is drastically different from reality (the data-mined view and what the experts think).

Companies don't fail due to lack of access to accurate information about the future. They fail when they don't strategically align their organization with future reality.

Discovering new information

One of the real opportunities from expert interviews comes when you expand the scope of questionnaires by asking follow-up questions. When I call an expert and review her responses with her, I always ask her why she believes specific things about the future. If you're good at using this technique (deep diving with your follow-up questions), you can often discover a treasure trove of new information.

Skilled intel people practice a strategy called *interrogating the data,* which consists of asking questions to find out the "why" behind something they already know. For example, suppose you find out (from publicly disclosed financial statements) that a competitor has increased its research budget. That information is of little or no use until you interrogate the data to determine its significance, if any. You can interrogate the data by asking your experts follow-up questions or by seeking answers to the following questions, using your own research:

1. What does this change mean?

2. What do the company's press releases reveal about their future product initiatives?

3. Do the company's annual reports leave any clues about new products or directions?

4. Has the CEO revealed anything relevant in recent speeches or interviews?

5. What about the company's 8K filing (its public disclosure of material changes at a company)? Has the company made any significant changes in key personnel?

Interrogating data helps you dig down to the point at which you can begin to really understand its meaning.

Improving Predictive Accuracy with Delphi Panels

A number of years ago, two researchers at The Rand Corporation developed a technique called the *Delphi method* to help achieve higher accuracy in predicting futures that involve high levels of ambiguity. Nobody really likes to define the Delphi method because it exists in numerous forms, but the process usually involves a moderator (you, for example) through whom a panel of experts communicates.

When conducting Delphi panels, don't let the experts communicate directly with one another. By acting as the gatekeeper, you can protect the anonymity of participants and prevent any of the more assertive participants from swaying the group's opinion. After completing separate interviews for the Delphi panel, you may want to add a group interview. By introducing group dynamics, you can often develop a deeper understanding of the issues and maybe even gain a surprise benefit from the impromptu nature of the conversation.

The process goes something like this:

1. **Send a questionnaire about a future issue (or issues) to six or so experts and collect feedback from all participants.**

   Don't introduce your own opinions or bias into the questionnaire. See the earlier section "Building an effective questionnaire" for details on how to avoid introducing bias into questions.

2. **Compile a summary of the responses that indicates areas of agreement and disagreement, making sure not to disclose anyone's identity.**

3. **Communicate your findings to all the experts and request additional feedback.**

   Explore disagreements among the experts; don't ignore them. If you dismiss the opinions of certain experts, they're likely to drop out prior to completing the process.

4. **Repeat Steps 2 and 3 to move the experts closer and closer to consensus until you finally achieve general agreement about the future issue(s) in question.**

   Step 4 has a lot of variations. Just keep in mind the goal: to facilitate movement to consensus about the future issue(s).

As most people find who work with the Delphi method, getting a group of experts to move toward agreement about an issue is very challenging. In some cases, the problem can be bias. In others, lack of knowledge among one or more participants may play a role. Sometimes experts are knowledgeable in current issues but uninformed about future developments in their field. The question is: How do you deal with that?

My solution has resulted in what I call *modified Delphi panels*. Here's what you do:

1. **Overpopulate your group of experts.**

   Instead of the traditional 6 experts that many people use, I begin with 10 to 12.

2. **Conduct separate interviews with all the experts on your panel via questionnaires, the telephone, or videoconferencing.**

3. **Evaluate the experts' responses.**

   As you look over the responses, you'll find that certain experts reveal themselves as the outliers — they don't seem to understand the reality of a specific issue, they have a strong bias, or they're simply unqualified to answer questions in a specific area.

4. **Eliminate the biased or unqualified experts from your final consideration.**

5. **Summarize the responses you received based on feedback from the experts who passed your competency evaluation.**

Modified Delphi panels work. Hundreds of studies and postmortems (evaluations done years after the work was completed) reveal that the approach is incredibly accurate on a consistent basis.

If you're interested in finding out more about the Delphi method, I suggest that you read *The Delphi Method: Techniques and Applications,* edited by Harold A. Linstone and Murray Turoff. You can download a free copy of the book as a PDF at http://is.njit.edu/pubs/delphibook.

Chapter 8

Tuning In to the Silent Conversation with Intuitive Listening

A good chunk of your research is likely to consist of audio/visual content — what people in your organization tell you, what you hear from the experts you interview, what you observe in focus groups, and what you hear and see when you're watching someone deliver a speech or presentation. Audio/visual content is becoming more and more prevalent through technology. You can now interview experts at remote locations via Skype, engage in videoconferencing on Google+, watch a speech delivered by a corporate executive in Prague from your office in Los Angeles through video streaming, or watch it a couple minutes later when it's posted on YouTube. At the heart of this newfound gold mine of information is *the silent conversation* — the unspoken message.

Regardless of whether you're talking to someone in person, over the phone, or via Skype, or whether you're watching a video of a speech or presentation online, you need to pay attention to not only what the person says but also how he says it. Certainly, words convey the bulk of the message, but posture, gestures, intonation, speech patterns, eye movements, and what the person *didn't* say influence the relevance and validity of the message and what it really means. In this chapter, I reveal the skills and techniques you must develop in order to become an intuitive listener, tune in to the silent conversation, and figure out the truth behind what people say.

Presenting Your Road Map to the Silent Conversation

One of the keys for success in CI is to be able to sense when anyone — a co-worker, a consultant, a competitor, or anyone else who's providing you with information — engages in an attempt to mislead you. Internally, politics can drive the use of misinformation for the purpose of personal gain. Even the experts you hire may be conflicted over providing you with important information. When you become skilled at listening to the silent conversation, your ability to gather and evaluate intel improves significantly.

Figure 8-1 gives you a bird's-eye view of what listening to the silent conversation involves. The rest of this chapter covers each component in greater detail.

Analyzing the silent conversation provides you with input about the person and the message that person is delivering. The analysis is never the final answer, but it's usually fairly accurate in alerting you to areas of possible misrepresentation.

Grasping the Real Conversation through Visual and Auditory Clues

You're probably pretty good at picking up on sarcasm, figuring out when someone's pulling your leg, or telling when a bad liar fibs. That's because human beings have the ability to accurately assess a situation and the true meaning of what's being said by paying attention to and synthesizing all the information being conveyed in a conversation.

Sure, some people are better at it than others, but interpreting clues isn't some sixth sense that only certain people are born with. It's a skill that you can learn by trusting less in the words themselves and paying more attention to what you see and a person's tone of voice and demeanor. In the following sections, I present a few exercises to help you develop your intuitive listening skills.

Don't ignore that funny feeling inside. Sometimes your intuition encourages you to question what you're hearing. Remember, intuitive insights tend to be a combination of all your listening skills, even if you're not consciously aware that something's not right. Always note when something just doesn't feel right and investigate a bit further. It may turn out to be nothing, but sometimes it can be quite revealing.

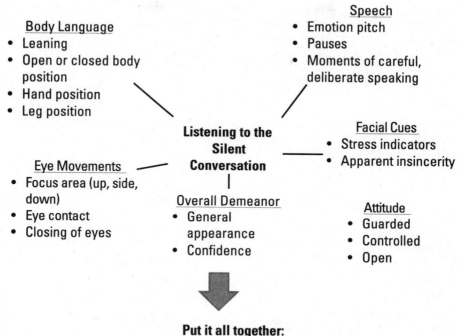

Body Language
- Leaning
- Open or closed body position
- Hand position
- Leg position

Speech
- Emotion pitch
- Pauses
- Moments of careful, deliberate speaking

Listening to the Silent Conversation

Facial Cues
- Stress indicators
- Apparent insincerity

Eye Movements
- Focus area (up, side, down)
- Eye contact
- Closing of eyes

Overall Demeanor
- General appearance
- Confidence

Attitude
- Guarded
- Controlled
- Open

Put it all together:
- What is your overall observation of the individual?
- Do the spoken words agree with the unspoken messages?
- Are any of your alarms going off?

Illustration by Wiley, Composition Services Graphics

Figure 8-1:
Listening to the silent conversation.

Watching conversations

One of the best ways to hone your intuitive listening skills is to watch conversations and ignore what the people are actually saying. Here's an exercise in conversation watching:

1. **Go to a public place, such as a café or coffee shop, with a friend.**

2. **Have a regular conversation with your friend, but while doing that, pick out two or three people near you who are engaged in conversation.**

3. **Without letting your friend know what you're doing, observe the other conversation.**

   - Use your peripheral vision only. Don't look at the other group or give your friend any indication that you're observing another conversation.

- Don't listen to the words. You can listen to each speaker's tone of voice, speech patterns, volume, laughter, sobs, or whatever, but ignore the words.

4. **Try to figure out what the conversation is about.**

- Is one of the parties upset?

- Is one of the parties being less than honest with the other?

- Is one of the parties more engaged, based on her body language?

- Is one of the parties trying to persuade the other?

Even though you're not following the words that each person is saying, you should begin to understand a great deal about what the conversation is about and how the people in the conversation feel about one another.

Most people who perform this exercise come away from it with an entirely new perspective on listening. What they discover, more often than not, is that the silent conversation conveys more truth than do the words. In other words, nonverbal communication conveys the real message.

Trusting your instincts when your alarms go off

Chances are good that at some time in your life, you ignored your instincts and lived to regret it. Maybe you trusted someone you had an uneasy feeling about or wandered into an unsafe neighborhood. Perhaps you received an e-mail message with a link that looked a little suspicious but you clicked it anyway and passed along sensitive information.

Whatever the case, to become skilled at intuitive listening, you need to start trusting your instincts a little more and trusting what other people tell you a lot less. Everyone has internal alarms that sound a warning when a situation doesn't seem quite right. Pay attention when those alarms sound.

The human system is an incredible combination of senses and intellect that warn of danger even before you're consciously aware of it. Finding how to listen to your internal alarms makes you more adept at figuring out the truth about others based on their unspoken communication.

To become more sensitive to your internal alarm system and start trusting it more, perform at least a couple of these exercises:

- ✔ **Think back to a situation in which you had an uneasy feeling about a person and ignored it, resulting in a bad decision on your part.**

✓ **Try to remember a conversation you had with someone who was saying all the right things but left you with a negative but uncertain feeling.** Did you respond with trust or seek out more information to confirm or refute your reservations? How did that turn out?

✓ **Think back to a time when you had an intuitive feeling about a situation that didn't seem quite right and discovered later that you should have listened to that intuition.**

✓ **Try to remember a conversation in which you had the impression that the person you were talking to didn't believe what he was saying and you later discovered that what he said wasn't true.** Many experienced bankers could tell you that they had a funny feeling inside when they approved a bad loan, and most of them wish they had paid more attention to that funny feeling.

It's okay to trust people, but follow Ronald Reagan's advice: "Trust but verify." If you have a feeling that what someone is saying isn't true, ask questions to test whether what the person is saying remains consistent or find other sources to confirm or refute what the person told you.

Spotting a fake competitor initiative

Competitors may try to fool you into making a mistake, especially if they know that you practice competitive intelligence and keep an eye on them. For example, suppose your company is trying to choose between two competing technologies. Both are expensive from a research and development standpoint, and you really want to make sure that you hedge your bet correctly. All of a sudden, you begin to pick up intelligence that your largest competitor is going to go with technology B. Their sales people begin to let it slip, and even their CEO mentions the supposed superiority of technology B in a speech.

To evaluate this supposed leak of information, or something similar, here's what you do:

1. **Assume they're lying.**

   This protects you at least until you can obtain confirmation that they're telling the truth.

2. **Investigate the frequency of leaks.**

   If you get several leaks over a short period of time, someone is probably orchestrating the leaks.

3. **If you have a video of a corporate official delivering one of the supposed leaks, watch it, paying close attention to messages from the silent conversation.**

Here are some clues to watch for:

- **Eye movements:** Did she look up and to the right or left? Did she look down when she first talked about Technology B?

- **Body position:** Did she lean forward when she talked about the new technology?

- **Word patterns:** Did she pause just before she started talking about technology B? Was her speech pattern more controlled and deliberate when she talked about technology B?

- **Facial expressions:** Did her facial expression change when she got to the point in the speech where she talked about technology B?

- **Openness:** Did her arms or hands indicate a closed or open position?

- **Sitting posture:** If she was sitting down, were her shoulders slumped slightly forward and was her overall posture open or closed? Was her body position assertive (leaning forward) or more negative (leaning back)?

In the next section, I explain how to interpret these and other nonverbal clues.

4. **Describe what you felt as you watched the video.**

   Can you honestly say that the person is being truthful and transparent?

Through this verification process, you arrive at one of two conclusions: that the speaker was being truthful *or* that the supposed leak was a smoke screen orchestrated to deceive. Chances are pretty good that whichever conclusion you reach, you have an 80 percent chance of being right, as long as you completed the verification process.

Trust your spidey senses

Spiderman relies on his spidey senses to tell him when trouble is brewing. Human beings don't have spider senses, but they can synthesize information and engage their rational minds to spot trouble. Consider the story of a police officer responding to a citizen's call about two people sitting in a car outside her house. This type of call was routine for the officer and his partner, but both men were on high alert before they ever got out of their car. Their instincts told them that something was wrong.

As the policeman stood there talking to one of the individuals in the car, all he knew was that

the person was a potentially serious problem. He noticed the man's eyes cut to the right, obviously trying to figure out where he was going to run. This visual signal was an additional alert to the officer who, after getting the man in handcuffs, discovered that the man was a felon with multiple warrants out for his arrest.

Moral of the story? Your intuition can tell you a lot, but you have to listen to it and trust it over the voices in your head that try to convince you to be more trusting of others.

Getting a Read on Body Language and Other Nonverbal Cues

Body language is one of the best resources you have to listen in to the silent conversation and figure out what a person is really saying. While speaking, people usually send signals indicating whether they're being open and transparent or closed off and guarded in their remarks. You can usually tell by interrogating the data, as I explain in Chapter 7, or in this case, interrogating the target — your observations of the person's posture and physical movements.

Reading nonverbal messaging isn't an exact science. Rather, it's about patterns. Seek patterns of behavior that seem to occur on a consistent basis and behaviors that run counter to those patterns. Never base your judgment on a single indicator.

In the following sections, I describe certain postures and physical movements and explain how to interpret them.

Don't focus on only one or two aspects of body language; pay attention to the composite of all aspects of the message — verbal and nonverbal. Observe patterns of behavior along with parallel behaviors. The accuracy of your interpretation hinges on your ability to engage your intuition, all your senses, and your intellect. Violating this rule often leads to incorrect conclusions.

Evaluating eye movements

You probably can't tell just by gazing into someone's eyes whether the person is honest or dishonest, but if you know how to interpret eye movement, you can tell whether a person is being creative or deceptive, feigning confidence, and so on. Be aware, though, that each individual has different places that their eyes go during a conversation. Interpreting eye movement isn't as simple as thinking that someone's lying if he looks up and to the left. For one person, up and left may indicate lying, but for another, it may simply indicate that the person is trying to formulate an accurate response. As you observe an individual, study where her eyes normally go after you ask her a question. Try to establish a baseline for the individual you're watching — where the person's eyes typically go in response to certain questions or topics — so you can tell when eye movements deviate from the baseline.

For every individual you observe, try to figure out which direction is associated with each of the following spaces:

✔ **The creative space:** Sometimes, a person who wants to make sure that her answer is correct looks up and to the right or to the left.

- **The deceptive space:** In most cases, but not always, a person's deceptive space is the mirror side of their creative space. That is, if their creative space is up and to the left, then their deceptive space is up and to the right.

- **The liar, liar, pants on fire space:** Many people look down when they're telling a lie, to avoid eye contact altogether. This type of deception is usually accompanied by other clues, such as slumping shoulders.

- **The fake confident look:** Some people try to fool you into thinking they're telling the truth by looking you straight in the eye. Be especially aware of accompanying behaviors, such as body position, to figure out if they're being truthful or deceptive.

- **Closed eyes:** When someone closes his eyes, ask yourself why. People rarely close their eyes purposefully. He may just need to rest his eyes for a moment, or he may be hiding something he doesn't want you to see, such as a lie. Be careful about reading too much into closed eyes, but take note of anything other than a blink.

Unmasking facial expressions

Most people can easily tell when someone is happy, sad, disinterested, worried, surprised, or confident just by looking at the person's face. Then again, some people can easily put on a brave face when they're terrified, appear confident when they're worried or happy when they're sad, or seem angry even when they don't really care. In short, a certain facial expression may be nothing more than a mask a person puts on to influence your opinion of him or her.

You need to be able to unmask facial expressions by cross-checking what a person's facial expression conveys against what you're picking up from other nonverbal signals and by being aware of the following caveats:

- **Smiles can be deceiving.** Some people smile at everyone, which could mean that the person is warm and friendly or that he's trying to hide his true motives. Usually, you can safely assume that a smile is a gesture of sincere joy and receptiveness, but if the smile conflicts with other nonverbal signals, it may be a facade. To gather additional clues, watch how the person interacts with others and whether the interactions seem sincere. If the person is smiling but appears impatient or hostile, something's hiding behind that smile.

- **A facial expression may change when you look away.** Try to catch a glimpse of the person's face when she thinks you're not looking. If her smile morphs into a sad or angry expression, you may want to question her sincerity in dealing with you.

In the earlier section "Watching conversations," I encourage you to practice intuitive listening in a café or other social setting. Try the same exercise, but this time try to read the conversants' facial expressions without them noticing and without actually listening to the conversation. What do their facial expressions tell you about what they're saying and how each person feels?

Tracking speech patterns

As a person is speaking, try to tune in to speech patterns — anything about the person's oral communication style that's distinctive. For example, pedantic know-it-alls lecture listeners and don't give them a chance to speak. Others speak very deliberately and slowly, taking time to carefully choose the words they use. Changes in speech patterns can also help you interpret the overall meaning and gauge the truth of what someone is telling you.

As you listen, tune in to speech patterns and remain sensitive to the following indicators:

- **Nonstop talking:** People who don't give others the opportunity to get a word in edgewise are trying to control the conversation. You often see this in debates and news interviews. Control behaviors often accompany a lack of honesty.

- **Pauses:** Pauses are difficult to interpret, because sometimes you can't tell whether the person is pausing to construct an inauthentic answer or to consider the question and carefully word an accurate response. After several responses to different questions, you can begin to identify the significance of each pause.

- **Redirection:** When someone doesn't want to answer a question or discuss a particular topic, she's likely to reinterpret the question and provide a response that really doesn't answer it or that changes the subject. Redirection can sometimes be subtle, so listen carefully and constantly evaluate responses for relevance.

- **Emotional pitch:** Changes in emotional pitch can tell you what a person is enthusiastic about, strongly believes in or against, feels defensive or confident about, and so on. Listen to the emotion behind the words. (For more about this, see the later section "Tuning in to emotional pitch.")

- **Rehearsed responses:** A rehearsed response sounds like canned laughter. It's robotic. Regardless of what the subject is, you need to know that a rehearsed response is something of high importance to the speaker. When you hear a rehearsed response, dig deeper to find out what the person really thinks or what's really going on.

✔ **Change in speech pattern:** A change in the way someone speaks may indicate that she is genuinely more or less enthusiastic about something or nervous about something. If the person starts talking faster and seems more animated about one technology than another, for example, she probably prefers that technology to others under consideration.

Always match speech patterns with other messaging indicators, such as eye movement.

Tuning in to emotional pitch

Some people have little emotion in their voice. They speak in a relative monotone, whether they just won the lottery or their house is burning down. The rest of us usually spice up our speech with emotion to help convey some feeling behind the message. When you're listening to someone speak, try to tune in to the underlying emotion. Here are a couple things to listen for:

✔ **Elevated level of emotion:** An elevated level of emotion may convey excitement, disappointment, anger, or enthusiasm.

Beware of feigned emotion. Elevated emotion can be used as a way of covering up how someone really feels.

✔ **Highly controlled voice:** In some cases, people try to purposefully lower their voice so they appear to be very calm and controlled. This is tough to maintain, so asking a series of questions that dig deeper into an issue can usually cause the controlled voice to crack under pressure.

Although emotional pitch may not convey a whole lot of meaning definitively, it's a good tool to use for identifying topics that call for further interrogation. Strong emotions are signals that you need to dig deeper to figure out the issues at the root of those emotions.

Evaluating hand and arm positions and motions

The eyes may be the windows to a person's soul, but the hands and arms also tell you a lot about what a person is really thinking. You can probably remember a conversation with someone who appeared calm and honest while at the same time wringing his hands. This type of behavior can indicate that the individual is highly stressed over the conversation. As you observe someone speak, try to pick up on what their hands and arms are telling you. What you see is often what it means, so keep the following details in mind:

- Open hands with palms showing usually means that the person is being open and honest.

- Watch the person's arms, too. Open arms typically indicate openness. If the arms are folded, however, the person is probably feeling defensive (or a little chilly).

- Watch for indicators of stress, such as clenched fists or the tightening of muscles that may indicate that the person is uncomfortable or feeling stressed by the topic of conversation.

- Take note when a person turns her palms down. If the conversation progresses in a way that makes the person feel more comfortable, she may turn one or both palms up.

When meeting a person, consider shaking hands to gather insight into the individual. You may be able to size up a person's attitude just by the way he shakes your hand:

- **Limp fish:** A limp handshake often indicates that the person isn't interested in engaging with you. They may feel uncomfortable and want to flee the scene as quickly as possible.

- **Firm:** A reasonably firm (but not painful) handshake can be an indicator of confidence and a desire to engage.

- **Painful:** Some people shake hands as though they're arm wrestling — to demonstrate their superiority. More often than not, a painful handshake is a contrived behavior, a symptom of a control freak or someone lacking in confidence trying to overcompensate. It often indicates a lack of integrity and insecurity or ego in excess.

Who initiates the handshake may also carry some significance. In most cultures, the person of higher standing typically initiates the handshake. If the individuals are on a level playing field, then the one who initiates the handshake is usually the more confident of the two.

Also take note of the duration of the handshake. Some people never seem to know when to let go. When someone extends a handshake beyond a normal, casual moment, you probably should take that as an indicator that they have a predisposition toward control behaviors. Similar to when someone gets too close (in your bubble zone), people who are overly controlling with a handshake alert you to a number of issues that relate to control behaviors, which often indicate a lack of honesty or a need to manipulate others. Always keep your mental radar trained on signs of control. Some people control by talking, others by dodging or procrastinating, and still others by being aggressive.

Always take cultural differences into account when evaluating any nonverbal communication. For example, in some cultures, holding out a hand that is supported at the wrist by the other hand is a sign of respect.

Reading leg positions and movement

Some leg positions and movements are no-brainers. If somebody's running away from you, that's a pretty good sign that the person wants to avoid you. If they're running toward you, they're about to embrace or attack you, depending on their facial expression.

When a person is sitting down, however, leg positions are more subtle indicators of how they truly feel. First, try to establish a baseline of how the person usually sits by noting how the person is sitting — legs crossed or not, both feet planted legs open, and so on. During the conversation, note any changes in leg position. Here are a few leg positions and movements that may convey a person's unspoken attitude:

- Crossed legs may indicate a defensive posture. The person feels distant or threatened.

- Moving the legs so that they're pointing away from you but are still close together may signal negativity or a lack of engagement.

- Sitting with legs close together and hands clasped together may indicate an effort to create a false impression; for example, trying to appear more contrite and sincere than the person really is.

Knowing what people are telling you when they lean

Posture sends a message. Whether a person is leaning forward or back, literally talking down to you, or rigid as a plank, their posture tells you something about their character and how they feel about you and whatever they happen to be saying. Run through this checklist when observing a person's posture:

- Begin by considering your first impression of the person's demeanor, which takes into account other aspects of their behavior.

- Notice whether the person seems to be leaning back, which indicates a lack of engagement or disinterest in the topic of discussion.

- Note whether the person seems to be leaning forward, which may indicate interest in the topic or aggressiveness.

- Look for changes in body position, which can often mean a shift in attitude. For example, when a person begins to lean forward during a conversation, it usually indicates that they're becoming more interested or committed to what's unfolding.

- Always put your analysis into context by considering everything you see and hear. For example, don't interpret posture out of context.

To become more sensitive to posture and what it means, read through the following scenarios. Each scenario describes a different posture and is followed by a brief analysis of what it might mean.

Scenario: Susan is highly motivated and driven. As you work with her over a period of months, you notice that when she answers questions about projects she's working on, she seems to sit up with her back very straight. Her demeanor is positive, but what does it mean when she straightens up in her chair?

Analysis: Susan seems like a bit of a perfectionist. Note that she responds physically to issues that relate to her personal image and job performance. The change in posture may mean that Susan wants to make sure that she's accurate in everything she says.

Scenario: John seems casual enough, but at some point in conversations he puts his feet up on his desk and leans back in his chair.

Analysis: People, especially men, lean back in their chairs and put their feet up for a variety of reasons. More often than not, it means that they're very relaxed and comfortable. That probably indicates that they're going to be very honest with you in the conversation. (Sometimes, though, it's just a sign that the person has back problems.)

Scenario: When Sam approaches someone who's sitting down, he often seems to arch over the person with his shoulders forward. It makes some people nervous. What's that all about?

Analysis: Sam is probably insecure and trying to counteract his insecurities by posturing as dominant. People who engage in this type of behavior can be highly manipulative. If that's the case, Sam is not to be trusted.

Scenario: Arnold is a guy who has a few tics. In a number of different situations, you notice that when he's asked certain questions, he almost always slumps forward, puts his hands in his pockets, and looks down as he answers. Why?

Analysis: Based on the behaviors just described, Arnold probably puts on a façade of being a person of high integrity. The truth, however, is that Arnold is exhibiting a pattern of dishonesty that you probably picked up on from the get-go. People like Arnold can be incredibly dishonest and self-focused.

Scenario: Roberta is the most agreeable person you've ever met. She never challenges anything anyone says. Her body posture is usually almost rigid, and it never seems to change.

Analysis: Roberta is probably sending you a very troubling message. She may be the type of person who will say anything to avoid conflict with others. Information provided by Roberta is probably useless in most cases.

Has someone burst your bubble?

Everybody likes to have a comfortable space between himself and others. Some people refer to it as *personal space;* others call it *the bubble*. When someone gets in your bubble, you immediately feel nervous or threatened. In some rare cases, people get too close because it's the norm in their culture, but more often than not, it signals aggressive behavior (which is why you become nervous in the first place).

When someone breaks the bubble rule (gets too close), be very suspicious of that person . . .

unless, of course, you're packed in like a can of sardines. If you have plenty of room behind you or to either side, retreat — step back or to the side to put some space between you and the other person — and then hope that they get your subtle message. If the person remains clueless and steps toward you to close the space, you may have to be more direct and say something like, "I need some space. Would you mind backing up a little?"

Identifying tension and stress

Being able to identify when someone's relaxed or tense is crucial in detecting potential misrepresentation. Why? Because indicators of stress almost always accompany misrepresentation. Regardless of whether you're interviewing someone in person or on Skype or watching the person deliver a speech on YouTube, your ability to identify stress can add a great deal to your understanding of what's being said. Here are a few indicators of stress to watch for:

- ✔ **Uneasiness:** Call it intuition or whatever, but if you're like most people, you can tell when someone is uneasy or anxious. Trust that intuition.

- ✔ **Stiff and tight:** When people are anxious, they tend to stiffen and tighten up. Their movements seem less fluid and more constrained, so they appear smaller.

- ✔ **Changes in eye movement:** If a person's eye movements change in response to specific important issues, that could be a sign of stress.

- ✔ **Changes in emotional pitch and speech patterns:** If the volume, tone, or pattern of speech shifts when talking about sensitive issues, the person is probably feeling some stress.

Determining the level of stress or relaxation can be incredibly helpful when analyzing information obtained through humint (human intelligence). The key is to understand just how good or bad the information you're getting is.

Analyzing audio and video

Keep in mind that nonverbal communication applies to more than just interviews and other face-to-face conversations. The information age, and the Internet in particular, has generated gobs of audio and video content for CI practitioners to collect and organize, including speeches on YouTube and corporate blogs, podcasts, and audio and video interviews, presentations, and conferences. A big bonus with recordings is that you can replay them over and over to focus on different nonverbal messages. When your research turns up audio and video online, analyze it by applying the techniques discussed in this chapter.

Keep an eye out for audio and video content on corporate websites and on YouTube. Search engines and people who post video on the web are getting much better at having audio and video content indexed with search engines, but content that's not text based may not show up in search engines.

Deconstructing the Message Itself

Although I talk about the silent conversation in this chapter, don't ignore the words themselves. Always look for the following clues in what a person says so that you're better equipped to figure out whether the speaker is lying, covering up something, or trying to mislead you:

- ✓ **Inconsistencies or contradictions:** If what you're hearing contradicts or is inconsistent with what the person has already said, that's a huge red flag that the person is telling a fib. Keeping the story straight is pretty hard when you're weaving a tall tale.

- ✓ **Illogical statements:** Based on what you know from your research and experience, does what the person said sound logical? You often hear judges talk about what a reasonable person would do. Apply that same test to what someone is telling you.

- ✓ **Too little detail:** Lies often lack detail because the liar knows that the more detail he provides, the more chances of slipping up. If during an interview you suspect that the person you're talking to is bending the truth, press for additional detail.

- ✓ **Too much information:** When people lie, they may go way beyond answering the question in the hope of overwhelming your brain with excessive detail.

- ✓ **Absolutes, such as *always* and *never*:** When making a point, some people try to exaggerate by using absolutes, which are rarely accurate.

> ✔ **Words such as *honestly* and *truthfully*:** If a person has to point out that they're speaking honestly, then chances are they're not.

Make sure that you really want to know the truth. As humans, we generally want to trust people, which is what con artists bank on. Carefully scrutinize the message itself, outside of the context of how you feel about the person in general. Look at the message in context and out of context to check it both ways.

Listening for What's Not Said

Sometimes, what a person doesn't say is more important than what a person does say. This situation comes up all the time in international diplomacy when a politician fails to address an international incident, issue a call for action, or publicly acknowledge the rights of a certain country or political faction. The same is true in business. When corporate leaders intentionally avoid commenting on a major issue, their omission can be very enlightening.

As you listen to interviews, speeches, and so on, consider what's said in the context of all the other information you gathered during your research. If an organization's leadership has gone dark (not said anything) about a key topic, then dig deeper to find out why.

Here are a few additional techniques to help detect the presence of a sensitive issue that's not being talked about:

> ✔ Observe the use of diversion or avoidance tactics that speakers use to intentionally redirect interviews or conversations around important topics.

> ✔ Note that the meter of a person's speech becomes more regular and deliberate, signaling that the respondent clearly rehearsed the response.

> ✔ Compare interviews, both audio/visual and in print, to see if the respondent used the exact same words (a canned response) when answering questions about a sensitive issue.

When you pick up on an area that appears to be sensitive, it's usually a clue that you need to dig deeper in that area.

Formalizing and Consolidating Your Observations

As you're analyzing a speech, interview, or presentation, jot down your observations so you can review the message and nonverbal cues as a whole and in context. During your analysis, ask yourself the following questions:

✔ What do I see?

✔ What does it mean?

✔ What should we do about it, if anything?

No two people are exactly alike. A single quirky mannerism can often provide you with a lot of information as you analyze an interview or a video clip.

Create a see-mean-do outline — a simple document with three main headings:

✔ **See:** Below the See heading, list everything you noticed during the interview, including main points, how transparent and forthcoming the speaker seemed to be, any alarms that went off, and so on.

✔ **Mean:** Below the Mean heading, jot down a list summarizing the important points from the speech, presentation, or interview in light of your observations.

✔ **Do:** Below the Do heading, write a short summary of what you think your organization needs to do in response to the information. (For more about see-mean-do analysis, see Chapter 3.)

Chapter 9

Validating and Organizing Data for Analysis

· ·

In This Chapter

▶ Sifting the good information from the bad

▶ Cataloging data for quick retrieval

▶ Rating your resources from best to worst

▶ Building your own CI library to facilitate distribution of intel

· ·

*T*he information age has ushered in a new age of misinformation and too much information (TMI). Companies now face the challenge of having to sift through mountains of information to find a few golden nuggets that are worthy of analysis. To further complicate the challenge, some organizations release false or misleading information. Most people miss the most obvious misstatements because they tend to assume that what they read or hear is true.

In this age of information overload, part of your job as a competitive intelligence pro involves

✔ Evaluating the information that's been collected to gauge its potential value and the credibility of the intelligence and the source

✔ Indexing the intelligence so that the people who need it later can easily find it

In this chapter, you discover how to separate fact from fiction and irrelevant from valuable data. I explain practical steps you can take to gauge the truthfulness and accuracy of information and weigh its significance. You also find out how to organize data for analysis.

Assessing the Quantity and Quality of Your Intelligence

When you have some information to work with, you're ready to begin the analysis process. The first step is to evaluate what you have, determine whether you have a sufficient amount of information, and assess the accuracy and quality of that information. If you have enough high-quality data, you're ready to input that data into your system, as explained in the later section "Organizing Data for Analysis," and then perform your analysis, as explained in Chapter 10. If you don't have enough high-quality info, you need to circle back to gather appropriate information (don't worry; I give you the advice you need in the earlier Part II chapters).

In the following sections, I explain what you need to do to process the data you collected and to determine whether you need to mine more data before moving deeper into the analysis phase.

Sizing up the volume of data

How much information is enough? I can't give you any hard and fast rules to determine how effective your research is, so let me answer your question with a question — three questions, in fact, that can help you find the answer on your own.

To determine whether the information you have meets the minimum criteria for effective analysis, answer these three questions:

- ✔ **Have you identified the key areas of information related to the company or topic you're investigating?** For example, assume it's 2013 and you want to gather information about where the cellular business is going. A search of the major competitors may be helpful, but a deeper dig into related technologies, especially those that are emerging in Japan and China, may provide you a lot more information about where that industry is really going.

- ✔ **Do you have sufficient breadth and depth of coverage on the topic you're studying?** Breadth and depth of research ensure that you consider issues related to your research focus:

  - **Breadth:** Cast a wide net to accommodate anything on the fringe that may be relevant. For example, if you're researching tablet computers, looking at just tablets may not give you the correct information. What impact will cloud computing have on the use of tablets? What about the portable keyboards for tablets? Will tablets of the future work just like desktops of today? Will they use cloud-based software? Will computers with head-mounted displays, such as Google Glass, supplant the need for tablet computers and even smartphones? You need to start thinking about how consumers are likely to use computers in the future and what features they'll consider most important.

- **Depth:** To perform in-depth research, follow all the underlying trails that branch off from your primary focus area. As an example, think about nanotechnology (miniaturization) of computers. If you track it far enough and dig deep enough, you may find indications that nanotechnology is likely to fuel the development of a new product called the *super tablet*. This "deep dive" research yields the most accurate and valuable information.

Don't measure the volume of data in pages or words or the number of articles you find. Sometimes, the best surprises come in tiny packages — perhaps an off-the-cuff comment by a competitor's CEO or rumors of an emerging technology.

✔ **Have you reached a point at which you're encountering repetitive information on the key topics?** At the beginning, the hunt for information is stimulating as you uncover valuable nuggets of new information. Near the end, though, you start to get the feeling of been there, done that. If your research continues to simply reinforce what you've already uncovered, your search is likely near its end because you probably found all the critical information related to the topic.

If you can answer yes to all three of these questions, you're ready to move forward to consider whether your information is time relevant.

Gauging the time relevance of your data

As I explain in Chapter 2, all the information you gather should be future focused; that is, it should help you predict the future and formulate strategies for gaining a competitive edge months or years down the road. Although you can use some old information and insights to predict the future (for example, a CEO's past decisions may provide insight into future decisions, as I point out in Chapter 12), fresh data is usually more reliable.

When gauging the value of the data you've collected, answer the following questions:

✔ **What percent of your information is less than 12 months old?** At least half of your data should be fresh — less than a year old for most areas of research.

Just because an article has a recent date on it doesn't necessarily mean that the information is fresh. Some experts may not be up to speed on the latest developments in their area of expertise. This is especially true in legacy situations — when a product or technology has been the standard for a long time. Compare several sources to find out what other experts are saying.

✔ **What's the life cycle of the topic you're studying?** Freshness is relative. Intel about some technologies can go out of date within six months, in which case at least 50 percent of your data should be no older than six months.

✔ **Are you picking up any weak signals that indicate an impending development?** *Weak signals* are bits of information about a subject that give you a hint about an emerging issue but provide little solid information; for example, assume that you discover that Richard Branson, Founder of Virgin Airlines, has hired an expert in computer storage technology. Because your company is in the storage business, you may want to find out if the expert is going to work on storage of the massive volume of data the airline must keep or, in typical Branson fashion, is he going to start a computer storage technology company? If he is, you need to know that as early as possible. By following up on that weak signal, you can possibly anticipate the future competitive move.

Always follow up on weak signals, which often indicate that something is brewing. For guidance on conducting weak signal analysis, turn to Chapter 11.

Testing for accuracy

As you gather information, you need to constantly question the veracity of statements and the people who make them. Following are some ways to test information for truth and accuracy:

✔ **Consider the source.** Information from reputable sources is more likely to be spot on than info from unfamiliar or recently established organizations and individuals. Ask yourself whether the source has a solid track record for providing accurate information.

Beware of Internet experts — newcomers on the web who promote themselves as experts in a given field. Perform a background check on the author to determine whether she has the proper credentials.

✔ **Reality test the information, regardless of the source.** Does what you're looking at make sense? Trust your instincts.

Be especially wary of any information you obtain online. The web has plenty of false and misleading information about people, companies, and politically charged topics. You can even find websites dedicated to calling attention to false claims, such as www.factcheck.org.

✔ **Check other sources to find information that confirms or refutes the information you have.** Ideally you'll be able to triangulate the information (confirm it with at least two other sources). Granted, this level of confirmation isn't always possible, but searching for additional sources is still important because you may find conflicting data, which tells you that you need to dig deeper.

If the information you're testing is in the form of an interview, speech, or presentation, don't forget to tune in to the silent conversation with intuitive listening to find out what the person is really saying. (Chapter 8 helps you brush up on your intuitive listening skills.)

Assessing quality: Depth and clarity

Depth and clarity are relative terms and difficult to quantify. One way to test for depth and clarity is to ask the following two important test questions regarding each source:

✔ **Does the source demonstrate a depth of knowledge related to the topic?** If the source seems to merely skim the surface, you may need to rely on other sources to plunge the depths.

✔ **Does the source demonstrate a reasonable knowledge of the key issues and nuances related to the topic?** Comparing sources on a topic provides a pretty good indication of which sources pay attention to details and present a clear picture.

Another way to test for depth and clarity is to use the information you have to craft your own *white paper* (authoritative report) on the topic. Through the writing process, you discover the quality of the information you have and any gaps — information that's missing but required to complete the paper.

Nobody has a magic formula for assessing depth and clarity of information. As you conduct your research, you discover different layers of information, each of which helps to evaluate other sources. You may need to eliminate some sources and explore new ones as you work toward developing a comprehensive picture of the issue you're investigating.

Measuring value

If you watch any stocks, you've probably heard experts mention that a future event "has already been priced into the market." In other words, knowledge of that event has a specific value that investors account for when buying shares. The same is true of competitive intelligence — information has value, and some information is more valuable than other information.

To get a general idea of the value of a certain piece of information, ask yourself the following questions:

- What does it mean?
- What's significant about this information?
- Can it help us sell more product, develop a new product, or implement a change that improves efficiency?
- Can it help us avoid a costly mistake?
- What are the potential ramifications on the future of our business?

As you ask and answer these questions, you can begin to assign a value to the information:

- **Low or no value:** The information applies to an issue that's no longer relevant.
- **Medium value:** The information can improve the organization, boost profits, or cut costs in some way that's worth investigating further.
- **High value:** Acting on the information is critical for the future success — and possibly even the future existence of your organization — or a significant opportunity exists to boost profits or slash the costs of doing business.
- **Potential value:** The information points to something promising, but you need to watch the issue and gather further intelligence over time until the fog of ambiguity clears.

Whatever you deem the value of the information, you now have some idea of what to do with it: Act on it, file it for later consideration, or dump it.

Organizing Data for Analysis

A large collection of data can quickly become unwieldy, regardless of whether you store it in a computer or a filing cabinet. As you begin to think about storing data, keep in mind that your ultimate goal is to be able to easily retrieve specific information whenever you or others happen to need it. So always keep your customers — all the people who will be accessing and using that information later — at the forefront of your mind.

The task you face is similar to what online shoe stores have to deal with. Customers may land on a site looking for running shoes, dress shoes, work boots, sandals, clogs, or other options. Each customer needs a specific size and width and probably wants a certain color. Shoes can be categorized as women's or men's or by brand name. Some shoes are designed for specific industries, such as the restaurant business, and may have slip-resistant soles, steel toes, or other special features. The best online shoe stores make searching easy for customers so that they don't spend hours browsing through shoes and checking whether each one they like comes in their size. For example, Safety Solutions (`www.safetysolutions.com`) has its own Shoe Configurator, a single form that shoppers can use to check off all the features they want in a shoe. Talk about good customer service!

In the following sections, I introduce and describe the various categories you may want to consider using to index your information. Keep in mind, however, that your categories may differ.

Classifying data by strategic sector

A few of the first categories to consider are strategic sectors and the critical success factors related to each sector. A *strategic sector* is a segment of the total market for a particular product; for example, if your company manufactures and sells laptop computers, you may have several strategic sectors, including business users, teachers, college students, and rocket scientists. *Critical success factors* comprise everything you need to do to satisfy the needs of any given strategic sector, as in the following examples:

- Business users (road warriors) may need laptops that are more compact, weigh less, run a long time between charges, and are physically durable. They also need processing power, speed, storage, and connectivity so they can take everything they need with them on the road and remain in contact with their home office.

- Teachers may be in the market for less-expensive alternatives that are easy to use and compatible with their school system's current technology.

- College students (and their parents) want something that looks cool and can access the college's Wi-Fi, run basic applications, play games, store and display photos, and store and play music and video. They also want something that will last for at least four years; to address this concern, many laptop retailers offer four-year warranties or service contracts.

- Rocket scientists need processing power, speed, storage, and connectivity so they can run complex programs that involve a lot of calculations.

It doesn't take a rocket scientist to realize that you need to segregate information according to each different strategic sector. Here's how:

1. **List the various strategic sectors that represent the people who buy your products and services.**

2. **For each strategic sector, list its critical success factors.**

   Analyzing sectors based on critical success factors is important because it enables you to focus on the unique needs and demands of consumers in each sector; if the demands/needs are different, the offerings must be different. If you try to make a product that's all things to all consumers, you could end up with two or more dissatisfied groups.

3. **Consider combining strategic sectors that share the same or similar critical success factors; for example, business users and rocket scientists may comprise a single strategic sector for power users.**

Indexing data by product

You probably already classify a lot of information by product, including sales data, production data, distribution details, and so on. Consider classifying other information by product, as well. For example, if you're gathering information and find out that a competing company has developed a less expensive knock-off of one of your top-selling products, you want to be able to pull up all the data about that product in order to devise a suitable response.

Compare information related to each product to find out which products are generating the most revenue, which are generating the least revenue, and why. These types of comparisons often serve as a starting point for competitive-analysis projects.

Classifying data by competitor

Although competitive intelligence isn't restricted to competitor analysis, as I explain in Chapter 1, you should keep a dossier on each of your competitors so you know what they're up to and what they're planning. Here are just a few ways that having sufficient competitor intelligence can benefit the CI analysis:

✔ Profiles of key leaders — their tendencies, characteristics, and history — can help you predict the direction their organization will take, especially when an industry is facing new challenges. (I explain how to profile competitor CEOs in Chapter 12.)

✔ Knowing the financial health (or weaknesses) of competitors may indicate to you the firm's ability or inability to engage in costly strategic initiatives.

✔ Having a handle on your competitor's product quality and market perception can provide important insights into how you can effectively exploit its weaknesses.

✔ Early warning of new competitor strategic initiatives can help you formulate a strategic response before it's too late.

Competitor information is often the most important from an operational standpoint. Understanding as much as possible about your competitors enables you to develop a list of most likely future moves by each competitor. This type of information can be invaluable to the strategic planning team.

Indexing data by technology

One of the most important aspects of competitive intelligence is determining which technology will emerge as the next standard. In most cases, companies can't afford to invest heavily in all possible technologies for each different area, and nobody wants to do that even if they can afford it! To save your organization a chunk of change, try to develop reliable (and predictive) inferences from competitive intelligence. When classifying data by technology, answer the following three questions:

✔ What are the prevailing current technologies?

✔ What are the weak signals telling you about future technologies?

✔ Do your technology categories cover both present and emerging technologies? If not, they should.

Most big events in any industry usually involve some aspect of technology, but weak signals are usually the only early warning signs of these impending big events. R&D, marketing, and strategy people in your company are your key internal customers in using this information. (I offer insight into weak-signal analysis in Chapter 10.)

Organizing data by geographical market

If you operate in different geographic markets, consider classifying information you gather according to the market it's most pertinent to. Different geographical markets often vary significantly in terms of economy, ideology, politics, legislation, media, environment, and legal and regulatory factors. You need to take these differences into consideration when indexing data.

Keep an eye on indirect competitors, too

A *direct competitor* essentially sells the same thing you do; for example, Disneyland and Universal Studios compete directly against one another, because they're both in the theme park business. *Indirect competitors* sell something different that still competes with you in terms of where potential customers choose to spend their money. Anything that families might spend money on to have fun together competes indirectly with Disneyland and Universal Studios, including a family trip, a cruise, a beach resort, or even a home entertainment system.

Spotting the direct competition is easy. Spotting indirect competitors is more of a challenge, but is still important, especially during times of economic instability, when your loyal customers may feel compelled to look for alternatives.

Indexing data by customer

If more than 5 percent of your organization's revenues are from a single customer, you need to create a special category or subcategory for each customer that meets that criteria. In addition, CI should have an active intelligence-gathering initiative centered on those key customers.

Classifying data by ten forces

Another way to index the information you collect is to create categories around the ten forces discussed in Chapter 2:

- ✔ Market
- ✔ Technology
- ✔ Economic conditions
- ✔ Ideological forces
- ✔ Political and governmental
- ✔ Media
- ✔ Psychological/social
- ✔ Moral/ethical
- ✔ Environmental
- ✔ Legal/regulatory

Maintaining an active library around the ten forces is very important for assisting the corporate level executive team, especially if your organization can't afford to hire an expert on each of the ten forces. For example, your company may not be able to justify hiring a full-time economist, but CI can maintain sufficient economic information to help the executive team in future planning.

Cross-indexing resources when they relate to different areas of analysis

Some sources may reference more than one category of information. For example, a document about distributors may mention a new technology that improves efficiency and cuts costs. The question then becomes whether you should index the data under distributors or technology. The answer? Index it under both; in other words, cross-index the data so it appears whenever someone searches for data on distributors *or* technology.

Cross-indexing systems vary depending on the storage and retrieval system you have in place. If you're using a fancy database program, you may simply have check box options for each category and subcategory you want to index for a specific piece of information. If you're using index cards or a spreadsheet application, the process goes something like this:

1. **Start with the title of the article.**

   The article title should appear at the top of the index card or in the first field of the spreadsheet or database record.

2. **Add information about the source, including its name and date.**

   If you're creating a spreadsheet or database entry, enter the source name and date in separate fields.

3. **Add your name or the name of the CI team member (analyst) who reviewed the source and supplied the information.**

4. **Add a major category to each index card or record in your spreadsheet.**

   Major categories may include competitors, suppliers, and distributors. In Figure 9-1, the major category is Competitors.

5. **Add relevant subcategories to each index card or record in your spreadsheet.**

   Subcategories may include technology, leadership, products, and acquisitions. Each index card or spreadsheet entry should contain one major category along with one or more subcategories. In Figure 9-1, the subcategories are Leadership and Technology.

6. **For each piece of CI you gather, add a summary or brief description of the source and information.**

   The summary or description helps you assess the relevance and value of the information for your current project. If you're storing this information in a computer database, the summary is often referred to as *meta data* — text that describes the information you're indexing. Meta data serves as tags to help find the information later.

Figure 9-1:
Cross-index every source that references more than one category of information.

Article: "Management Change at Big Blue"
Source: *Forbes* magazine Feb. 15, 2014
Analyst: Janis Jones
Category: Competitors; Leadership, Technology
This article provides an overview of the meaning of recent senior management changes at IBM along with commentary about some of IBM's current R&D work in the area of analytics offerings as well as some of their systems-based organizational performance software.

Illustration by Wiley, Composition Services Graphics

Products and technology are usually closely related, so always consider possible cross-indexing of product and technology categories.

Make a habit of indexing at the point and time of analysis. In other words, as soon as you realize that a source mentions more than one research area, create a record for all relevant areas. Otherwise, you forget about it later, and the item gets lost in the thousands of intelligence documents you have on file.

Using a Resource-Scoring System as a Final Quality Check

As you evaluate sources, articles, white papers, and so on, assign them a score of A, B, C, D, or F to indicate how reliable and useful you think the source and the particular piece of information is. Scoring helps you and others develop a feel for the relative value of different sources and quickly determine how useful a specific piece of intel is likely to be. Assign three scores and a composite:

✔ Score the source of the article or other item.

✔ Score the author.

✔ Score the content of the article or other item.

✔ Assign a composite score that accounts for both the source and the content.

In the following sections, I explain the scoring system in greater detail.

General source score

When you obtain information from a third party, score the general source (the type of data and the context in which it was gathered). A general source can be a trade show presentation that's historically been very revealing or a specific publication. For example, if you receive a CI report from one of your internal marketing people about a presentation that a competitor delivered at a recent event, you may be able to assign a source score based on how valuable similar information collected under similar circumstances has been in the past.

Give a low score if the information comes from journalists or analysts who got it from organizations that may want to influence it. Analysts and journalists sometimes go easy on certain organizations that feed them stories or grant interviews because writing is easier when someone is feeding you information. Unless the journalist or analyst conducts an independent investigation, the integrity of the reporting is questionable.

Information that's freely presented at trade shows and conventions is often grade C or D material. It's highly suspect, if not intentionally designed to mislead, and you really shouldn't use it as a *prima facie* (accepted as true until proven otherwise) source. The only real value of such information is that you could use it to try to figure out what the organization's true motive was in making the information available.

Author score

Grade-A experts and analysts are consistently accurate in their predictions. These are your go-to guys and gals. Rate them accordingly. For example, for a number of years, I followed an analyst who often covered technology companies. Over time, I discovered that he was consistently accurate and reliable. I gave him an author score of A so that everyone who used the CI data we got from him knew that it was likely to be accurate and useful. Superior authors are usually experts in the field, and they may be analysts who've already done the heavy lifting to ensure accuracy, depth, and clarity.

Over time, you may also encounter less reliable experts and analysts — people who seem to be out of touch or out of step with what's going on and have a poor track record of predicting where certain markets are headed. Additionally, some publications and other media outlets have been known to sell out to organizations that advertise with them. Assign low ratings to these folks so the rest of the people in your organization remain skeptical when accessing their information.

Article score

The article score represents the actual value of the information you collected — the content of the publication, speech, presentation, or interview you conducted. When assigning an article score, consult your intuition and then give your opinion of just how good the article or other information really is.

Composite (overall) score

To determine a composite score for the source, don't simply add the three scores and divide by three. The composite score is actually just an abbreviation of your three ratings; for example, BAD:

B General source quality, fairly high

A Quality of the author's historic work, very high

D Quality assessment of the article itself, sub-standard

As you look at the above scores, note that the analyst rated the quality of the article as a "D" (substandard). In this case, the publication and the author are trustworthy, but the author's conclusions simply don't triangulate with other sources. Thus, the analyst wants the reader to know to approach the conclusions in the article with skepticism.

Low scores serve as red flags, alerting your organization that the source and the information are questionable and should be approached with skepticism.

Building credibility through scoring

Over time, scoring sources and specific intel affects your credibility and the credibility of the entire intel team. It's sort of like being a movie critic; if you pan good movies and praise lousy ones, eventually people stop listening to you, so you need to get it right. These scores can be incredibly useful to the end-users of the information in your organization. It saves them the time and effort of verifying information and gives them the confidence to act on high-quality intel. Scoring also adds a dimension of professionalism to the work of the CI unit and its people.

Developing a CI Library

The ultimate goal of collecting and organizing information is to create a library that puts all that information and insight at your fingertips. What such a library looks like and how it works varies according to each organization's needs and resources. Some organizations dedicate a room to CI, complete with filing cabinets and some sort of indexing system that helps users locate resources, very similar to a traditional library. Other organizations may scan articles into a database. Still other companies have war rooms where they store intel and meet for planning sessions during times of crisis (see Chapter 11 for details on creating an intelligence war room). Dedicated CI software is also available, including Comintelli's Knowledge XChanger, Fuld & Company's SharePoint Competitive Intelligence Portal, and Cipher Systems' Competitive Intelligence software. You may even consider storing information on an internal web (intranet) or tap the power of cloud-based computing.

When choosing a setup for your CI library, consult with IT and other departments to find out what your organization already has in place. Adding features and capabilities to existing software and infrastructure may be easier and more cost effective than introducing something new that you have to build from the ground up.

Whatever approach you take, make sure that your CI library has the following features:

- A simple data-entry function so everyone in the organization who has the proper authorization can add intel

- Easy browsing, searching, and retrieval capabilities

✔ Central location so everyone in your organization who needs the information can easily access it

✔ Easy maintenance, especially in terms of finding and removing old information that's no longer useful

✔ Security so only those people who have authorization to use the information can access it

Consider creating two databases — one for information and another where contacts or sources can go to collect information. Your contact database may organize sources by area of expertise. Consider entering information about each contact, such as where and when you met, the last time you communicated to one another, which companies the person is most knowledgeable about, and so on.

Consider rounding out your library with the following additional resources:

✔ Books about your competitors, if available. Successful businesses often become the focus of books, and the business grants the author internal access to its personnel and maybe even internal documents. Such books often provide valuable insight into a company's management, philosophy, and future plans.

✔ Books with a general information focus, including the following

• *CIA World Factbook* (updated annually)

• *Statistical Abstract of the United States*

• World atlas

• *Pocket World in Figures*

✔ Trade journals

✔ Industry white papers

✔ Books that deal with planning on topics such as scenarios and war gaming

✔ Books that deal with intelligence (visit www.scip.org for a list of recommended titles)

Part III
Turning Data into Meaningful Intelligence

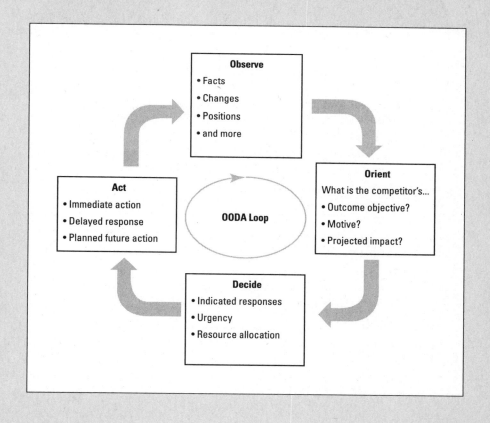

OODA (observe, orient, decide, act) loops are just one way of analyzing CI data you gather. Find out all your options with a free article available at www.dummies.com/extras/competitiveintelligence.

In this part . . .

- ✔ Examine the information you gather with SMD analysis and OODA loops to transform facts into insight — and find out what the heck SMD and OODA stand for.

- ✔ Craft intelligence briefing documents that have a good chance of convincing the management team to take action.

- ✔ Monitor the ten global forces that are likely to impact your organization so that you can capitalize on opportunities and avoid threats.

- ✔ Get a good understanding of your competitors and their CEOs so you can predict what they'll do before they do it.

- ✔ Brush up on the characteristics of different market types, including emerging and mature markets, so you can spot and forecast industry trends.

Chapter 10

Intelligence Analysis 101

· ·

· ·

You've collected a mountain of information. Now what? Until you make sense of that information, it's relatively useless. The next step is to analyze it and transform it into actionable intelligence — to develop insights into what that information means, why it's important, and what your organization needs to do in order to benefit from it.

That's what this chapter is all about. First, I lead you through an exercise to determine whether you have the innate abilities and requisite training to conduct analysis. (If you don't, you need to recruit someone who does or develop the skills internally.) I spend the rest of the chapter explaining how to conduct analysis — how to review what you collected and extract the most crucial information, transform information into actionable intelligence, and create briefing documents that have a good chance of convincing upper management to take action.

Determining Whether You're a Natural Analyst

Some people are born analysts. They're curious, perceptive, skeptical, and persistent. Their brains are wired to connect seemingly unrelated bits of information. They seem to possess a sixth sense. But what they really possess is a distinct set of qualities and skills that I describe in the following sections. Even if you don't have these qualities yourself, you may be able to acquire them through training, practice, and the advice I give in the next sections.

Natural curiosity

Curiosity drives research. Without it, you're content with what you already know, and you'll never achieve the breadth and depth of information required to produce quality intel.

If you're not naturally curious, you can get the same results by remembering to interrogate the data, as I explain in Chapter 7. In other words, as you review information, ask questions, especially the question *why*. If you read something that interests you or that you suspect is important, jot it down and try to find out more about it. Pretend you're on a treasure hunt and follow your leads, wherever they happen to take you.

Don't be misled by intentional leaks and other misinformation. Always combine curiosity with skepticism, as explained in the later section "Skeptical attitude toward information."

Hypervigilance

Hypervigilance is the quality of always being on guard. Police officers and children of alcoholics often develop hypervigilance as a defense mechanism to protect themselves from dangers and threats. As you may have guessed, hypervigilance isn't necessarily a good thing. It produces anxiety, interferes with a person's ability to trust people and build relationships, and dooms a person to live in constant fear. In CI, however, hypervigilance makes you keenly sensitive to opportunities, threats, and claims that just don't seem to make sense.

If you're not naturally hypervigilant, start thinking about what could possibly happen to put your company out of business. Ask your CEO and other executives and managers within your organization what keeps them up at night. Ask yourself what your company's competitors could possibly do to put your company out of business. As you conduct research, you're likely to encounter consumer trends and emerging technologies that pose a threat to your organization and make you more sensitive to dangers in your industry and the markets in which you do business.

Hypervigilance on the streets

After about two years on the street, almost all police officers develop hypervigilance as a result of constant exposure to danger. Trusting anyone other than their partner could be a fatal mistake, so when they're on the job, they can't afford to let their guard down.

As a CI professional, you need to develop the same mind-set. Your organization is constantly in danger from a host of factors you have no control over. When you're on the job, you need to remain aware of the potential threats and opportunities that surround your organization.

Tendency to notice things in information that others overlook

Natural analysts often pick up on details that the average person tends to miss. If you're a perfectionist, you're likely to have this ability, because you notice when something is out of place. The CIA often hires people with advanced degrees in fine arts or literature because they have the ability (natural or trained) to observe nuances in information. (People who have an innate ability to extract key bits of information make up only about 2.5 percent of the population.)

A good way to work on developing attention to detail is to start with an attitude that you don't believe anything you hear or are told. Also, read widely, which you naturally do as you conduct research. As you dig up information about the same issue from multiple sources, you gain valuable insights from different perspectives that help you focus on what's most important. As you read and hear information, interrogate the data. Ask yourself what each piece of information means and why it's relevant or significant to your current investigation. If something seems out of place, avoid the temptation to merely skip over it or omit it. Instead, focus on it until you understand how it fits or why it doesn't.

Ability to see the big picture as well as the details

Some people are natural systems thinkers. They can count cards, calculate probabilities in their heads, and spot patterns in everything from diagrams to behaviors. Great sailboat racers have that same ability in that they generally have a mental map of the racecourse and a real-time ability to see competitors' positions.

If you're a big-picture person, you have the ability to draw accurate inferences from a collection of data, quickly determine what those inferences add up to, analyze all the possible outcomes, and determine a course of action that's most likely to produce positive results.

If you're more inclined to see the nitty-gritty details than the big picture, go ahead and focus first on the details and then step back from them and look at the big picture. You may need to review the information three or four times from different perspectives over the course of a couple days.

Summarize the data in one to three sentences. Sometimes, forcing yourself to summarize the information you've gathered enables you to pull all the disparate pieces together and develop a big-picture view.

Skeptical attitude toward information

The best analysts know to approach information with a healthy dose of skepticism. The Internet has made passing off fiction as fact and faking credentials far too easy. In addition, the volume of information available today often obscures false claims and misleading information. Analysts assume that everyone's a liar until proven otherwise and that every article is bogus until they can validate it with information from another independent source.

To develop a skeptical attitude, don't trust anyone or anything you read and ask *who, what, when,* and *why* about each issue you're researching and each source you're investigating. (For more information on this technique I call *interrogating the data,* turn to Chapter 7.)

Eighty percent of communication is nonverbal, so when you acquire information from an interview or video recording of someone speaking, give more consideration to what you observe than what you hear. Skepticism regarding people as well as information consistently leads you to achieving higher-quality intel. Check out Chapter 8 for more about deciphering nonverbal communication.

Capacity for skimming large volumes of information

Research requires reading a lot of material, much of which is useless, so you need to be able to skim text very quickly and pick out valuable details and insights. Doing an initial scan can save you a lot of time by eliminating useless information quickly.

Here are a few other techniques to help you develop the ability to skim articles and other printed material. For additional techniques, see the later section "Taming the 800-Pound Information Gorilla."

- **Read any summaries.** Summaries often appear at the very beginning or end, providing you with the gist of the article.

- **Look for headings.** Headings are like labels telling you what's covered in each section.

- **Rely on standard structures.** Most articles present the main idea in the first paragraph, restate it in the last paragraph, and present support in between. Start by reading the article's title and first paragraph. If the article seems to be relevant to your current investigation or highlights a potential opportunity or threat, read it more closely.

- **Highlight or note key information.** As you read, highlight or jot down important ideas and key information. Doing so helps you retain the information and makes finding it later much easier.

If you're a slow reader who ponders everything you read, you may need to recruit someone who's a natural speed-reader. Look for someone who can skim through a long article in less than five minutes and recount the main ideas or who can skim through a business book in ten minutes and tell you exactly what the book is about.

Talent for crystallizing blocks of information into a focused idea

In some cases, you may be analyzing hundreds or even thousands of pages from numerous sources. Natural analysts can synthesize that information to draw a single insight from it or develop a recommended course of action in response to it. People who have advanced degrees in literature, philosophy, fine arts, and similar disciplines often have the training and experience required to perform such synthesis. Exam questions and essay assignments in these fields of study often challenge students to compare and contrast two or more works — an excellent exercise for developing an ability to synthesize information.

One way to develop the ability to synthesize information is to engage in see-mean-do (SMD) analysis, as explained in the later section "Creating Actionable Intelligence." As you conduct research, ask yourself, "What do I see? What does it mean? What should we do in response?" SMD analysis forces you to draw conclusions from details.

Another approach is to put a sticky note on the front of an article (you can do this electronically on a summary sheet, as well). Try to summarize the main idea in one or two short phrases. When you get ready to write up your final analysis, these sticky notes prove invaluable. (See the later section "Using sticky notes to capture key ideas" for details.)

Logic and critical thinking

Your brain is the best tool you have for producing quality CI, so put it to good use by thinking logically and critically rather than emotionally. Logical thinking enables you to see the data for what it is instead of reading into it. Critical thinking consists of questioning the veracity and accuracy of the information.

Developing logical and critical thinking often starts with self-diagnosis. List three or four opinions that you hold regarding an issue you feel really strongly about. Then ask if any facts clearly support your view. Ask a couple trusted friends to consider the same issues and present any facts they have to support their opinions. Based on the feedback, assess your opinions as emotional or factual. This exercise should give you a good idea of exactly how you're thinking and what you can do to become more objective.

Avoid emotional thinking, which leads to ego trips, bureaucracies, and political organizations that are incapable of making rational, fact-based decisions. (When you have to fight with your boss to convince him to do the right thing, your organization is in serious trouble. When an organization becomes a calcified bureaucracy, it's well on its way to failure because it can no longer adapt to the ever-changing environment in which it operates.)

Taming the 800-Pound Information Gorilla

As you gather information, you soon realize that it becomes as unwieldy, massive, and overwhelming as an 800-pound gorilla. You'd think technology could take the lead in data analysis (and it certainly is making some inroads via analytics), but a human being still usually needs to be involved in reading and studying all information before it gets entered into the CI system, if for no other reason than to determine whether the information is valuable enough to keep.

In the following sections, I introduce you to a technique I've used to successfully train hundreds of people to skim articles in a matter of minutes (as opposed to hours), to determine the relative value of the information, and to extract key details. I also explain how technology can help reduce one area of your workload — through analytics.

Developing your scan technique

To process information more efficiently, you need to develop a technique for skimming through articles and extracting key facts, figures, ideas, and opinions. I've developed a three-pass technique, which I describe in the following sections, that is highly efficient and effective.

First pass: Get a general idea of the topic

The goal of your first pass is to simply gather a general idea of what the intel you're reading is about. The best way to do that is to read the way writers write. Writers tend to follow a formula for writing, starting with a descriptive title. The first paragraph usually introduces the key ideas, body paragraphs support those key ideas, and the final paragraph recaps or reinforces the key ideas.

When performing your first pass, proceed as follows, spending no more than two minutes skimming through the article:

1. **Read the title.**

   The title usually clues you in on what the article is all about.

2. **Study the first and last paragraphs of the article.**

   The first paragraph usually contains the *thesis statement* — the main idea or the point that the author sets out to prove in the article. The final paragraph usually restates the point or summarizes the article.

   Look for a three-point outline that's common in business writing and usually appears in the first and last paragraphs. A *three-point outline* merely states the three key ideas that the author sets out to address in the article.

3. **Read any headings to find out what's covered in the body of the article.**

   Headings are like road signs telling you what to expect.

Second pass: Pick out the main ideas and key details

Now that you have a general idea of what the article is about, read to pick out the main ideas and important details:

1. **Grab a yellow highlighter or notepad (if you're reading the article online).**

2. **Skim through the article again, highlighting or jotting down key ideas and important details.**

3. **Watch for the *golden moment* of the article, where the writer sums up the main point.**

   For example, as you study a white paper on the diffusion rates of online television, the writer comes to the conclusion that online programming is at least five years from being commercially viable.

Third pass: Summarize the intel in your own words

On your third pass, you should be ready to summarize the article in your own words:

1. **Quickly read through the article (two minutes max).**

2. **Write a one-paragraph summary of the article.**

   This one-paragraph summary can also be referred to as a *sticky-note summary;* see the next section for more details on creating sticky-note summaries. When you're working with an electronic database, the same summary is considered *metadata* (data about data).

Using sticky notes to capture key ideas

A major data-mining investigation may yield more than a thousand articles, and you're not likely to remember what each article covers a few days after reading it. Unless you have total recall, you probably won't remember much of what you read even a few hours or a few minutes after reading it!

A great way to improve your retention and help refresh your memory later is to write a sticky-note summary of each article you read and store your summary along with a copy of the article. You can do this whether you're using a paper system or storing articles electronically, although in the case of electronic files, a sticky-note summary is more commonly referred to as metadata.

Take the following steps to create and use sticky-note summaries and/or metadata:

1. **Perform your three-pass review of the article.**

   I explain how to perform a three-pass review in the earlier section "Developing your scan technique."

2. **Copy or scan the article or item you're indexing (or at least its title page).**

3. **Compose your sticky-note summary, being careful to use descriptive keywords.**

4. **Stick your summary to the front of the article or add it to your database entry for the article.**

   If you're working on a project that has numerous articles, create stacks of articles based on your classification of each article (competitors, technologies, customers, products, and so on). See Chapter 9 for more about organizing and storing information.

   When using a paper filing system, if an article applies to two or more categories, file the cover page with your sticky-note summary under the primary category it applies to, copy the title page with the sticky-note summary on it, and file it under other categories it applies to.

Letting analytics do some of the work for you

Analytics is meaning-based computing; that is, it works like the human mind to identify patterns in data and to display data in meaningful contexts. When you read articles, you have to do all the work. With analytics, computers do the heavy lifting and help you expand the breadth of your research coverage. Here are a few ways that analytics can help you tame the 800-pound information gorilla:

- Analyze high volumes of blogs, tweets, social media, and other online data.
- Search an internal database of articles to find only the most relevant articles and filter out the rest.
- Conduct analytics-based searches of private (paid) databases such as Lexis-Nexis.

Wrapping your brain around metadata

You can find some of the best examples of metadata at your local library. In the old days, libraries used card catalogs to index all the books in their collections. Each card in the catalog included the title of the book, its author, the Dewey decimal code for finding the book on the shelves, and a brief, one-paragraph description of the book — the metadata.

A more common use of metadata is to describe content on the web. Every page on the web has metadata that's typically invisible to users but that search engines can see to help them properly index the page. Metadata for web pages may include keywords, tags, and meta descriptions.

What's important is that the metadata accurately describes the contents of the article, page, book, photograph, or other item in a way that helps people (or search engines) find it later.

Search for topics on Google to harness the power of analytics-based searches. Older search engine technology relied primarily on keyword matching to present search results, so if you were searching for "GSM" (a cellular phone protocol), the search results would contain only those articles that mentioned GSM by name. Analytics-based search engines, on the other hand, figure out that even though you're searching for GSM, you're probably interested in reading articles about other cellphone protocols, such as CDMA, and its search results include entries for articles that mention these other protocols.

Shop carefully for analytics services and software. Quality varies widely and different vendors tend to be narrowly focused in some areas. For more about shopping for an analytics solution, check out Chapter 6.

Creating Actionable Intelligence

The best approach for converting information into actionable intelligence is what I call the see-mean-do (SMD) approach, introduced in Chapter 3:

- ✔ What do I see?
- ✔ What does it mean?
- ✔ What should we do?

Take a piece of paper and draw two vertical lines on it to create three columns of equal width (see Figure 10-1). At the top of the first column, write "What do I see?" at the top of the second, "What does it mean?" and at the top of the third, "What should we do?" I explain what to do with each column in the next sections.

When you consistently apply the SMD approach as detailed in the following sections, you soon discover that the quality of your analysis and the output of actionable intelligence is significantly enhanced.

What do I see?	What does it mean?	What should we do?
1.	1.	1.
2.	2.	2.
3.	3.	3.
4.	4.	4.
5.	5.	5.
6.	6.	6.
7.	7.	7.
8.	8.	8.
9.	9.	9.
10.	10.	10.
11.	11.	11.
12.	12.	12.

Figure 10-1: See-mean-do form.

Illustration by Wiley, Composition Services Graphics

Observation: What do I see?

Whenever you first look at a piece of information, jot down a list of what you see, being very careful not to read anything into it, make any judgments about it, or draw any conclusions from it. List the facts as stated in the article, speech, interview, or whatever source you're looking at. *Note:* This step of untangling strands of information is crucial to conducting quality analysis — even when it gets a little tedious.

For example, suppose a short newspaper article reports that a major competitor is going to build a plant in Bentonville, Arkansas. In the "What do I see?" column, write the following:

> Competitor B is going to build a new manufacturing plant.

> Competitor B's new manufacturing plant will be in Bentonville, Arkansas.

Keep your facts straight and keep them separate, as in this example. By separating the facts, you improve your ability to analyze each claim, as explained in the next section. This is a very simple example. In some cases, you may have dozens of observations in the "What do I see?" column.

Debunking the "some people have it, and some people don't" myth

Many CI professionals embrace the notion that "some people have it, and some people don't" regarding the ability to analyze information and transform it into actionable intelligence, but that's a myth. Converting information into intelligence and using it to determine a recommended course of action is a business skill that any intelligent and talented individual can learn with the proper training.

That some people have a knack for performing analysis is true, but if you limit yourself to people who have those special abilities, you're probably missing out on a lot of knowledge and talent. What's important is to have a solid process in place — a technique for analyzing the information you gather — and apply that technique consistently. Consistency leads to high-quality intel, regardless of the individual who's conducting the analysis.

Don't try to interpret what you're seeing during the observation stage. The biggest mistake that unskilled analysts make is leaping to conclusions before they've done a good job of looking at each piece of information. Save the interpretation for the *mean* part of the see-mean-do approach.

Interpretation: What does it mean?

When you have a list of observations, you're ready to interpret what the facts mean by asking your Why? questions. Continuing with the example facts from the preceding section, here are the Why? questions you may be inclined to ask:

- ✔ Why is Competitor B planning to build a new manufacturing plant?
- ✔ Why is Competitor B building said plant in Bentonville, Arkansas?

To answer these two questions, you probably need to circle back and perform additional research. Competitor B may be planning to build a new manufacturing plant for any number of reasons, including the following:

- ✔ It's planning to close an existing plant somewhere else.
- ✔ It's planning to ramp up production to meet a future increase in demand.
- ✔ It's developing a new product that its current manufacturing facility isn't equipped to produce.
- ✔ It's moving forward to take advantage of emerging technology.
- ✔ It's trying to slash manufacturing costs by moving to a new area.

Jot down all these possibilities in the "What does it mean?" column of your SMD sheet.

Likewise, Competitor B may have its sights on Bentonville, Arkansas, for any number of reasons, including the following:

✔ Workforce availability and affordability

✔ State or local tax incentives

✔ Geographical location nearer to suppliers or distributors (or both)

✔ Fewer costly regulations

Jot down all these possibilities in the "What does it mean?" column of your SMD sheet, grouping them according to the "see" event they apply to. In this example, you have two "see" events — the fact that Competitor B is building a new plant and the fact that it plans to do so in Bentonville — so you should have two sets of reasons in the "What does it mean?" column. Breaking down observations and reasons is important; the new plant may indicate a new product or process, whereas the fact that it's being built in Bentonville may indicate a new strategy, perhaps to target a certain customer.

You can begin to see why keeping your facts separate in the observation stage is so important. By keeping your facts separate, you can ask and research the answer to two distinct questions and obtain all the information you need to draw accurate conclusions.

Look for patterns. For example, you may find out that Competitor B has also assigned a marketing executive to its Bentonville office. Why would it do that? As you begin putting all the information together, you may be able to conclude that the competitor is preparing to pursue a client called Walmart, which is headquartered in Bentonville, Arkansas.

Drawing two or more conclusions from your observations is not unusual. What's critically important to the process is that you begin to develop a picture of exactly what a competitor's intentions are and why a competitor is engaging in the observed behavior. This step in the process enables you to create incredible depth of understanding.

Action: What should we do?

The first two steps of SMD analysis give you insight into what's happening and why. Now you need to decide what to do about it. How should your organization evolve to take advantage of the new reality or defend itself against a perceived threat?

I can't provide much step-by-step guidance here because each situation is so unique. Even the example I present of Competitor B with Walmart in

Bentonville is loaded with variables. If your company has been trying to get Walmart as a client, then Competitor B's plans could gum up the works and require you to ramp up your efforts. If Walmart is already a client, then you may be facing a competitor that's planning a full-frontal attack against your company or planning to introduce a new, innovative product as a back-door entry point to gain a foothold with Walmart. Each possibility presents different challenges that your strategy must address.

What to do? Here's where you have a great opportunity to strengthen your internal ties with key members of your intel team. Here's one approach to do just that:

1. **List four or five responses that your organization may consider implementing.**

   Record these responses in the "What should we do?" column of your SMD sheet.

2. **Create a one-page overview of the issue that asks one representative from each department (including finance, marketing, advertising, product development, and brand management) to rank the responses from best to worst.**

3. **Ask each rep to explain her reasoning for the rankings.**

4. **Ask each rep to summarize any thoughts about the competitor, the product, or any other relevant issues.**

At the end of the process, you've demonstrated value for the CI work and received input from each constituency. The combined input should allow you to propose a solution that may already have some level of acceptance within the organization simply because of the collaborative approach you used. For additional suggestions on how to develop buy-in for a CI initiative, see Chapter 16.

Gaining Insight from CI and OODA Loops

To add another important dimension to your CI analysis work, consider *observe, orient, decide, act* (OODA) *loops.* In the mid-1950s, Colonel John Boyd created OODA loops for the purpose of revolutionizing air combat strategy. His approach consisted of training pilots to predict what enemy fighter pilots would do based on their purpose, intent, and objectives. Properly trained pilots flew one to two steps ahead of their enemy counterparts, as if they knew what the enemy would do before the enemy did it! Today, OODA loops are used in business as well as military applications.

Although SMD analysis is effective and sufficient for most CI needs, OODA loops such as the basic one shown in Figure 10-2 add the dimension of competitor motive to provide an additional layer of understanding. In the same way OODA loops changed air combat, OODA loops can change your effectiveness as a CI analyst in predicting future events. In the following sections, I explain each stage of the OODA loops process.

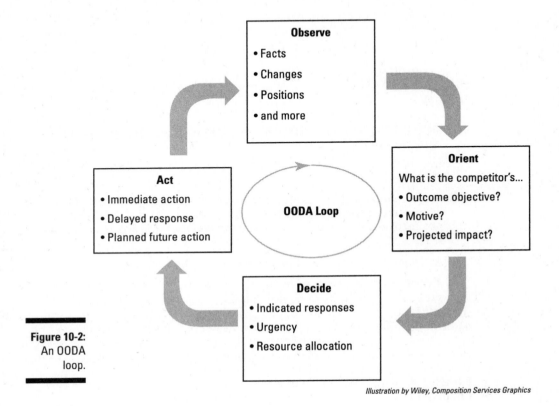

Figure 10-2:
An OODA
loop.

Observation: What do you observe?

The observation stage of the OODA loop is identical to that of the *see* stage in SMD analysis, which I describe in the earlier section "Observation: What do I see?" Here, you list everything you're seeing as basic statements of fact; for example:

> Competitor B is going to build a new manufacturing plant.
>
> Competitor B's new manufacturing plant will be in Bentonville, Arkansas.
>
> Competitor B is closing a plant in Pasadena, California.
>
> Walmart is in Bentonville, Arkansas.

Here's why OODA loops can be so helpful:

- Because OODA loops are not time constrained, you can effectively apply them during a meeting or in any time frame necessary, such as on the spot when the organization is trying to create a response to a new competitor initiative.

- By using OODA loops and adding the orient step to your analysis, you generally reach more insightful and predictive conclusions that others who use a different approach.

Orientation: What are their motives?

The orientation aspect of OODA loops enables you to skip forward in your thinking and consider where a competitor is really going. When taking this orientation step, think about the competition's purpose, motives, or objectives. Ask your Why? questions:

- Why is Competitor B planning to build a new manufacturing plant?
- Why in Bentonville, Arkansas?
- Why has Competitor B gone public with this information?

Beware of responding to orchestrated leaks. For example, a competitor may launch a false rumor just to see how you react. By stopping to evaluate the meaning, purpose, and ultimate goal the competitor may have for leaking the information, you often end up one move ahead. You can then formulate a calculated response that doesn't reveal anything about your core strategy or that even misleads your competitors.

Decision: What should we do?

At stage three in the OODA loop process, you must decide what to do in response to the insight you've gained. You basically have three options here:

- **Act immediately.** If you deem that what you observe is a high-impact event, you need to respond immediately to take advantage of the opportunity or defend against the threat.

- **Monitor the situation.** If all you have to work with are weak signals (hints of impending activity), you need to continue to monitor the situation and conduct additional research to determine whether the weak signals lead to high-impact events.

> ✔ **Do nothing.** Not all intel needs to be acted on. You may discover that a competitor is pursuing an opportunity that has little chance of success. Doing nothing frees up your resources to pursue more promising opportunities while your competitor squanders its resources.

Action: Execute your response

Strategic initiatives that involve change fail roughly 80 percent of the time due to resistance to change and, ultimately, inaction. With that in mind, you need to be sure that you do your part to convince your executive team to implement recommended changes:

1. **Create a one-page summary document that clearly details the urgency and impact of the issue.**

   See "Briefing the Decision Makers," later in this chapter, for pointers on crafting this document.

2. **Brief your team of internal sponsors (hopefully all the way up the organization to the executive level) and get their buy-in for further analysis and, ultimately, action.**

Loop back

You've done OODA, now it's time to loop back and do it again. The whole idea of an OODA loop is that if you perform all the steps correctly, you change the environment in which you operate, so you need to go back to the beginning and observe the new conditions. With OODA loops, you fine-tune your response and continuously adapt to the ever-changing environment.

Briefing the Decision Makers

If you keep track of world events, you soon realize that the major players base their decisions on the best intelligence they have at the time. They approve spending or cuts, increase or slash taxes, form alliances, and wage wars based on what their advisors and analysts tell them is going on and the probable outcomes of available choices.

As a member of the CI team, you play the role of advisor, providing your organization's decision makers with the information and insight they need to implement positive change. Because of this, you must be skilled not only at analysis but also at communication. You need to lay out your case in as convincing a manner as possible and present the information in an easily accessible format. You also need to get your recommendations into the hands of the right people at the right time. In the following sections, I explain how to accomplish all this and more. (In Chapter 16, I offer additional guidance on how to build consensus and shepherd a CI proposal through your organization.)

Creating a CI briefing sheet

Before you contact your organization's decision makers, prepare a competitive intelligence briefing sheet. Whether you use the briefing sheet presented in Chapter 5 or one of your own creation, make sure that it includes the following details:

- ✔ **Classification:** Indicate the relative sensitivity of the information: highly classified (so sensitive that only executives should see it), confidential (highly sensitive but important for more people to see), sensitive (internal eyes only), or general (not sensitive).

- ✔ **Priority:** Indicate the urgency to take action: urgent, important, or normal (FYI). Another option is to use a 1-2-3 rating system:

    - **1: Critically important, drop everything!** Use this rating when you have strong signals from very reliable sources that call for an urgent response. Use this rating rarely so it has impact when you really need it.

    - **2: When-you-get-a-free-moment urgency:** The executive team really needs to consider this within the next few weeks, but urgent action isn't necessary.

    - **3: No urgency — continue to monitor:** The information is provided for briefing purposes only. No action is necessary.

    I know a company that uses the 1-2-3 rating system for most of its internal messages. If a senior executive is in a meeting and receives a text message flagged with a 1, he knows it's important enough that he needs to step out of the meeting. This system has proven highly effective in communicating the importance of information.

- ✔ **Your name and today's date:** Include your name and today's date for obvious reasons.

- ✔ **Summary (see):** Compose a one- to two-paragraph summary of the information, primarily your observations.

- ✔ **Insight/significance of information (mean):** Compose a few sentences that give meaning to the information or put it into context.

- ✔ **Your recommendation (do):** Add your recommendation. What do you think the organization needs to do in response to the opportunity or threat you described?

  Be assertive. Any recommendation you make should be a clear call to action. If your recommendation sounds wishy-washy, circle back to do additional research until you can convince yourself that action needs to be taken and what that action is.

- ✔ **List of sources:** Include a list of sources that the decision maker can consult for reinforcement to add credibility to your report.

Distributing your briefing sheets

After creating your briefing sheets, you need to distribute them to the decision makers on a need-to-know basis. Team up with the executive team to create a need-to-know distribution list. Group people on the list according to classification levels, such as

- ✔ **Highly classified:** Executives only
- ✔ **Confidential:** Executives and management only
- ✔ **Sensitive:** Everyone in the company

Have a system in place to change a person's classification so that if an individual is promoted or submits his resignation, for example, his access to sensitive information is changed accordingly.

Remember the three-second rule

Book publishers are well aware of the *three-second rule*: Buyers make a buy/no buy decision within three seconds of looking at a book's cover. A similar rule applies in the corporate setting; you have a matter of seconds to communicate information and convince an executive or manager of the urgency to take action. One of the realities of conveying information to incredibly busy people is that 90 percent of them won't get past the first page; they read only the executive summary — the first page — so make your briefing sheet count.

Chapter 11

Applying Advanced Intelligence Analysis Techniques

You've mastered the basics. You can conduct see-mean-do analysis like a pro, you've tamed the 800-pound information gorilla, and you can do loopty-loops with OODA loops (all of which I cover in Chapter 10). Now you're looking to take your CI game to the next level.

Well, you've come to the right place. In this chapter, you discover how to tackle the challenge of ambiguity, tune in to weak signals and find out what they really mean, perform strong signal analysis, engage in triangulation to test your intel, and build a war room that's conducive to top-notch analysis and strategic planning.

Addressing the Challenge of Ambiguity

Conducting CI is similar to dating. It would be much easier if you had clear, unambiguous signals to work with. Unfortunately, reality isn't so clear-cut. People intentionally — and sometimes unconsciously — lie and mislead. Opportunities and threats come and go. And the complexity of a situation can quickly become overwhelming. In the midst of ambiguity, CI professionals are still expected to dig up dependable information that's highly predictive. Fortunately, by developing an awareness of the sources of ambiguity, you can begin to improve your foresight and your track record for predicting future outcomes.

As you step up to the challenge, consider the three primary sources of ambiguity:

- ✔ Complexity
- ✔ Velocity
- ✔ Blind spots

In the following sections, I address each of these sources in turn. I also give you a couple tactics for reducing the amount of ambiguity you have to deal with and discovering how to trust your instincts.

When most organizations fail at CI, they do so because the organization's leadership and planners (as well as CI personnel) haven't accounted for the complexity of a situation and/or the velocity of change.

Developing an understanding of complexity

When conducting CI, you're aiming at a moving target. To have any hope of hitting it, you need to aim in front of it. That's where complexity comes into play. Think of complexity as the number of moving parts in any given situation you're researching — the issues, forces, and variables that come into play.

If you're lucky, you're dealing with only one or two issues, forces, or variables, and your job's pretty easy. More often than not, that's how a typical CI assignment starts out, but it rarely remains that easy. Soon you discover that you're now dealing not only with five major competitors but also with dozens more that are popping up in developing countries. In some cases, the governments of those countries are instituting policies that create favorable conditions for their companies to compete in the global marketplace. To make matters worse, emerging technologies that you thought wouldn't be a threat for several years are nipping at your heels and the rate of new product introduction is likely to double in the next 24 months.

The more moving parts you need to account for, the greater the complexity and the more challenging it is to explain what's going on, predict what's about to take place, and plan an effective response. Figuring out how to deal with multiple factors, changing velocity (see the next section), and increasing levels of uncertainty are critically important if you're going to be successful in developing meaningful intelligence.

As the level of complexity rises, the level of predictability tends to drop. In other words, as the number of moving parts increases, your ability to do solid predictive modeling with your CI data is compromised. Try your best to stay on top of changes in your industry and the markets in which you compete. Otherwise, the changes are likely to become overwhelming at a point when it's too late to respond effectively.

Understanding and gauging velocity

Velocity (or *diffusion*) refers to how fast a change occurs. How soon will competitors in your industry adopt a new technology or approach? How long will consumers be using smartphones and iPhones before a new gadget arrives on the scene to replace it? When will brick-and-mortar retailers be relegated to the history books?

Whatever changes your industry or organization faces, you need to have a somewhat reliable timeline in place so you can plan for changes that are destined to occur. The importance of accommodating for the velocity of change can't be overstated. If a company anticipates that a new competitive product will arrive in four years but consumers adopt it in just two years, the outcome can be disastrous. An inability to anticipate such changes often leads to an extended period of diminished earnings, if not an outright crisis.

Accounting for human blind spots

Challenges posed by complexity and velocity aren't all that difficult to overcome until you add the human element into the equation. Human beings have blind spots that prevent them from seeing the complexity in a situation and accounting for the velocity of change. Blind spots are at the root of the difficulty when predicting outcomes and executing initiatives. Following are a few examples of the types of blind spots people may have:

- ✔ **Paradigm blindness:** Writer and scientist Thomas Kuhn detailed the reality that most people reject information if it's different (dissonant) from their existing understanding of reality. In other words, human beings (except for the 2.5 percent of the population I call *pathfinders* — visionaries who embrace change) are generally incapable of recognizing change.

  Pathfinders are the only people who can see reality without bias. As a result, they're your insight into the future and critically important to your success. (For more about pathfinders, see Chapter 15.)

✔ **Complexity blindness:** A concept first introduced by Newell and Simon called *bounded rationality* (and later adopted into strategic thinking by Henry Mintzberg and Ralph Stacey) hypothesized that the human mind is simply incapable (or bounded) when it comes to making sense of complex situations. Most people want to shut down and ignore that information. The key is to engage, analyze, use your intuitive capabilities, and patiently develop an understanding of what is really going on.

✔ **Blindness to unfamiliar solutions:** According to prospect theory, decision makers often choose a solution that won't solve the problem at hand, simply because they're unfamiliar with the necessary fix. For example, suppose a firm has a problem with cycle time — the time required to complete a process such as placing an order. Solving the problem probably requires knowledge of process mapping or process engineering, but the people looking at the problem aren't knowledgeable in those areas, so they suggest something like creating a new mission statement. A new mission statement won't help, but it's something they know how to do, so that's the "solution" they recommend.

For your organization to overcome its blind spots, everyone in the organization needs to engage in *systems thinking* — an approach that develops an understanding of how all factors influence one another in your market. SMD analysis and OODA loops (which I cover in Chapter 10), as well as war gaming and scenario development (which I cover in the later "Creating an Intelligence War Room" section) are all approaches that leverage systems thinking as a foundation. Additionally, they're all effective, to varying degrees, in overcoming resistance to change.

Old habits die hard

In his classic article "Gunfire at Sea," Elting Morison tells the true story of British artillery procedures at the end of the horse-drawn artillery era. With their new truck-attached guns, the British artillery units simply couldn't fire fast enough to be effective in battle. They took a film of an artillery unit in action and noticed that before each shot, crew members would run 30 feet back from the gun, clench their fists, and fire. Commanders didn't understand why that procedure was in place. They asked an old artillery officer to come view the film.

After showing him the film, they asked him why the gun crew was running 30 feet back,

clenching their fists, and then firing. "Oh it's simple," he said, "They're holding the horses." In other words, the crew members were following the same procedures that had been in place since the days of horse-drawn artillery, never realizing the purpose of their actions.

This same phenomenon occurs in the business world, where people are blind to the most obvious things simply because they assume that nothing will ever change. To avoid the trap of getting stuck in old, meaningless ways of doing business, you need to constantly question whether the old ways still make sense in the current reality.

Clearing up ambiguity with the interrogation technique

CI is constantly trying to develop actionable intelligence from incomplete or highly limited information. To reduce ambiguity and improve clarity, start with the information you have and then interrogate it (analyze it through questioning) to fill in the gaps. The interrogation technique is part of a deep-dive approach designed to reveal additional details that are relevant to a situation you're analyzing. Begin by asking the five Ws and one H: Who? What? When? Where? Why? How?

Suppose your intelligence discovers that a major competitor has recently added a senior vice-president named Alexis Medina. She's given the nondescript title of SVP Global Markets. Little else is provided except that she came from a different industry and worked her way up in the consumer-products division of the firm. She has an MBA from a prestigious university and has more than 12 years of experience in her previous field.

To flesh out Alexis's profile and understand why she has been hired in as SVP Global Markets, interrogate the information you already have by asking the five Ws and one H. (Pay close attention to the motivations of both parties when you get to the why and how questions.)

- Who is she?
- What's her area of expertise? What's her mission?
- When was she hired?
- Where has she served in the past?
- Why was she hired and why now? Why has she been named SVP Global Markets? Why would she accept this particular position?
- How has she been successful in the past? How is your competitor likely to use her experience and skills?

On the surface, Alexis's background may appear to be fairly straightforward, but suppose you discover that she did a stint with a major security agency where she was able to use her mastery of Mandarin Chinese. You dig deeper and find out that Alexis is the daughter of a former U.S. diplomat and spent eight years of her childhood in Taiwan. You also learn that one of her key accomplishments in a previous job was to develop key outsourcing relationships in China.

This information and your knowledge of the current sourcing strategies in your industry sector alert you to the possibility that your major competitor may use Alexis to move a significant amount of its manufacturing offshore, most likely to China. Such a move, you realize, could drastically alter the industry's cost structure. Furthermore, if your key competitor made such a move and was able to surprise you, you'd stand to lose market share and profits.

The first round of questions is only the beginning. Continue to interrogate and scrutinize your answers to challenge your conclusions, identify subordinate issues, and reveal new possibilities. Pretend you're a child trying to understand the reasons behind your parents' decision. After every answer, ask Who? What? When? Where? Why? or How? until you run out of questions and have a clear idea of the strategy that drove your competitor to execute a specific change.

For example, here are some follow-up questions you may want to ask about Alexis and why your competitor hired her:

✔ Do any other sources confirm or challenge the initial conclusion that Alexis was hired to outsource production to China?

Always triangulate information and conclusions to confirm or challenge your initial findings. You must be able to back up your intel with information from at least two other sources. (See the later section "Using Triangulation to Test Your Conclusions" for more about triangulation.)

✔ Was Alexis hired to use her consumer products background and language skills to help the company compete in the Taiwan and China markets instead of outsourcing production?

✔ Does Alexis know other languages, such as Spanish or Portuguese? If so, is your competitor possibly planning to harness her skills to pursue markets or outsourcing opportunities other than those in Taiwan and China?

Before concluding that you have the right answers to your CI questions, be sure you can answer yes to each of the following questions:

✔ Have you followed all the clues that the interrogation process uncovered?

✔ Have you been able to investigate to the point that you believe you have the correct answers (or implications) about the subject under study?

✔ Have you dug deep enough to be confident in your understanding of the direct and indirect implications of your information?

✔ Are you comfortably confident in your conclusions?

After clearing up the ambiguity related to a certain question or issue, you're in a better position to brief your organization's decision makers on the intel and its possible implications. If you're still not completely confident in the intel or your conclusions, you may need to do some additional research.

Having an inkling that something bad will happen

On September 2, 2001, I was giving a presentation to a group of 40 people about using systems thinking to understand and predict future events. I made a statement that later came back to haunt me: "It's not an issue of *if* but only an issue of *when* America will experience an attack from radical religious forces."

The attack on the World Trade Centers and the Pentagon occurred on September 11, 2001, and America lost 1 million jobs in 30 days as a result of that catastrophe.

I didn't predict the 9/11 tragedy. Nobody but the terrorists who planned it knew it would occur, and U.S. intelligence agents had only ambiguous information and a lot of it to work with. However, you do need to be able to predict the probability of such events and what's likely to happen as a result so that your organization can develop contingency plans.

Trusting your instincts

Appreciating just how capable you are in dealing with large volumes of information, when most if not all of that information is fuzzy, is vitally important. The human mind is still the most sophisticated processing entity around. It has the ability to make sense out of massive amounts of information. The only question is whether or not you're willing to listen to what your mind and the continual flow of intel are telling you.

Here's a simple set of steps to help you maximize and trust your innate abilities:

1. **Allow your mind to process or think about all the information you've dug up.**

2. **Allow that processing to continue by asking the "What does this mean?" question as you observe different sets of data.**

3. **Be especially observant as you begin to develop intuitive indicators about what the information might mean.**

4. **Complete the process by crystallizing those intuitive indicators into a conclusion.**

If you ever have a "funny feeling inside" regarding a particular situation, more often than not, you'll come to realize that your intuition was correct.

Implementing the Issue-Management System

CI serves as your organization's radar. As you monitor the global environment, you begin to pick up signals — some strong, some weak. When you pick up a signal, the first task is to classify it as strong or weak. Then you analyze the impact of the information at hand to determine whether it will have a high, moderate, or low effect on your organization so that you can respond appropriately. Figure 11-1 shows the steps of the issue-management system, which can be summarized by these key points:

- ✔ **Strong signals indicate a level of certainty.** If impact analysis reveals that the issue is high or moderate, then urgent action is necessary. Events that have a predicted low or unknown impact call for continued monitoring or no action at all.

- ✔ **Weak signals are ambiguous and usually involve issues that are at least six months into the future.** Depending on the predicted velocity of change, the firm usually has time to figure out what the weak signal indicates and preemptively prepare for the event.

In the following sections, I explain how to perform impact analysis for strong and weak signals.

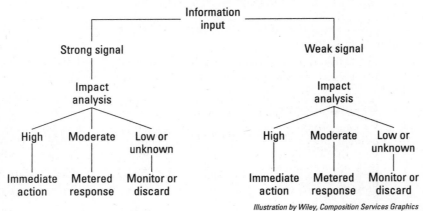

Figure 11-1: The issue-management system.

Illustration by Wiley, Composition Services Graphics

The CI team leader should work closely with the organization's leaders to determine the probable impact and urgency of any intel. The CI team leader must serve as a trusted advisor. The decisions of if, when, and how to respond to the intel are in the hands of the executive team.

Performing strong-signal impact analysis

A signal is classified as strong when it's a clear and reliable predictor of a future event. The strength of the signal has nothing to do, however, with how important that event is. After picking up a strong signal, the next step is to assess the probable impact of the event on your organization. Choose between the following three ratings:

- ✔ **High impact:** A golden opportunity or serious threat has arisen or is imminent (less than a few months out). Immediate action is necessary to exploit the opportunity or avoid the threat (or minimize the fallout), and what needs to be done is fairly clear.

- ✔ **Moderate impact:** A good opportunity or moderate threat has arisen or is imminent, and you have more time to plan a response. Planning generally involves other departments, including marketing, advertising, and research and development (R&D), depending on what's involved.

- ✔ **Low or unknown impact:** The event is unlikely to present a good opportunity or pose a serious threat to your organization. You may choose to ignore the event entirely or keep an eye on it to see if the impact value changes over time.

Strong signals, by definition, are an indication that your intelligence is substantial and that the resulting opportunity or threat has a very high probability of occurring. However, always be willing to verify the validity of your conclusions and avoid the temptation to accept strong signals as facts at first glance. Perform your due diligence to test their validity and importance. Triangulate — make sure that you have at least two other credible sources that hold the same opinion of the projected outcome. See Chapter 9 for more about validating information you collect.

In the following sections, I provide additional guidance on gauging the urgency of strong signals and preparing a response.

Gauging your response

When something qualifies as a strong signal, that refers only to how predictable an emerging event may be. The event may have little or no impact on your organization. Your response is directly proportional to the expected impact of the event, but you may still need to consider the costs and benefits of your response:

- ✔ **Weigh the costs of taking action against the costs of not taking action.** In some cases, the cost to preemptively prepare for a future event may significantly exceed the impact cost. Answer the question, "Is this event worth responding to?" This is also an opportunity to try to calculate the opportunity cost or, conversely, the damage that may occur if the event is not addressed proactively.

✔ **Look for alternatives.** Is there a way to work around the issue? For example, if you're looking into adopting a new, expensive technology, you may have several options to consider, including the following:

- **Upgrading the technology that's already in place:** This solution is the least expensive but also possibly the most risky if the velocity of change is extremely fast.

- **Using proven leading-edge technology:** Wait until someone else invests the big bucks in the bleeding-edge option (see the following bullet) and buy yourself some time to see how that plays out for your competitor. In the meantime, costs may drop and other better or more reliable technologies may become available. This is the middle-of-the-road solution from a risk and cost standpoint. The key is velocity — the amount of time you have to formulate a response.

- **Investing in bleeding-edge technology:** Invest the big bucks to gain a momentary advantage. This solution is the most costly but may be necessary if failing to implement the technology will give a competitor a significant momentary advantage.

Assessing the urgency of strong signal intelligence

To determine the urgency of strong-signal intelligence, consult the following three groups:

✔ The executive team, including the CEO, because executive team members have access to information about future strategies and plans that could influence just how urgent a response to intel may be

✔ The internal support team, which should include senior managers

✔ CI team members, who should include people from every key functional and product area of the firm

Gauging the urgency of strong signals may be difficult for the CI team, especially if the team doesn't have a complete picture of the firm's future strategy. Senior management, marketing, and R&D have been known to keep major developments and plans secretive. Even plans for a new product may be kept hidden from the CI team.

If possible, CI needs to be kept in the loop regarding all the organization's strategic areas of operation. Just imagine the damage that can result if your company releases a product without knowing that a competitor has a superior version in the works. CI must know about internal plans so it can monitor for any events that may undermine them.

Weak signals can have strong impact, too

In the months leading up to January 1, 2000, the world was abuzz about how computers and software that had no ability to recognize any date past December 31, 1999, would respond to the new year. Y2K became a major issue for everyone from owners of home computers to the owners of large power-generation plants. Some people discounted the seriousness of the issue, but computer consultants enjoyed a period of incredible revenues as they worked with major industries to help them configure their old software and computers so that they could recognize dates after the turn of the century.

Although signals were strong that computers and software had this problem, the signals were weak regarding the effect on functionality. Speculation and fear reigned supreme. Nobody really knew how serious or widespread the damage, if any, would be. Yet the economic impact was significant, lifting the entire computer industry.

A good way to keep the CI team on track while the executive team keeps highly sensitive information confidential is for the CI team to provide a fairly frequent briefing document to a senior executive who's "in the know." That way, the CI team can be "guided" in its work without having access to the top-secret stuff the executive team is working on.

Keep executives and decision makers in the loop when you have strong-signal intelligence, just in case they have any confidential information that can shed light on the urgency of the intel. (See Chapter 10 for more about briefing decision makers.)

Engaging in weak-signal impact analysis

Weak signals characterize the nature of about 98 percent of the information a CI team receives. And although these signals can be ambiguous, weak-signal analysis can be the source of the real gold in the intelligence gathering and analysis process. To determine whether weak signals point to gold or fool's gold, you need to assess the possible impact of the event on your organization. As with strong-signal impact analysis, you have three options:

> ✔ **High impact:** When weak signals point to high-impact issues, you need to give your executive team and R&D and marketing folks a heads-up immediately so they can assess the situation and collaborate with CI to obtain additional information.

> ✔ **Moderate impact:** Depending on the anticipated event, you may want to loop in the executive team or continue to monitor the situation and perform additional research until you detect stronger signals.
>
> ✔ **Low or unknown impact:** You can usually ignore events that have low or no impact on your organization. If the impact is really fuzzy, continue to monitor the situation.

The more preemptively you can deal with change in your current operating environment, the better your chances of capitalizing on an opportunity or steering clear of catastrophe. But be careful about responding too soon or too dramatically. A miscalculated response can be costly.

Using Triangulation to Test Your Conclusions

As you gather information, you naturally begin to draw conclusions about what you're seeing. That's what see-mean-do (SMD) analysis is all about (as I discuss in Chapter 10). As you draw conclusions, however, you should test those conclusions through *triangulation* — seeing how they stack up against the opinions of others and any additional information you can find. Try to validate your conclusions with information from at least two other sources, as I explain in the following sections.

Don't dismiss findings that challenge your conclusions — or toss your conclusions just because initial findings don't support them. When you find disagreement between sources, use it as an opportunity to dig even deeper so you can ultimately confirm or reject your assessment. Interrogate the data, as explained in the earlier section "Clearing up ambiguity with the interrogation technique."

Testing your findings with analysts or trade publications

When you think you're ready to give your recommendation, think again. See what investment-firm analysts have to say about the situation you're investigating. Investment-firm analysts are particularly useful for providing a reality check and testing the quality of your intelligence. (For more about checking analysts' opinions, see Chapter 6.) If you can't find any relevant analyst insights in publications, try to contact the analysts directly to find out what they think about the specific issue you're investigating.

Also check trade publications, but bear in mind that they may be less dependable. Reports may be biased due to close relationships between organizational insiders and publication staff, especially if the organization pays for advertising in the publication. Seek out the opinions of independent reporters and analysts.

Comparing your findings to those of industry experts

Another way to perform a reality check is to take a second look at what the industry experts have to say. In Chapter 6, I advise you to read white papers written by consulting firms or individuals who are experts in a particular field or industry. The Gartner Group, for example, is a dependable intel resource for trends or future developments in technology areas.

Modified Delphi panels, presented in Chapter 7, are also an excellent source for expert opinions. Consider following up with panel members you interviewed during the information-collection stage to confirm or challenge your assessment.

Confirming your findings with internal intelligence

When seeking confirmation, don't overlook the sources closest to you — internal intel. Many of the people in your organization are industry experts, and everyone should be a source of information. Check with your internal intelligence sources to see what they think and to find out whether they have any information that may call your assessment into question. (For more about tapping internal intelligence sources, check out Chapter 5.)

Seeking out opinions from people inside your organization brings the added benefit of building support for any future change initiative. And that organization-wide buy-in is incredibly valuable in selling the results of your CI to senior executives.

Creating an Intelligence War Room

If you've watched any old war movies, you've probably seen depictions of war rooms. These rooms are usually spacious, with maps draped on the walls and a large table that the military officers stand around to study the fields of battle and simulate troop movements.

An intelligence war room serves a similar purpose, but it looks a little different — more like a conference room. Rather than maps of the battlefield, your intelligence war room probably has a whiteboard and a projector screen for presentations. However you choose to furnish it, your intelligence war room serves two primary purposes:

- ✔ It's a central location for key players to meet to discuss urgent events and formulate strategic plans.
- ✔ It's a kiosk for intel and related information.

In the following sections, I offer guidance on how to set up a physical war room and a virtual war room, how to populate both with white papers and competitor profiles, and how to use your intelligence war room to engage in simulations and crisis management.

Setting up a physical facility

A conference room or similar space is ideal for use as an intelligence war room. It just needs the following furnishings:

- ✔ A conference table and chairs so people can sit around and bounce ideas off of one another
- ✔ One or more computers and filing cabinets for storing and accessing your organization's intel. If you use digital storage (and you should), you can use
    - • Local or network database storage
    - • Secure, cloud-based storage of all information at a remote service facility (numerous companies operate highly secure server operations where a company can store and access its critical information)

 Digitize any critical physical data (paperwork, photos, audio and video recordings, and so on) and back up digital data at a different location so you can recover it in the event of a fire or other disaster.

- ✔ Videoconferencing and document-sharing capabilities to consult with offsite experts
- ✔ Back-up communications capabilities in the event of local power outages
- ✔ A whiteboard
- ✔ A projector and screen for presentations

Unlike a standard conference room, your war room must be secure to prevent unauthorized access to sensitive intelligence. If you can't keep the door locked, at least encrypt and password-protect the information and keep any filing cabinets locked. Also, make sure that at least two people have access to the information, just in case something happens to one of them.

Creating a virtual war room

Even if your organization has a physical war room, it also needs a *virtual war room* — an online version where the CI team and decision makers can meet even when they're on the road or working from remote locations. With rare exception, executives are frequent travelers, and in many cases, they may not even have a physical office at the firm's home base.

Except for the conference room, table, chairs, and filing cabinets, your virtual war room needs the same amenities as its physical counterpart: secure storage (and a remote backup) of intel that's accessible for everyone involved, videoconferencing and document-sharing capabilities, backup communications, a virtual whiteboard, and a way to deliver and share presentations.

Populating your war room with white papers and competitor profiles

No war room is complete without a collection of white papers about key issues and profiles of competitors and their CEOs. In Chapter 12, I explain how to profile competitor CEOs. In Chapter 13, you find out how to create competitor profiles.

In addition to getting your hands on relevant published white papers, for key issues that are of critical importance to your organization, you should also compose white papers that organize and summarize all the intelligence related to those issues. A solid white paper includes the following:

- An introductory abstract of the material in the paper

- An organized discussion of the key elements of the issue

- A summary and conclusion that reveals the most probable outcomes (if they can be determined) or any specific developments that may indicate a need for urgency or further study

White papers serve a number of purposes. Most important, the CI author of the paper may be able to bring a much higher level of analysis to the overall research. Second, because a white paper is a synthesis of many articles in most cases, a 5- to 15-page summary of all resources can be invaluable to a time-constrained executive who has little time to make a decision. For pointers on writing white papers, check out *White Papers For Dummies* by Gordon Graham (Wiley).

Preparing to respond to crises

A main purpose of having a war room is to have a place where key players can quickly gather to respond efficiently and effectively to an emerging crisis, but simply having a room, whether it's physical or virtual, isn't enough. You need to have an emergency plan in place and have key personnel practice dealing with different scenarios so your organization is prepared to avert a crisis — or at least limit the fallout from one. In the following sections, I describe two ways to facilitate a successful response to a crisis.

Composing crisis policies and procedures

Making good decisions in the midst of a crisis is always difficult if you haven't previously decided what your priorities and processes are in the event of such an emergency. The quality of decisions and outcomes is often determined by the preestablished policies and procedures put in place long before an incident occurs. Here's how you can take the lead in helping to create a manual to guide your firm's leadership in the event of a crisis:

1. **Query your internal support network (especially the senior managers) to determine what crisis policies and procedures are currently in place.**

2. **Obtain support from key decision makers about creating a draft crisis policy and procedures document.**

3. **Work with your support team as you draft a proposed policy and procedures document.**

   Your policies and procedures document must include the following:

   • A comprehensive list of all mission critical assets, processes, resources, and people, including anything required for business as usual (either on-site or at a remote emergency site)

   • The location of a remote, secure place that can be used to immediately move people to and set up ongoing operations

   • A list of all functional areas that must be involved in making sure that all mission critical issues and areas have been identified

   • Descriptions of the types of crises and the level of urgency required to convene a meeting

- Which personnel (titles) will be involved in the meeting to deal with the crisis

- Steps for dealing with specific crises; for example, what to do if a key member of the product development team leaves or is unable to perform his duties

4. **Obtain final sign-off on a crisis policy and procedures document and then make that document a permanent resource in your war room.**

In some organizations, this exercise may become incredibly political and fraught with challenges. In the event that you're unable to get consensus with CEO approval, consider creating a case file that includes how other companies have handled crisis events and the procedures they have in place.

Conducting simulations

When you have your policies and procedures written up and distributed to decision makers and other key personnel, put them to the test by conducting simulations (think of simulations as fire drills). Such simulations are usually mandated by senior management, which helps overcome any internal resistance you may encounter. Following are some examples of crisis scenarios you may want to simulate:

- ✔ A customer just posted very negative comments about your organization on five different heavily trafficked business rating sites.

- ✔ One of your leading competitors just acquired your primary supplier.

- ✔ One of your main distributors just decided to stop carrying your product.

- ✔ The global economy crashed.

Take a lesson from the navy

Many people aren't aware that U.S. Navy battleships have computers on board that contain as many as 5,000 simulations, randomly programmed so that the ship's crew has frequent exposure to dealing with various types of emergencies. Here's how it works:

- ✔ The computer spits out an emergency scenario, such as a fuel spill on the deck of an aircraft carrier.

- ✔ The emergency is declared, and the entire ship's crew performs all the procedures specified for dealing with fuel spills.

- ✔ After the exercise is complete, the commander and staff perform a postmortem analysis to iron out any wrinkles and identify what could have been done better.

Like the Navy, your organization needs to test its crisis-readiness regularly to stay sharp.

Tylenol: A study in successful crisis management

In September and early October of 1982, seven people died in Chicago after taking Extra-Strength Tylenol capsules that had been laced with potassium cyanide and placed on the shelves of local area merchants. The news spread quickly, and sales of Tylenol and other pain relievers tanked. Consumers were understandably terrified.

The Tylenol story has become the gold standard of crisis management for companies. Here's what Johnson & Johnson, the manufacturer's parent company, did:

✔ It immediately acted with only one priority in mind: Save lives. No consideration was given to profits, downplaying the crisis, or improving the company's public image. The company came clean and immediately went public with a national request that no one take any Tylenol and requested the immediate return of all Tylenol to its distributors and ultimately to the company.

✔ It designated the CEO as the voice of the company. He focused on communicating the important message about returning the capsules and was involved in little more than being the spokesperson for the company.

✔ Behind the scenes, the entire management team along with law enforcement handled the details of investigating the incident and making sure that all the procedures for returning the capsules were executed with precision.

✔ Johnson & Johnson offered a $100,000 reward for information leading to the capture and conviction of the "Tylenol Killer."

The outcome: Although the criminal who poisoned all those people was never caught, Johnson & Johnson proved itself trustworthy and compassionate in the eyes of consumers. Because of the integrity and efficiency that the Tylenol executives had demonstrated in limiting the damage from the tainted medicine, Tylenol became a mainstay product when it was rereleased into the market. Additionally, the public equally welcomed the introduction of tamper-proof containers.

From an organizational standpoint, the creation of simulations can be very useful. As you run through various simulations, you may discover who really needs to be involved, problems with your communications system, an inability to access critical data during times of crises, and so on. Finding out about problems during a simulation is a lot better than finding out about them in the midst of a crisis.

Engaging in War Games and Scenario Building

A good portion of CI involves speculation and playing "What if?" You engage your mind and the minds of others in trying to imagine what the next big thing and next little thing will be. You try to figure out when the industry is likely to adopt an emerging technology or adapt to a fresh round of government regulations. You try to anticipate various crises and envision how your organization is likely to respond . . . and how it should respond.

Two ways to engage and challenge your imaginative powers and those of others are through war games and scenario building, as I explain in the sections that follow. *War gaming* is a form of simulated competition. *Scenario building* involves thinking and planning about future events in a specific area of interest. (Depending on the number of people involved and the approach that's taken, war gaming and scenario building may be conducted inside or outside the confines of the war room.)

Conducting war games

The idea of war games is to create a hypothetical competitive situation and then have two or more teams engage in battle. This simulated warfare helps you gain insight into how your competitors will respond and how well your own strategic initiatives are likely to play out on the battlefield. War games can be a real eye-opening experience, especially when senior executives take on the roles of your organization's competitors. Often, when they see how a particular issue plays out in the simulated reality of a war game, they're much more receptive to the idea of implementing the changes required to remain competitive.

Here's how it works:

1. **Define the competitive issue or scenario you want to study.**

   Your scenario should involve key players, including direct competitors and possibly even indirect competitors that may have an impact on the issue you're studying.

2. **Assign players to competing teams.**

   How you set up the teams may vary a great deal. For example, you may have two teams, one representing your organization and the other representing a rival, or you may have two or more teams, each developing a different product idea.

   When assigning players to teams, consider the following:

   - You want to assemble a fairly large group of players from your organization. The more participants you have, the more you'll learn, and the more buy-in you're likely to get when the time comes to implement a solution.

   - If you're creating teams that focus on different areas (such as product innovation and sales), assigning individuals to areas that are outside of their usual area of responsibility is usually best, because it forces them to think more creatively. For example, assign your senior sales executive to the team that's focused on product innovation.

- Brief senior managers in advance that they should avoid taking control or leading any of the teams. The influence they hold over the group could stifle creativity and expression and negate the value of the game.

3. **Give the scenario to the teams, explain who they'll be competing against, and describe the current conditions (context) in the industry segment, product segment, or other area of study.**

   Encourage and foster an environment of friendly competition. War games are designed to challenge a paradigm (and blind spots) by getting everyone caught up in winning and beating the other teams. You want people to harass and razz other teams in fun. As players engage in simulated battle, miracles of learning naturally occur.

4. **Give the teams one hour to develop a strategy that they believe is the best for the company they're representing.**

5. **Give each team five minutes max to share its strategy with the whole group in a short presentation.**

6. **After the teams have shared their strategies, send them back for another hour to develop a new strategy based on what all the other teams have done.**

7. **Repeat Steps 5 and 6 through at least four cycles.**

   A single war game may last up to eight hours. Each iteration creates another level of learning. Some companies have been known to pay upwards of $100,000 a day to have this kind of experience staged for them.

8. **Debrief the group.**

   After wrapping up your war games, work with the group to begin to develop a consensus document about what's really going to happen in the area you studied.

War gaming needs to be a fun exercise. When the players realize that they're free to act as competitors, their competitive juices take over, and the output of the process can be pretty incredible. Case in point: As your organization engages in war games, it's likely to benefit from

- ✔ Some pretty incredible creative thinking about what can and in some cases will happen in the segment under study

- ✔ Long-term positive impact on the organization overall

- ✔ Insights that help executives overcome paradigm blindness and make decisions that are much better aligned with reality

Engaging in scenario development

Scenarios have been very helpful to companies that deal with high levels of uncertainty and within industries that involve high volatility. Scenarios offer a number of potential benefits that are helpful in the following areas:

- ✔ Managing resistance to change
- ✔ Developing contingency plans for unexpected events
- ✔ Leading a team through an in-depth analysis of possible future events

Here's a simple approach for building scenarios:

1. **Identify area(s) for study.**

2. **Analyze the area of study around the forces or variables that can impact the outcome of each area under study.**

3. **Gather intelligence about each of the key issues that appear to impact the issue or area of study.**

4. **Create three scenarios that best describe the range of possible outcomes.**

   Some examples include

   - Worst case, expected case, best case

   - Sales decline, sales maintain current levels, sales increase

5. **Work each scenario into a story, such as: Bob's (the CEO) Worst Day Ever, Business as Usual, and Bob's Best Day Ever.**

After you create three scenarios or three stories, consider sharing them internally with individuals who may have important information and insight to add. Doing so allows you to fine-tune the different scenarios for more accuracy.

Don't forget the power of modified expert panels (see Chapter 7). If the issue justifies spending to obtain outside input, get outside industry experts to select a most probable outcome and keep a record of their comments so others can consider their reasoning.

Chapter 12

Profiling the Competitor CEO

. . . .

In This Chapter

▶ Measuring the agility of an organization's leadership

▶ Predicting how an organization's leaders will respond to change

▶ Gauging an organization's risk tolerance

▶ Evaluating a competitor CEO's approach to product development

. . . .

Individuals are products of their past and creatures of habit. Based on their past behaviors, the size of their egos, their aversion to risk, and other factors, you can generally predict how they'll respond in any given situation. For example, based on the media's labeling of a politician as liberal or conservative or a hawk or a dove, you can often predict the way she'll vote on a particular issue.

The same holds true in the world of business. By studying a company's CEO or an organization's culture, you can often plot its future course. Do it well, and the result is almost as good as having the opposing team's playbook a week before the big football game!

In this chapter, I guide you through the process of profiling an organization's CEO and the corporate culture that drives the organization so you can begin to predict with some degree of certainty how your competitors will respond to changes in your industry and in market conditions.

Sizing Up Your Competition

Competitors always pose a threat to your organization, but just how serious a threat does each competitor pose? Size and market share aren't always the best indicators. You need to look behind the scenes to find out which competitors are the most creative and capable of adapting to the ever-changing landscape. In the following sections, I explain how to size up your competition in three distinct areas:

- ✔ CEO
- ✔ Leadership's ability to change direction
- ✔ Corporate culture

Then I explain how to create a composite assessment (agility index) to determine which of your competitors poses the greatest threat. Along the way, you discover how to use the assessments in other ways to predict how a competitor is likely to respond when presented with an opportunity or a challenge.

Ratings of CEOs, corporate leadership, and corporate culture, as well as the agility index, are based on extensive research conducted in part by the late by H. Igor Ansoff and his associates and in part by yours truly. These assessments have been successfully used hundreds of times and have demonstrated a very high predictor of organizational outcomes (including bankruptcy).

Completing and using the seven-factor CEO profiling assessment

One of the quickest and easiest ways to profile a CEO is to complete the seven-factor CEO profiling assessment. It's based on hundreds of studies of organizations of all sizes (Fortune 100 down to small entrepreneurial firms) and has shown consistent results in gauging the predictability of CEOs and the organizations they lead.

To get started, choose a competitor's CEO and research and study him until you have a general idea of how he operates. CEOs of Global 1000 companies are high-profile people who usually have plenty written about them, so you should have no trouble gathering the necessary information. If you're investigating the leadership of an organization that isn't publicly traded, you can gather information primarily from human sources, including local business groups, former employees, competitors, customers, local journals, trade associations, and so on.

Now rate the CEO on a scale of 1 (highly negative) to 5 (highly positive) for each of the following seven factors. This is purely a judgment call based on your opinion.

____ Personal ethics and philosophy

____ Attitude toward subordinates

____ Humility

_____ Seeks the best for others

_____ Attitude toward creativity

_____ Attitude toward risk

_____ Iconoclastic tendencies (willingness to challenge the status quo)

Here's a fun exercise to test your ability to profile CEOs. Rate the following CEOs based on the description I provide for each one (write the total score, maximum 35, on the line to the left of each description):

_____ The CEO of Company A is the ultimate numbers man. He has little time for people or motivation. He won't hesitate to cut personnel to save money. Former employees characterize him as incredibly competitive and even brutal. He's also known for his willingness to push legal limits to the max.

_____ The CEO of Company B is the ultimate people person, who has very high expectations for everyone in the organization. She's the classic leader who inspires others to achieve what they never believed was possible. She expects people to be creative and believes that failure is often the steppingstone to success.

_____ The CEO of Company C is the ultimate egomaniac. Six security people accompany him at all times. All employees of this Fortune 500 company have been told to exit the elevator if he gets on and not to make eye contact with him. His personality traits result in a workforce that lives in fear and will do anything to avoid mistakes or failure.

_____ The CEO of Company D is the ultimate creative force in his company. He's known for occasional rages at employees, but is also so creative that he has a ten-year track record of creating highly innovative products that continually break sales records.

Assuming that you have your own CEO scores in place, read on to see how I scored these individuals and my reasons for each rating:

14: The CEO of Company A is capable of getting hard-nosed short-term performance out of his people, but he is clearly not a team builder. He makes all the decisions at his company and is probably unwilling to listen to advice, heed warnings, or seek out creative ideas. With little regard for ethics, his company is likely to get into legal trouble or suffer from poor PR.

30: The CEO of Company B values her subordinates, embodies humility, and expects excellence, making her the most formidable of her peers from an overall corporate performance standpoint. Her ability to motivate others and listen to what they have to say makes predicting what she'll decide very difficult.

So who are these CEOs?

Here are the names of two of the CEOs I analyze in this chapter:

Company B's CEO is Mary Kay Ash, the former CEO of Mary Kay Inc., the global cosmetics company. Her leadership created an organization that is continually at the forefront of product innovation, and her ability to inspire others has resulted in a high compounded growth rate for a long period of time.

Company D's CEO is the former head of Apple, Steve Jobs. Instead of leveraging the intellectual capital of his people, Jobs was simply a creative genius when it came to anticipating customer needs and trends. His untimely death in 2012 left the company with a creative void, which the current CEO is working to correct.

The identities of the other two CEOs will remain anonymous for obvious reasons.

7: The CEO of Company C may have been a skilled leader in getting his company up and running, but he's a train wreck waiting to happen. The fear of failure he has instilled in his subordinates will ultimately stifle their creativity and lead the company into becoming a change-resistant bureaucracy. The good news for you is that this CEO's actions and direction are very predictable.

17: The CEO of Company D will probably score low for most factors except creativity and iconoclastic tendencies. The company will probably develop some highly successful products but will have trouble retaining talented people. If the CEO leaves the company, it will be in serious trouble, losing its sole creative force.

Using the assessment to gauge predictability

A CEO's assessment score provides insight into how predictable a CEO's decisions and actions are and how a CEO is likely to act in specific situations. After performing an assessment, use the total score as a key to understanding and predicting the CEO's behavior:

- **7–10:** A score this low usually indicates that you're looking at a my-way-or-the-highway CEO, who makes all or most of the decisions and bases them pretty much on the numbers. The CEO's behavior is very predictable because he's not open to input from subordinates and other external sources. Due to the CEO's inflexibility, you can expect high turnover in the company as subordinates experience frustration.

- **11–20:** A CEO with an assessment score in this range makes most or all of the key decisions but is more receptive to influence from external sources. (Which sources they are depend on scores for the individual factors.) You can expect the organization to devolve into some level of bureaucracy, exhibiting status-quo thinking, slow decision making, and behind-the-curve responses to changes in market conditions. Because the CEO's style probably contributes to turnover, expect a lack of consistency in how well the organization is able to execute strategy.

✔ **21–30:** CEOs who score in this range can be somewhat unpredictable. They're usually management-by-objective types (goal-oriented, not inspirational or motivational), but they may be capable of leveraging some of the intellectual capital of others in their organization. In the case of CEOs who score in this range, your analysis of each of the seven factors (and the implications of each) are important in predicting their behavior.

✔ **31–35:** CEOs who score above 30 are the most formidable. They're classic leaders rather than managers (empowering as opposed to controlling). They inspire creativity and risk taking, encourage everyone in the organization to take the initiative, and are very fast and efficient at making decisions. Because so many people are involved in the decision-making process, predicting the organization's behavior is nearly impossible. Organizations like these are agile, creative first movers.

Using the assessment to predict behaviors

Although the composite score provides a good indication of how predictable a CEO or organization is, scores for the different factors can help you understand and predict how the CEO is likely to respond in any given situation. For example, if a CEO scores high on all factors except personal ethics and philosophy, you know that the CEO won't hesitate to break or bend the rules to further her goals.

Consider the CEO of Company C, whom I introduce earlier in this chapter — the ultimate narcissist who has little regard for others. This CEO's priorities go pretty much like so: Me first, profit second, everything else third. He's an emotional thinker rather than a logical one, so when you're trying to predict what he'll do, consider the emotional aspects of the situation. For example, if he has an opportunity to show up a competitor, he's likely to do so, even if he has to overspend to do it.

Conversely, the CEO of Company B looks at the situation logically. Her priorities look like this: Customers first, personnel second, me last. She's going to place customers and her company at the forefront of every decision, even if she has to make a personal sacrifice. She's not interested in self-promotion.

Use your CEO assessment in tandem with see-mean-do (SMD) analysis and observe-orient-decide-act (OODA) loops. In SMD analysis, your CEO assessment can shed light on what certain activity means and what your competitor is likely to do — how your competitor will respond. When using OODA loops, CEO assessments can help you *orient* your organization in relation to how you predict your competitors will respond. (For the full scoop on SMD analysis and OODA loops, see Chapters 3 and 10, respectively.)

Assessing leadership's ability to change direction

Most organizations are stuck in a rut merely because leadership has forgotten how to turn the wheel. Unfortunately for them, the ability to change direction in response to changes in the industry or in market conditions is vital for an organization to survive and thrive.

As you profile CEOs and the organizations they lead, assess their ability to change direction so you have an overall idea of how much of a threat they really are. Rate each of your competitor's leadership teams on a scale of 1 to 5 in the following areas:

____ **Leadership style** (1 = very controlling; 3 = management by objectives; 5 = inspirational, empowering)

____ **Attitude toward risk** (1 = risk averse; 3 = risk tolerant; 5 = encourages risk taking)

____ **Attitude toward subordinates** (1 = discounting/demeaning; 3 = expecting compliance; 5 = supporting/empowering)

Total your scores to come up with a composite score and use the composite score to predict the firm's ability to execute strategy:

✔ **3–5:** The organization is generally incapable of executing meaningful, significant change initiatives.

✔ **6–10:** The organization is generally capable of slow, deliberate change.

✔ **11–15:** The organization is capable of radical change and execution of key initiatives. Anticipate rapid response from the organization with a high level of innovation empowerment at all levels.

Assessing corporate culture to predict behavior

Every organization has a personality. Some are buttoned-down, nose-to-the-grindstone sweatshops, and others are abuzz with laughter and creativity; some are roll-the-dice risk-takers, whereas others focus on tradition and consistency; some are focused on long-term results, and others capitalize on short-term success; some encourage and reward individual ingenuity, whereas others encourage and reward group efforts.

Developing an accurate understanding of a competitor's corporate culture can help you predict a lot about an organization's ability to execute strategic initiatives. In fact, a lot of research in this area compares the success of firms with adaptive versus nonadaptive cultures.

To assess a competitor's corporate culture, rate the following areas on a scale of 1 to 5:

____ **Attitude toward change** (1= defends the status quo; 3 = indifferent toward change; 5 = embraces change)

____ **Value of employees** (1 = devalues employees; 3 = indifferent toward employees; 5 = highly values employees)

____ **Rewards and incentives** (1 = rewards historic performance; 3 = rewards productivity; 5 = rewards creativity and risk taking)

Total your scores to come up with a composite score and use the composite score to predict the firm's future behavior based on its corporate culture assessment:

- ✔ **3–5:** This score reveals a competitor with a classic frozen bureaucracy, indicative of future organizational failure.

- ✔ **6–10:** A score in this range is typical of companies in the middle of the pack. Depending on whether the score is closer to 6 or closer to 10, you can expect the competitor to be very slow to moderate in terms of responsiveness and execution.

- ✔ **11–15:** Companies that score in this range are typically rock-star organizations — the most agile and creative. Assuming that the firm's strategy is solid, it's probably in the top 10 percent of its competitive segment.

Putting it all together: The agility index

To determine an organization's overall ability to cope with and capitalize on change, total its CEO, leadership, and corporate culture scores (for a possible maximum score of 65) and divide the result by 65 to get the percentage score. Use the following key to size up your competition's ability to respond creatively to change:

- ✔ **90–100:** Industry leader in agility, your worst competitive nightmare

- ✔ **80–89:** Very high agility

- ✔ **70–79:** High agility

- ✔ **60–69:** Responsive, with moderately fast execution

- ✔ **50–59:** Middle of the pack in agility at best

- ✔ **40–49:** Substandard agility, usually a follower in its sector

> ✔ **30–39:** Slow on the uptake, lacks the ability to respond and execute
>
> ✔ **20–29:** Incapable of formulating a meaningful response

Spotting Patterns in Leadership Behaviors

Although all intel needs to be future focused, you can predict a great deal about how a person or organization will react based on how it responded to similar challenges in the past. In the following sections, I explain how to study patterns to predict future behaviors.

Gauging a CEO's decision-making predictability

How a CEO and the organization he leads makes decisions can often help you gauge how predictable the organization is. For example, if a CEO always consults with the board of directors, the CI team, and other key players within the organization prior to making a decision, predictability is low, because anything can happen. On the other hand, if the CEO is insular and rarely seeks out input from others, you can usually predict his decisions based on past decisions. Here are some descriptions of real-life CEOs along with assessments of the predictability of their decisions:

Leader 1 listens to the board of directors but generally is so forceful that the board rarely challenges his proposals or decisions. This leader's blind spot is the people factor, and most decisions can be tracked to numbers and cost strategies.

Leader 2 tends to be a collaborative, people-focused CEO, but the board of directors for this Fortune 100 company frequently overrides her proposals with demands to cut costs and increase short-term profits (to elevate the stock price). Conflict with the board is likely to compromise your ability to predict the organization's behavior based solely on the CEO's behavior.

Leader 3 frequently appears in the company lunchroom to spend time with employees and conducts monthly conference calls with employees (anonymous) from around the world. This leader has a history of making decisions that focus first on employees and customers. Predicting this CEO's decisions and direction can be difficult because they rely so heavily on input from others.

Leader 4 has been known to tell financial analysts that they shouldn't buy her company's stock due to their insistence that the company's salaries and benefits for lower-level employees are simply too high. Along with all the company's executive team, she answers her own telephone instead of having an administrative assistant on staff. This leader also has an incredible ability to focus on what's best for the customer. Leader 4 is very much a challenge-everything leader, which (except for her focus on employees and customers) makes predicting this leader's decisions difficult. Her approach has permeated this public company, and the firm has an agility index of 90 percent.

Recognizing the key behavioral patterns and decision-making approaches of competitor CEOs is important. CEOs with seven-factor assessment scores lower than 10 (out of a possible 35) tend to be egocentric decision makers. (I fill you in on the seven-factor assessment in the earlier section "Completing and using the seven-factor CEO profiling assessment.") They may be very smart people, but emotional factors drive their decisions, as in the case of cutting costs to achieve an arbitrary goal rather than doing what's in the organization's best interests overall. Predicting decisions made by CEOs who score in that range is pretty easy.

CEOs who have an agility index of 45 or higher are much more difficult to predict. They tend to be much less egocentric and less emotional because of their tendency to involve themselves in collaborative decision making. Due to their fact focus and their understanding of the motivational role of people (employees and customers), they're tough to predict and make formidable competitors.

Analyzing control patterns

Occasionally, an organization is led by a CEO who's part creative genius and part control freak. For as long as that person is in charge, the organization thrives. More often than not, however, the CEO is all control freak with no creative genius thrown in. As a result, the organization has no creative drive; it doesn't come from the CEO, and the CEO stifles any of his subordinates' creativity. As a result, the organization's decision patterns become very predictable.

To determine how much of a control freak a CEO is, answer the following questions:

- How much control does the CEO exert when making key decisions?
- What's the turnover rate for subordinates relative to the turnover rate in similar organizations? (High turnover is often a sign that a my-way-or-the-highway CEO is in charge.)

✔ How creative are the ideas coming out of the organization? (Lack of creativity is often a sign that the CEO isn't very creative and doesn't listen to people who are.)

✔ Does the CEO actively seek out the opinions of others internally?

✔ Does the CEO include the board of directors in the decision-making process?

Consider your answers as a whole to arrive at a verdict of how controlling the CEO is or isn't. Then take a look back at the CEO's seven-factor assessments score, which should confirm the answers to these questions.

Analyzing the role of the board of directors

Close collaboration between the board of directors (for publicly held companies) and the CEO is a good sign that the CEO listens to the opinions of others. A board that seems invisible or that is in conflict with the CEO could be a sign of trouble. When reviewing the SEC filings of a publicly held company, tune in to any insight about the CEO and board of directors, and look for answers to the following questions:

✔ How stable is the board in general? What's the turnover rate?

✔ Do you observe any "churn" (high turnover) among the independent directors?

Every public company is required to have a majority of *independent directors,* who aren't members of management, haven't worked as consultants for the company during recent years, and have demonstrated no conflict of interest related to their board involvement. When internal strife appears in the form of the departure of independent directors, be sure that you determine what's going on at the company. It could be very important.

✔ Do you observe any indicators of conflict between the board and the CEO of the company? (If problems exist, you can usually find them noted in analyst reports.)

Examining an organization's approach to making decisions

The agility index, which I mention in the earlier related section, provides a very accurate indication of how an organization makes decisions and how well it can execute new initiatives. For further confirmation of the results of the agility index — and to gain a clearer understanding of how an organization makes decisions — answer the following questions:

✔ **How instrumental is the CEO (and has she been historically) in the final outcome of decisions as compared to the board of directors?** The CEO can ultimately force her view on corporate management, and in most cases, the board of directors. Investigate the CEO's historic behavior related to just how hard she pushes toward a personal view in making a decision.

Conversely, if you determine that the board of directors exercises its power over major decisions, you need to understand how each party thinks and make a judgment as to which one (the CEO or the board) will prevail.

The more iconoclastic (willing to challenge tradition) a CEO or board of directors is, the bigger the potential threat to your company. It all gets down to how customer focused each party is. That characteristic in the CEO/board adds a great deal of uncertainty for your organization, similar to an organization with a high agility index.

✔ **Can you identify any historic patterns of decision making that may relate to how the firm will make decisions in the future?** If so, what do the patterns show?

✔ **Does the organization have a strong, well-defined set of values that controls decisions and behavior throughout the firm?** Look to the organization's mission statement and for other clues. Does the organization generally act in accordance with its principles?

Reality-test your information. An organization may tout itself as "customer first," but your research may reveal that the company has a poor record of following up on consumer complaints. *Remember:* Actions speak louder than words.

Assessing Organizational Propensity toward Risk

The old saying "No risk, no glory" applies to all fields of endeavor, including business. The bigger the risk, the bigger the chances of failure or success. You can often predict an organization's decisions based on the level of risk it tends to take in the area of product innovation:

✔ **Level 1:** Continually improves existing products.

✔ **Level 2:** Seeks to innovate in the existing product area — looking for the next little thing and rarely the next big thing

> ✔ **Level 3:** Engages in both *related innovation* (the first two levels) and *unrelated innovation* (totally new and different product areas)

Note that the level of risk rises with each level of innovation. In many ways, Steve Jobs might be best described as the leader who was willing to engage in unrelated diversification, succeeding in several different industries: computers, cellphones, and even the music industry.

Knowing your competitors' propensity toward risk significantly improves your ability to predict their likelihood of pursuing future initiatives. In the following sections, I present two different approaches for assessing an organization's attitude toward risk.

Using historical innovation efforts to predict future efforts

Assuming an organization hasn't had a recent shake-up in its leadership, you can often predict its future course according to any changes in direction it has made in the past. As you research your competitors, keep a list of products they've introduced to the market over the past couple years. You should see one of the following three patterns:

> ✔ **One-hit wonder:** The organization won big with its first product and hasn't done anything creative since then.

> ✔ **Me-too innovation:** The organization introduces a new product only in response to innovative products introduced by its competitors. This organization is likely to remain behind the curve.

> ✔ **Existing product innovation:** The organization continues to improve its current products but rarely, if ever, introduces a new product line and only when forced to by its competitors.

> ✔ **First mover:** The organization almost always beats its competitors to the punch, leaving them questioning, "Why didn't we think of that?"

As you examine your competitors' history of innovation, keep an eye on their agility index. A company with a poor history of innovation would require a significant improvement in its agility index in order to move from being a me-too innovator to a first mover. For example, suppose your intelligence indicates that a competitor has decided to emulate 3M and create internal initiatives to stimulate high levels of related and unrelated diversification. A quick look at the company's agility index reveals just how capable the firm is of executing that initiative. If its agility index is 27 percent, for instance, it has little chance of success unless, of course, it takes big steps to overcome its deficiencies, such as replacing the CEO or hiring a leading expert in critical technology. (For help determining a competitor's agility index, see the earlier section "Putting it all together: The agility index.")

Before you put too much stock in a CEO's history of innovative decisions, do an in-depth analysis of the state of the firm:

✓ If the firm has stable earnings, you're safe in predicting future actions based on the past.

✓ If the firm is in a declining stage, approach the CEO's history of innovation with some degree of skepticism because the CEO may try to change direction to turn things around.

✓ If the firm is in crisis stage, don't be surprised if the CEO totally changes her approach to innovation. After all, desperate times call for desperate measures.

Mining annual reports

A publicly traded company's annual report tends to be more about self-promotion and less about painting a true picture of the state of the firm, but you should still keep an eye on these reports to stay abreast of any changes in the organization that indicate a change in direction related to risk taking and innovation, such as the following:

✓ A change in leadership from a risk-averse CEO to someone who has a track record of making bold decisions or vice versa

✓ A decision to invest significantly more or less in research and development

✓ Hiring of innovative designers, programmers, engineers, and so on

Perform a variance analysis of the firm's income statement and balance sheet. In other words, look at how the numbers have changed from one quarter to the next. For example, if a competitor's R&D costs increase by 25 percent, that variance can indicate that the firm has adopted an entirely new strategic approach. By calculating changes as percentages, you can quickly pick up on how the firm is allocating its funds (and possibly better understand its strategies).

Evaluating a CEO's Product-Development Philosophy and Approach

Some CEOs seem to have a product-development philosophy that can be summed up as, "If we build it, consumers will buy it." They invent a new product, load it with bells and whistles, and hand it over to marketing and sales to sell. When it flops, they blame marketing and sales or, even worse, consumers. Some companies that fit this mold are successful: Twenty percent or more of the products they roll out are big hits, and that's enough to keep them afloat.

Companies achieve greater success, however, by taking aim at true opportunities and gaps in the market before pulling the trigger. Organizations that aim first usually have a customer-focused approach to product development. They work closely with consumers throughout the product-development cycle to determine what prospective customers really want and need. This approach takes longer, but it leads to greater innovation and consistency in success rates for new products.

How do you find out whether your competitors are product focused or customer focused? First, consult your salespeople; they have firsthand knowledge of which competitors are beating them and how. Second, conduct a basic investigation of a competitor's history of introducing new products to the marketplace. Look into how successful the organization's new products are. An organization that consistently hits doubles and triples and occasional home runs is usually customer focused. Organizations that strike out a lot and only occasionally hit home runs tend to take a product-focused approach.

Seeing how your competitors have historically innovated (incremental product improvement; a frequent next-little-thing approach; or a next-little-thing combined with an occasional next-big-thing approach) helps you understand exactly what you're dealing with and enables you to predict their future innovation approach. In the following sections, I present a few other considerations you need to make in order to evaluate a CEO's product-development philosophy and approach.

Differentiating between PR and the CEO's real opinion

Every organization on the planet likes to think of itself and promote itself as innovative and cutting edge, but few of them walk the walk. Take everything an organization says about its innovative nature with a grain of salt and dive deep in your research to determine whether the organization's actions back up its claims. As you perform your research, use it to answer the following questions:

✔ Does the organization invest in intellectual capital (research directors, brand managers, and other thought leaders)? Do these investments or lack thereof align with the CEO's statements?

✔ Do the firm's financial statements align with the CEO's statements?

✔ Historically, has the CEO tended to make statements that were designed to mislead, or have they been highly predictive of what the firm actually did?

Sizing up a CEO's ability to think outside the box

Trying to figure out a CEO's ability to think (and act) outside the box can be difficult. Here are a few ways to assess a CEO's ability to think creatively and implement creative ideas:

- ✔ Look at the CEO's seven-factor assessment score (see the related section earlier in this chapter). A score of 30 out of a possible 35 points indicates that the CEO is very capable of thinking outside the box. A score of 25 indicates a moderate capacity for creative thinking and behavior.

- ✔ Interview the CEO's former co-workers, who can usually tell you about the CEO's ability or tendency to think outside the box and receptiveness to creative ideas.

- ✔ Study historical data to see how creative this CEO's past decisions and actions have been.

A CEO doesn't necessarily need to be creative. By surrounding herself with creative people and letting them influence her decisions, she can foster a corporate culture of creativity that's just as good if not better than what a highly creative CEO can accomplish.

Assessing a CEO's willingness to move assets to new areas

Some CEOs get stuck in the rut of tradition, focusing on the organization's history of success in a particular sector, its core competencies, and where it tends to excel in relation to its competitors. That type of thinking and leadership often dooms an organization to being left behind by more innovative competitors.

The most radical CEOs take a portfolio approach to internal resources, including cash, liquidity, talent, and skills. In other words, they act as though they're managing an investment portfolio. As they spot opportunities or threats, they're more willing than your average CEO to shift resources in response and extend beyond their historical comfort zone to pursue opportunities. These individuals can be dangerous competitors if you happen to be operating in a sector in which they have identified a major growth opportunity.

As you research the competition, look for evidence of each competitor reaching out beyond its traditional areas of success to expand its reach, and you'll usually discover CEOs who are willing to shift assets to pursue momentary advantages. For example, General Electric has an excellent track record for getting rid of lower-performing products in order to invest in higher-opportunity areas.

Gauging a CEO's risk tolerance

A CEO's risk tolerance is usually fairly indicative of an organization's propensity toward risk and its drive to innovate. To gauge a CEO's risk tolerance, consider the following:

- **The CEO's seven-factor assessment score:** The higher the score, the more willing he is to take risks.

- **The CEO's historic risk-related behavior:** High rollers are usually high rollers in all aspects of their lives.

- **Information you've found in industry and other publications:** A story about a CEO making a bold move to seize a momentary advantage reveals a great deal about his attitude toward risk.

Going toe to toe rather than toeing the line

When Dave House took over as the new CEO of Bay Networks, the company was in trouble. One of his first statements to his employees was a bit of a shocker: "If you are not willing to fight with me for what you believe in, you might not be right for this company." Stories of his early months at Bay Networks became the subject of some major publications. They told of junior managers standing toe to toe with House, disputing a decision with him. After the fight was over, House would reach out and shake the hand of his opponent and thank him for his willingness to argue for a different view.

Many people attribute Dave House's successful transformation of the firm's culture to the successful turnaround of the company.

The moral of this story is that a CEO's management style can dramatically influence how an organization operates. Knowing Dave House's management style, an analyst can accurately predict that regardless of the organization he leads, everyone in the organization will have a voice and be encouraged to contribute and fight for their creative ideas.

Chapter 13

Creating Competitor Profiles

. . . .

In This Chapter

▶ Profiling competitors' marketing and innovation strategies

▶ Using a future competitive index to see how you stack up against the competition

▶ Forecasting how competitors are likely to act and react

▶ Keeping an eye on the competition's evolution (and your customers' health)

. . . .

You probably know which organizations directly and indirectly compete against you, but you may know very little if anything about their inner workings and how much of a threat they really pose to your organization. To get a better feel for who your competitors are and how formidable they may be now and in the future, create a profile for each of them, as I explain in this chapter.

Few organizations currently understand or use competitor profiling to gain information advantage and put it to use in formulating strategies. That's their loss and your gain. By harnessing the power of profiling, you equip your organization with superior knowledge as well as predictive abilities that others simply don't have. You also gain the ability to target your strategic initiatives. By understanding where each competitor's weakness is, you can often spend less to attack those weaknesses, and your competitors who have those weaknesses will have to overspend just to catch up.

If you're using competitive profiling like the seven-factor assessment I present in this chapter and your competitors aren't using any sort of competitor profiling, you're going to see important competitive issues much sooner than they spot them, assuming they ever do.

Introducing the Seven-Factor Profile

Nobody can tell you what consumers will be buying, which competitors will be leading the sector, or which product will be the next big thing three years down the road. As a CI professional, however, the quality of your analysis is measured by its predictive power. To be of any use, it needs to be able to answer questions such as these:

✔ **What's the probability of vertical integration in any given sector in which we do business?** *Vertical integration,* also referred to as *disintermediation,* consists of combining two or more stages of a production process traditionally performed by separate companies into one company.

✔ **Which competitors are most capable of discovering the next big thing?**

✔ **What pricing strategies will characterize the sector within the next three years?** Product differentiation? Image differentiation? Commoditization? The biggest mistake you can make is to miss the shift to *commoditization* — when no distinct difference exists between products, so they tend to be priced the same and all you have left to stand above the crowd is your image. For example, computer processors are usually introduced as a differentiated product (the newest, best thing), but within a matter of months, they become commodity products (replaced by the next best thing).

Ask whether the future will allow you to differentiate based on product. (If you can't differentiate based on product or superiority, then your strategy must shift to differentiating based on image — positioning of the product).

✔ **Which noncompetitors or technologies could move into this sector?**

✔ **What length of product life cycles (and rate of innovation) will characterize this sector in the future?**

Enter the seven-factor profile, an approach that has proven to be highly predictive of future competition. More than 400 actual projects have been completed (including studies of 200 Fortune 500 companies), and the indexes have been consistently accurate.

The seven-factor profile shows you how your organization stacks up against the competition and reveals which competitors you really need to pay attention to (and those you can pretty much ignore, at least for the immediate future). It enables you to evaluate how competitive a market sector or any organization in that sector will be in three years based on the following seven factors:

✔ Marketing

✔ Innovation

✔ Management

✔ Culture

✔ Structure

✔ Decision systems

✔ Strategic planning

As a bonus, the profiles you create may also provide valuable insight that leads to new strategic initiatives.

What's the matter with SWOT?

For many years, CI has relied on SWOT (strengths, weaknesses, opportunities, threats) analysis to evaluate the competitive landscape. Although SWOT is still widely used in some intelligence circles, shortcomings in the approach may lead to highly flawed conclusions. Here are just a few problems with SWOT:

✔ It tends to be present focused rather than future focused. Looking at current products, strategies, and capabilities sheds little

or no light on what your organization needs to become in order to succeed in the future.

✔ It usually avoids or misses the complexity and the velocity of change in the future competitive context.

✔ It has little or no predictive power.

SWOT is best used as a starting point — useful for certain short-term applications but much less so for formulating long-term strategies.

Calculating the Future Competitive Index for a Market Sector

When you're playing king of the mountain, you need to know where you stand in relation to the other players so you can formulate a strategy for beating them. In the business world, for example, if your top three competitors introduce new products every 24 months, you know that you need to develop new products along the same timeline or faster to remain competitive.

To gauge just how competitive your competitors will be over the course of the next three years or so, calculate the competitive index for the market sector you're focusing on. The competitive index reflects a composite measurement of your company's competition in the areas of aggressiveness in marketing and innovation — the first two factors in the seven-factor profile. In the following sections, I explain how to figure the competitive index and tell you what the numbers mean.

Obtaining ratings and calculating the competitive index

The future competitive index looks at two aspects of marketing — advertising and sales — and two aspects of innovation — R&D (research and development) and new product introduction. You and others rate how aggressive you predict the competition as a whole will be in each of those four categories in the months and years to come on a scale of 1 to 5 (1 = passive, 2 = stable, 3 = slightly aggressive, 4 = aggressive, 5 = highly aggressive). Here's how to collect information and calculate the index:

1. **Find out internal management's view by recruiting 10 to 20 individuals (not senior executives) who work in different areas of your organization to rate your organization and its competitors on the four factors listed.** If you don't have 10 people, get input from as many as you can. You can use the future competition questionnaire shown in Figure 13-1 to gather input.

2. **Gather information from external sources (publications), as explained in Chapter 6, and assign ratings based on your research.**

3. **If you have the budget and time, get some expert opinions.** Consult experts and expert panels, as I explain in Chapter 7, to see how they would rate your organization and its competitors.

Future Competition Questionnaire

Sector: North American Cell Phone Market for Fully Integrated Devices (FIDs)
(US and Canada)

Please complete this questionnaire and submit it to the CI department. DO NOT include your name. Your input is confidential.

Please rate how aggressive you think competitors in the North American Cell Phone Market for Fully Integrated Devices (FIDs) will be over the course of the next three years. Enter a rating in each of the following four blanks on a scale of 1 to 5 with 1 = passive, 2 = stable, 3 = slightly aggressive, 4 = aggressive, and 5 = highly aggressive.

Marketing

_____ Advertising
_____ Sales

Innovation

_____ Research & development
_____ New product introduction

Figure 13-1: Future competition questionnaire.

---

4. **Summarize (average) the ratings of marketing aggressiveness from each group and record the results on a chart, as shown in Figure 13-2.**

5. **Summarize (average) the ratings of innovation aggressiveness from each group and record the results on a chart, as shown in Figure 13-3.**

6. **Combine your results into a single chart, as shown in Figure 13-4.**

    Note that the chart tracks three views: Internal view (what people inside your organization think), publications view (what your research tells you), and experts view (the collective opinion of any experts or expert panels you consulted). The chart includes a legend that breaks down the scores for these three views.

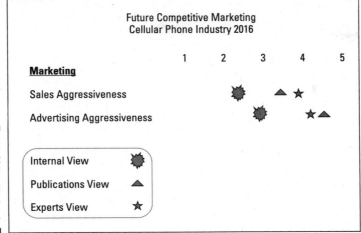

Illustration courtesy of Jim Underwood

Figure 13-2:
Chart
sales and
advertising
aggressive-
ness.

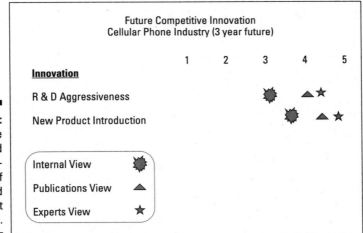

Illustration courtesy of Jim Underwood

Figure 13-3:
Chart the
perceived
aggres-
siveness of
R&D and
new product
introduction.

7. **Based on the three ratings (internal, publications, and experts), choose a rating that you think most accurately represents how the sector scores in each of the four areas listed and place an X on the chart to mark your ratings, as shown in Figure 13-5.**

Internal management's view is usually the least accurate, because it usually suffers from blind spots and bias. The view you derive from publications is probably more accurate, and expert views are usually the most accurate. However, accuracy varies according to your sources. Only you can determine the relative accuracy of each source to determine your own rating.

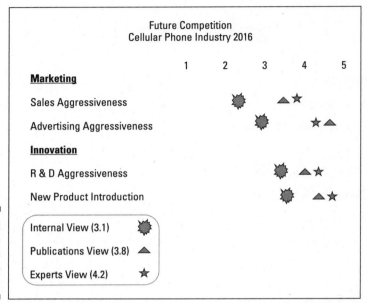

Figure 13-4:
Combine
results into
a single
chart.

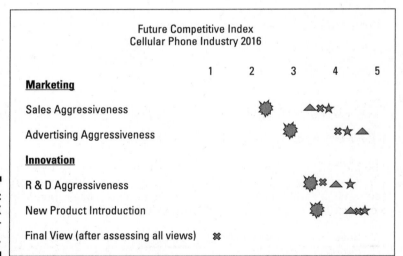

Figure 13-5:
Place an X
to mark your
rating.

8. **Create a chart that shows only your final estimate of the most accurate view of the competition's future marketing and innovation ratings, as shown in Figure 13-6.**

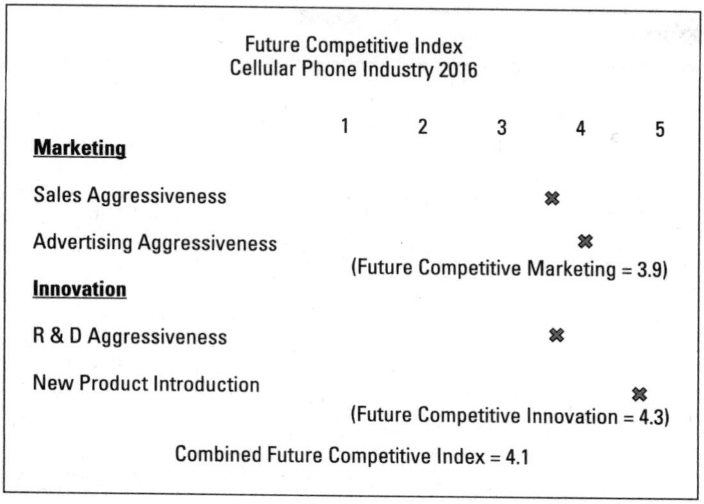

Future Competitive Index
Cellular Phone Industry 2016

	1	2	3	4	5
Marketing					
Sales Aggressiveness				✖	
Advertising Aggressiveness				✖	

(Future Competitive Marketing = 3.9)

Innovation

R & D Aggressiveness				✖	
New Product Introduction					✖

(Future Competitive Innovation = 4.3)

Combined Future Competitive Index = 4.1

Figure 13-6:
Chart only
your rating.

Illustration courtesy of Jim Underwood

9. **Calculate the average for marketing and the average for innovation.**

   In this example, the future competitor marketing index is 3.9, and the future competitive innovation index is 4.3.

10. **Average the two indexes from Step 7 to determine the future competitive index.**

   In this example, the competitive index is 4.1. (3.9 + 4.3 = 8.2 ÷ 2 = 4.1)

Examining the implications of a market sector's competitive index

The future competitive index calculated in the preceding section serves as a benchmark or baseline that offers insight into just how competitive the sector is and what an organization needs to do to survive and thrive in such a competitive environment, as shown in Table 13-1.

Table 13-1	Future Competitive Index Implications
Benchmark	*Implications*
0–1.99	This level of competition rarely occurs. An index in this range generally indicates that the firm is competing in a highly monopolistic sector. At that level, the demand for the product generally exceeds the existing supply.

(continued)

Table 13-1 *(continued)*

Benchmark	Implications
2.0–2.99	Generally, competitor moves are predictable, and change is slow enough that a follower strategy, as well as benchmarking of products, works fairly well.
3.0–3.99	As the competitive index passes 3.0, the environment becomes much more competitive, and the velocity of change accelerates. As the index approaches 3.99, complexity rises, and the level of predictability becomes very low.
4.0–5.0	At this level, product commoditization occurs and attempts to differentiate from the competition begin to fail; the only competitive differentiator is price. The industry usually has more competitors than product demand requires, which usually results in industry consolidation. Expect vertical integration to occur because competition at this level usually results in extreme pressure on profits.

Using the marketing and innovation indexes to inform strategic decisions

By carefully examining marketing and innovation ratings for a market sector, you can tell where your competitors will be allocating their resources and where you need to step up your efforts. Refer to the chart in Figure 13-6 and note the following:

✔ The sector as a whole will invest fairly aggressively in sales (3.8) and advertising (4.1).

✔ The sector's emphasis on research and development is fairly high at about 3.8.

✔ The competition's new product introduction appears to be extremely high at 4.8. At this level, competitor product innovation may have a significant impact on shortening the product life cycles in the sector.

So what does all this mean to your organization?

✔ The future competitor marketing index of 3.9 indicates that you have some room to achieve a momentary advantage in this area. By increasing your efforts and expenditures in sales and advertising, you may be able to increase market share.

✔ The sector's emphasis on R&D (3.8) means that you should probably monitor your own R&D spending and be prepared to increase it to at least the baseline level for competitors in this sector.

✔ Because new product introduction is likely to be aggressive, you need to watch for sector disruption in the future. This high index could pose a significant threat to your company if you don't keep up the pace.

Profiling Your Key Competitors' Organizational Attributes

Looking at a sector's competitive benchmark and the ratings for individual competitors gives you a broad view of how competitive your competitors will be over the next three years or so, but you can't always trust those ratings when studying them in a vacuum. To obtain a clearer idea of what you're up against, examine the benchmark and ratings in the context of your competitors' organizational attributes, which comprise the remaining five items of the seven-factor profile:

  ✔ Management

  ✔ Culture

  ✔ Structure

  ✔ Decision systems

  ✔ Strategic planning

In the following sections, I lead you through the process of rating your own organization and each of your competitors in these areas.

Management

Based on your research and the assessment of management that I help you conduct in Chapter 12, rate management for each of your competitors based on the following five-point scale:

  1 = Highly controlling

  2 = Controlling

  3 = Goal oriented

  4 = Moderately empowering

  5 = Highly empowering

Culture

Based on your research and the assessment of culture that I help you conduct in Chapter 12, rate the corporate culture for each of your competitors based on the following five-point scale:

1 = Rigid: averse to change

2 = Nonadaptive: resistant to change

3 = Moderately adaptive: slow to change

4 = Adaptive: highly adaptive to change

5 = Proactive: iconoclastic, create the future

Structure

Assess each competitor's structure using the following scale:

1 = Hierarchical: bureaucratic, inflexible

2 = Traditional: mostly bureaucratic, rarely flexible

3 = Divisional: moderate level of flexibility

4 = Matrix structure: cross-functional relationships, very flexible

5 = Matrix, bicentralized, empowered, highly flexible

Decision systems

Based on your research, rate each competitor's decision systems (how they make decisions related to speed and horizon/time frame), using the following five-point scale:

1 = Internally focused: incredibly slow

2 = Internally focused: slow

3 = Internal with some external focus: moderately slow

4 = Externally focused: fast with future-focused decisions

5 = Externally driven: light-speed decisions, proactively future focused

Strategic planning

Figuring out how competitors plan their strategy can be very difficult. Many don't talk about how they plan, so you can't get that info. By observing an organization over time, however, you can often figure out how the organization "thinks." For example, 3M's strategic planning focuses about 20 percent of its efforts around nonlinear thinking; that is, the company likes to force people out of the box when thinking about the future.

On the following scale of one to five, rate each of your competitors in the area of strategic planning based on your observations:

1 = Little or no formal strategic planning

2 = Strategy basically involves the budgeting process

3 = Historically focused on perceived competencies, resources, and advantage

4 = Future focused, creativity driven, and innovative

5 = Focused on asset maximization: nonlinear, systems thinking

Strategic planning at level 3 and below tends to be focused on historic patterns, competencies, product areas, and budget concerns. As the approach becomes more externally focused, the firm's leadership is more willing to innovate outside of historic areas of competence for the purpose of discovering novel, high-growth opportunities.

Using Seven-Factor Profiles to Predict Future Competitor Actions

Assuming that you've read the previous sections in this chapter, you have all the skills you need to create seven-factor profiles for your organization and your competitors. Simply rate each organization on a scale of one to five in each of the following areas based on the internal view, publications view, and experts view:

- ✔ Marketing
- ✔ Innovation
- ✔ Management

- ✔ Culture
- ✔ Structure
- ✔ Decision systems
- ✔ Strategic planning

Rating sectors and competitors isn't a one-shot event. To maintain a steady succession of momentary advantages, you need to keep your competitive index and seven-factor assessments up-to-date according to the following guidelines:

- ✔ Update your seven-factor assessments every 12 months and maintain them as part of your competitive intelligence library.

- ✔ Update your future competitive index at least once every 12 months. *Note:* If the velocity of change in an industry sector accelerates, you may need to update the index more frequently.

Now that you have seven-factor ratings for your organization and all the organizations you'll be competing against in a specific sector, you're ready to put those ratings to work in the following practical applications:

- ✔ Maintain a constant awareness of the key aspects of each competitor.

- ✔ Conduct highly accurate and insightful SWOT analysis.

- ✔ Predict future competitor initiatives and each competitor's most probable move when a major event occurs in the sector.

- ✔ Detect weaknesses in the industry overall that you can possibly take advantage of.

- ✔ Identify each competitor's strengths and weaknesses so you can minimize your investment in crafting your strategy to deal with each one.

- ✔ Predict with reasonable accuracy the winners and the losers.

- ✔ Target organizations that may be prime acquisitions candidates.

Look at each company's scores in relation to the sector's competitive index. Companies that rate –1 below the sector's competitive index in all or most areas will generally have a difficult time competing in the future. If all or most of an organization's ratings fall –1.5 below the index, it's a prime candidate for failure in the future unless it takes steps to improve its numbers.

Figures 13-7 and 13-8 show the seven-factor ratings of two companies, which I call Filbert and Macadamia, competing in the same sector. The vertical line labeled *Competitive Index* represents the benchmark for the sector. Each of the seven factors is rated on a scale of 1 to 5.

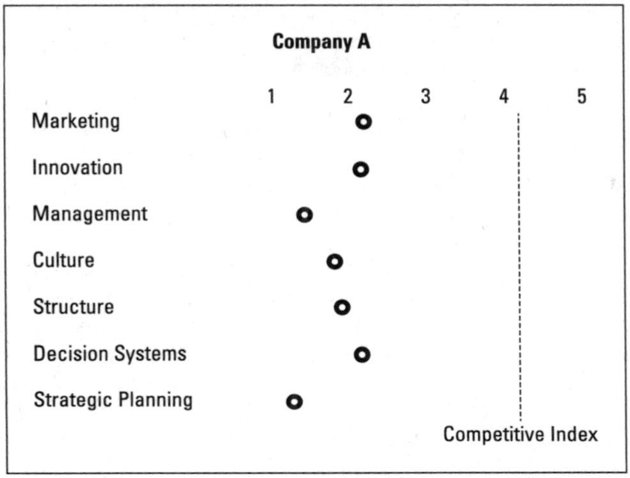

Company A

	1	2	3	4	5
Marketing		○			
Innovation		○			
Management	○				
Culture		○			
Structure		○			
Decision Systems		○			
Strategic Planning	○				

Competitive Index

Figure 13-7: Filbert's seven-factor profile.

Illustration by Wiley, Composition Services Graphics

Company B

	1	2	3	4	5
Marketing				○	
Innovation					○
Management				○	
Culture				○	
Structure				○	
Decision Systems					○
Strategic Planning					○

Competitive Index

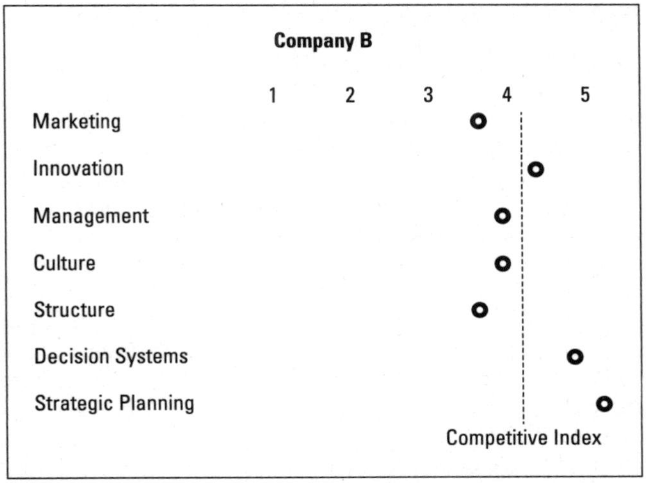

Figure 13-8: Macadamia's seven-factor profile.

Illustration by Wiley, Composition Services Graphics

Filbert (Company A) is a publicly traded company. Over the years, the firm has been able to develop a few good products. However, with a mere glance at its seven-factor profile, you can quickly see that the company is woefully below the sector's standard (represented by the competitive index line). The firm is almost incapable of executing strategy, especially if it involves some level of novel change. Even if the firm were able to develop some new products, the profile reveals that the current organization is incapable of executing those strategies.

Conversely, Macadamia's (Company B's) profile is indicative of a very robust organization. It, too, is a publicly traded company, but it's much more closely aligned with the future competitive index.

When you begin to compare seven-factor profiles in this way, you need little or no imagination to spot the future winners and losers. In this case, you could pretty much ignore Filbert (for now) and focus your attention on competing with Macadamia — a formidable foe.

Don't dismiss any competitor, regardless of how low its scores happen to be. Situations can change via takeovers, adjustments in personnel, changes in strategy, and so on. Continue to monitor low-scoring competitors so you're not blindsided by a dramatic turnaround.

Keeping in mind the seven-factor assessment when reading financial reports and considering threats can shed a lot of light on conditions in your sector. I describe how in the following sections.

Reading financials with a seven-factor eye to identify the biggest threats

Numbers can be very deceptive when reviewed out of context. For example, if you're examining only financial reports, Filbert could come out on top simply because it has chosen to cut costs to boost current profits. Macadamia, on the other hand, may be showing net losses over an extended period of time as it ramps up to introduce and market a whole new line of innovative products. The company that stands to win the future is more likely to come out on top eventually.

To spot emerging threats from a competitor, review its financial statements in the light of its seven-factor assessment. There could be a forward-thinking reason behind the competitor's financials.

Predicting the most probable competitor thrusts

Seven-factor ratings can help you identify what area a competitor is strongest in and weakest in so you can spot the most and least probable and serious threats that a competitor poses to your organization.

Threats are most likely to arise from a competitor's area of strength. For example, although Macadamia is relatively strong in marketing, it's even stronger in innovation and strategic planning. You can expect the organization to respond to a competitive situation by rolling out more novel products before it engages in upping marketing expenditures. That kind of information can be critically important to your strategic-planning teams.

Keeping Tabs on Your Customers

Competitive intelligence often focuses on competitors, but you also need to keep track of your customers. After all, if your top customers begin to sneeze, you're the one who's going to catch the cold. Use the same profiling technique I describe in the earlier section "Profiling Your Key Competitors' Organizational Attributes" to evaluate your customers. The more you practice using this technique, the better you become at picking winners and losers and spotting which customers and competitors are headed for trouble.

To monitor the health of your customers, do the following:

- **Maintain seven-factor profiles on your top five to ten customers.** Compare profiles from year to year so you can pick up on important changes and warning signs.

- **If a key customer is a publicly traded company, run key financial ratios, including the *current ratio* (current assets divided by current liabilities).** Current assets are generally those that can be turned into cash within 30 days; current liabilities are those that are due within 30 days. The current ratio gives you an idea of a company's *liquidity,* which is its ability to pay off its current liabilities.

    Figure 13-9 is a simple example of the Jones Company, whose current ratio is trending in the wrong direction. Between 2009 and 2014, the ability of the firm to cover its current liabilities dropped from 2.5 down to 0.7. In other words, in 2009, it had the ability to pay off all current liabilities to the tune of 250 percent of what it owed. But by 2014, it could pay off only 70 percent of its current payables as of December 31.

    Keep a five-year running chart that allows you to visually compare the year-by-year changes that occur in each customer's current ratio.

- **Maintain an intelligence file on each of your key customers.** Changes in management, merger rumors, or other factors can have an impact on the future of those customers and your business.

Intel on customers can be very valuable for executive decision making. In some cases, if intel reveals that a customer is in trouble, digging up additional information may identify a customer as a prime takeover target.

Jones Co.					
	Dec. 31, 2014	Dec. 31, 2013	Dec. 31, 2011	Dec. 31, 2010	Dec. 31, 2009
Current Assets	$10,000,000	$8,000,000	$7,000,000	$6,000,000	$5,000,000
Current Liabilities	$15,000,000	$8,000,000	$6,000,000	$4,000,000	$2,000,000
Current Ratio	0.7	1	1.2	1.5	2.5

Chapter 14

Spotting and Forecasting Industry Trends

To stay on the cutting edge, companies need to be able to spot and forecast industry trends, which vary depending on the type of market. Spotting trends and predicting where markets are headed enables companies to avoid future calamities while taking advantage of emerging opportunities.

In this chapter, I explain special considerations you need to make depending on the nature of the market you're analyzing, such as whether you're looking at a fragmented, secondary, emerging, mature, declining, or global market.

Exploring Trends in Fragmented and Secondary Markets

Before you start examining trends in fragmented and secondary markets, you need to understand the nature of these market types:

> ✔ A *fragmented market* is one that's populated by multiple, often smaller players rather than a couple dominant players. It's frequently characterized by emerging products or technologies.

✔ *Secondary markets,* often referred to as *aftermarkets,* are extensions of primary markets that typically appear in one of the following forms:

- **Original equipment manufacturer (OEM) replacement parts:** Many manufacturers earn significant profits from the sale of replacement parts for items they manufacture, including cars, home appliances, and airplanes.

- **Aftermarket parts:** Third parties manufacture products for the purpose of replacing OEM parts, usually with less-expensive options.

- **Customers other than those a product was designed for:** For example, jewelry makers may use toolboxes and tools designed for general use.

- **Used parts:** For example, a used oil-field pump jack is often viewed as a great buy (versus a new one), because a pump jack often has a useful life of 100 years.

Fragmented and secondary markets are often the most susceptible to rapid acceleration in the velocity of change for various reasons, so you really need to stay on your toes in these markets. In the following sections, I explain what you need to monitor closely.

Navigating fragmented markets

Fragmented markets tend to be dominated by smaller firms that serve local customers. Competition isn't quite as stiff as in national and international markets, and profit margins are higher. Organizations that operate in fragmented markets often have to follow different rules for success than do their national and international counterparts. When you're analyzing fragmented markets, keep the following points in mind:

✔ **Fragmented markets tend to be vulnerable.** Because of the massive size of external (often global) competitors, you have to be constantly vigilant of competitor thrusts into those markets.

✔ **Fragmented markets are often subject to uniquely different issues than global markets are.** For example, governmental regulations have changed various aspects and requirements for products in California. If you're looking to expand operations into a specific location, get up to speed on any regional issues that may impact business.

Fragmented markets have different rules of the game and can be somewhat volatile in nature. CI's ability to keep upper management informed about fragmented markets is a key to successfully competing in these markets.

When competing in fragmented markets, clarify your understanding of the market by answering the following questions:

- **Why is the market fragmented?** Understanding why the market is fragmented is very important. The market may involve an outdated distribution system with wholesalers in the middle of the value chain. It also may be an area that requires some level of personalized service. Numerous other factors may be involved, and discovering those factors may reveal opportunities for your company.

- **What are the *growth* prospects for the market or sector?** Compare the growth prospects for different market sectors and try to identify sectors with moderate- to high-growth prospects. Sectors with higher growth prospects are those in which your organization has the opportunity to gain the first-mover advantage and claim a bigger share of the market.

- **What are the future *profit* (profit margin) prospects for the market or sector?** You always need to think about growth prospects in the light of future profit margins. Highly competitive markets are at a greater risk of diminished profit margins. Look at the competitive index for the market or sector (I tell you how to calculate this in Chapter 13). If the index approaches or rises above 4, the increased level of competitive behavior is likely to drive down profits, even in markets or sectors that have moderate to high future-growth prospects.

- **Does the market still offer some first-mover opportunities?** The first companies to enter a market or sector usually profit the most. After all, if a certain fishing hole has already been fished out, you're probably only going to land a few bluegills. If your sector has been fished out, your best bet is to paddle out to areas with the biggest opportunities and the least amount of competition. CI can be instrumental in helping your organization capture a series of next little things and next big things on a continual basis, driving profits higher and your competition crazy.

Usually only one company captures the first-mover advantage, and that's usually where you want to be. However, sometimes you can actually gain an advantage by being a fast follower; that is, not being the leader of the pack but being in the pack of early adopters. Fast followers often take advantage of lower entry costs by allowing the leader of the pack to invest in the high cost of development and then simply following the trail blazed by the leader. The earlier you try to enter, the higher the rewards, but the higher the cost, too.

- **What are the geographic considerations of the market?** Sometimes regional markets exist due to high transportation costs or government regulations. Changes in any of those factors can change the attractiveness of the fragmented market. The factors you need to consider depend on whether you're dealing with an existing or emerging market:

- **Existing market:** Conduct additional research to identify the key drivers that led to fragmentation. When you understand what those drivers are, you're ready to begin thinking about the potential value of the market.

- **Emerging market:** Consider approaching emerging products with the same trepidation you have when considering the adoption of new technologies. You rarely want to be on the bleeding edge, which can be very costly. Instead, try to use CI to place your organization on the leading edge, where you can gain first-mover advantage on a budget.

✔ **What's the probability of market consolidation?** In other words, does an opportunity exist for a company to acquire a number of competitors for the purpose of becoming the dominant player in the market? Keep an eye on the following factors when looking for opportunities in fragmented markets that are undergoing change:

- Changes in local laws, regulations, or attitudes

- Trends toward vertical integration in the sector

- Positive economic trends that may drive the market

- Consumer expansion

Fragmented markets tend to get targeted by large national or international companies because they're typically less competitive and offer higher profit margins. The Walmart phenomenon changed the makeup of almost every business in the United States within a few decades and is now affecting global markets as well. *Vertical integration* or *disintermediation* (dissolution of supply chains) is a sure sign that frame-breaking change is already occurring in a sector.

✔ **Do any technologies drive this market? If they do, how important is each technology from a competitive standpoint?** Technology often triggers an unexpected tsunami in a market, particularly a fragmented one. For example, although the move from brick-and-mortar to online stores didn't happen overnight, the technology that made it possible caused a radical shift in how consumers shop and buy many products and services.

✔ **What's the typical *product life cycle* — the amount of time from a product's introduction to its modification or steep decline — in this market?** Fragmented markets tend to be less competitive (lower competitor index), so product life cycles are typically much longer (and more profitable) than in markets subject to national or international competitors.

Larger national and international competitors typically spend the R&D dollars so that they can remain competitive by continually launching new products. In most cases, this doesn't happen in fragmented markets until the larger competitors decide to try to capture increased global market share by attacking those markets.

Beware of the 800-pound gorilla factor

Highly fragmented markets are always susceptible to consolidation of some sort. Why? Because more often than not you have a massive network of players involved in a highly inefficient manner in bringing products to consumers.

In the late 1970s, for example, mass merchandising began penetrating different markets. At that time, more than 12,000 small office-products firms were doing business in the United States. Almost all were small, owner-operated businesses. As the big-box concept hit that market, almost all those 12,000 companies went bankrupt or were forced to close. Additionally, the entire distribution chain of wholesalers in the industry was devastated. And it all occurred in fewer than 48 months.

✔ **Are any new players entering the market?** New competitors can blind-side you in any market or sector, even in fragmented markets. Apple demonstrated to the world that it's possible to identify a high return opportunity and to acquire the resources and capabilities to radically impact a market. Steve Job's success is not novel, but it's still not "business as usual" for a lot of competitors. A lot of companies, such as Texas Instruments, have engaged in similar unrelated diversification and have ended up causing major disruptions in markets. Additionally, they've made a lot of profit doing it.

✔ **Do any of the ten forces (economy, ideology, politics, media, regulations, and so on) impact the market?** Regardless of the type of market in which you're doing business, you need to keep an eye on the ten forces that are likely to impact the sector and your business. (See Chapter 2 for the details of ten-forces analysis.) The best strategy in the world won't avert the challenges of a tsunami or a volcanic eruption like Mt. Pinatubo. When global forces are at work, the firm must clearly be in adaption mode if it is to succeed.

Staying on top of secondary markets

Secondary markets may be one of your company's most profitable areas, but they may also pose a significant threat to your profits when third parties try to swoop in and claim their pieces of the pie.

To keep tabs on secondary markets, here's what you need to do:

✔ **Be aware of your company's key profit producers.** In many cases, the most profit from the sale of a product is the sale of replacement parts, not the original product. Those fat margins can be tempting for agile competitors who specialize in aftermarket parts.

Take a lesson from the aircraft industry

A major aircraft manufacturer was known to make incredible profits on the sale of spare parts for its aircraft. In one case, 25 years after a product was introduced, the company was still racking up fat profits from spare parts sales.

That market deteriorated when a group of small-parts manufacturers convinced the government to change spare-parts regulations for aircraft to allow them to build equivalent parts, using the same manufacturing standards, and sell the parts at substantially lower prices. The aircraft manufacturer took a major hit, and your organization may too if you don't prepare for competition in secondary markets.

✔ **Keep tabs on your secondary market competitors.** Find out who they are, how agile they are, and how willing they are to invest in producing your aftermarket components.

✔ **Watch for companies who compete on price alone.** They often enter a market by offering high discounts, which can rapidly erode profits in a sector.

✔ **Maintain an active intelligence file on all your secondary-market competitors.** See Chapter 13 for guidance on how to profile your competitors.

Keeping Pace with Emerging Markets

In its broadest interpretation, an *emerging market* is one that arises where no such market existed previously, usually in the context of the global marketplace. For example, when analysts talk about emerging markets, they're often referring to Brazil, Russia, India, and China. An emerging market may also arise out of a new use for a product, as in the case of corn being used to produce ethanol. In the United States, the federal government's mandate that gasoline contain 10 percent ethanol fueled an emerging market for biofuels.

Keeping your finger on the pulse of emerging markets in the global business world enables you to preempt competitors by

✔ Planning and perhaps even starting to execute your response before the market fully emerges.

✔ Mitigating the financial damage that may result from an emerging market that draws profits away from your traditional market. By knowing about the emerging market, you can start to reduce the damage before the event begins to impact your bottom line.

When conducting analysis on emerging markets, focus on key drivers. What are the forces that drive the emerging market you're observing or expecting? Key drivers may include anything from technology to economy to government regulations or even consumer sentiment. After you identify the key drivers, you know exactly where to focus your future CI efforts.

When you spot a declining market, look for an emerging market in another area. A declining market is usually the product of an emerging market.

The following sections help give you tips on spotting emerging markets that aren't the real deal and ones that are.

Watching out for counterfeit shifts

Keep an eye out for *counterfeit shifts* — emerging markets that are artificially manufactured. An example of a counterfeit shift is the market for ethanol in the United States. As pointed out in "The Great Ethanol Scam" (by Ed Wallace of *Bloomberg Businessweek*), very little hard data supports the government mandate for using ethanol:

- ✔ Ethanol-fuel mixes produce more smog than non-ethanol gasoline.
- ✔ Ethanol decreases gas mileage by up to 20 percent or even higher in blends that are more than 10 percent ethanol.
- ✔ More than 1 gallon of ethanol is required to produce 1 gallon of ethanol.
- ✔ Ethanol damages fuel systems.

To spot a counterfeit shift, answer the following three questions:

- ✔ Does the basic data contradict what's happening?
- ✔ Are political forces at play?
- ✔ Could any other unseen factors (other than market forces) be driving the shift?

If the answer to any of the three questions above is "yes," you need to be wary. It's important to remember that global economic forces will tend to destroy a counterfeit shift at some point.

As an analyst, you need to determine how long the counterfeit shift will last; in this case, whether the mandate will continue and for how long. The problem is, you can't predict how fast or when a counterfeit shift will succumb to reality, so you need to maintain a *dual-track strategy*. Here's how:

- ✔ Maximize your profit by carefully riding the wave of the counterfeit shift.
- ✔ Run a parallel planning effort that focuses on the product or service that will probably end up as the winner.

Keep in mind that the CI team's role is to act as trusted advisor. You may suggest a dual-track strategy, but the decision on how to respond lies in the hands of your organization's leaders. Keep senior management informed of the risk issues as well as the most probable replacement if and when the counterfeit shift ends.

Maintaining focus on future developments and trends

Predicting future developments and trends is often difficult, simply because they often involve forces and factors that are novel as opposed to an extension of the past. A great way to start gathering information about the future is to consider next-little-thing and next-big-thing analysis. Here's one approach:

1. **Make a list of your prime competitors, and then try to figure out the answers to the following questions about each competitor:**

   - What are the next little things I expect this competitor to create?

   - What are the next big things I expect this competitor to develop?

2. **Answer the following questions about the industry or sector as a whole:**

   - What are the next little things I expect to emerge in this industry?

   - What are the next big things I expect to emerge in this industry?

   - What next little things and next big things keep your CEO up at night?

Playing "What if?" to prepare for out-of-the-blue developments

You can't predict or anticipate every change that can possibly occur in an industry or a specific market. Here are a couple examples of discoveries that appeared out of the blue and resulted in seismic shifts:

✔ A number of years ago, researchers published a report claiming that oat-based products could lower cholesterol. The news caused an immediate shift in the production of baked goods and consumer food items.

✔ The Texas City, Texas, explosion in the 1950s led to the discovery that a certain type of chemical fertilizer when combined with a simple petroleum product could explode with equal force of dynamite. This out-of-the-blue event nearly destroyed the dynamite business for decades.

Although you may not be able to predict out-of-the-blue developments, you can prepare for them by playing "What if?" What if a new use is discovered for one of our products? How would we find out about it? How would we respond? What if a discovery or a new product makes our product obsolete? What do we need to do to stay in business if that occurs?

Tracking Changes in Mature Markets

A *mature market* is one that levels off, leaving little room for growth or innovation. Although mature markets may seem highly predictable, CI still needs to monitor activity in these markets with an eye toward the future. In the following sections, I show you what you need to keep your eye on in a mature market or sector.

Examining key life cycles

To analyze mature markets, you need to become somewhat of a biologist and study the life cycles of products, technologies, and demand. Each provides a different perspective and different level of insight into possible changes in the future of the market. In the following sections, I explain what to look for.

Product life cycles

Understanding product life cycles is critical to knowing when you need to introduce new products. If all your products are in the maturity or decline stage and you have nothing new in the works, your company needs to seriously ramp up its R&D efforts.

A product's life cycle typically lasts from about 18 months (in markets with a competitive index of 4 to 5) to seven years or so (in markets with a competitive index of 1 to 2). (For more about the competitive index, see Chapter 13.) The cycle progresses through several stages, as shown in Figure 14-1:

- ✔ **Product introduction:** Sales start out slow and steady.

- ✔ **Growth:** Sales grow steadily and fairly steeply.

- ✔ **Maturity:** Sales level off.

- ✔ **Decline:** Sales drop as the product becomes obsolete and consumers move on to other products that pique their interest.

Consider two aspects of a product's life cycle: total length (in months or years) and which stage the product is in at any given time. If you calculated the competitive index for a market sector, you can use that index to estimate the duration of product life cycles for any given market sector, as shown in Table 14-1.

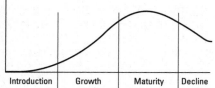

The Product Life Cycle

Figure 14-1:
The life
cycle of a
product.

Introduction | Growth | Maturity | Decline

Illustration by Wiley, Composition Services Graphics

Table 14-1	Estimating Product Life Cycles
Competitive Index	**Product Life-Cycle Duration (Estimate)**
< 2	6–7 years or more
2–3	3–5 years
3–4	2–3 years
4–5	18–24 months

Technology life cycles

Although you may not be able to predict the duration of a particular technology's life cycle, you need to be aware that every technology eventually becomes obsolete. Constantly monitor the market for any emerging technologies that may replace current technologies.

Consider how music playback technology has changed over the years. Vinyl records had an 80-year history of being used to store and play back audio, but audio CDs (which have only been around since 1982) are already being challenged by MP3s. And many technologies change significantly faster than audio playback has, so be sure to stay in tune with existing and emerging technologies that affect your sector.

Demand life cycles

Like product life cycles, demand life cycles are predictable and tend to be more generic in nature; for example, replacing people with technology. The demand life cycle is generic because it doesn't specify a certain technology. In fact, thousands of technology and product life cycles will occur over the duration of that particular demand life cycle.

Another good example of a demand life cycle is the demand for a natural resource such as coal. Heating or cooling a house requires energy from some outside resource, such as coal, heating oil, natural gas, or electricity, which is often produced by burning coal. However, the demand could drop drastically if other forms of renewable energy become commercially viable, such as

- ✔ **Zero-point or free energy:** Energy that certain elements or combinations of elements produce while at rest. Think of it in terms of having a battery that never needs to be charged.

- ✔ **Solar energy:** Some companies are developing roofing materials that have built-in solar cells, making it much easier, cheaper, and more attractive to add solar energy panels to a home.

- ✔ **Hydrogen energy:** Researchers are working on ways to make hydrogen fuel cells that are economical and safe. Although most of the research seems to be going on in the auto industry, hydrogen is also being considered for powering homes.

When cheap, clean, renewable energy resources become available, the demand for coal and other fossil fuels is likely to drop.

When a demand life cycle is approaching its final decline phase, the results to companies that depend on the demand for that solution may be catastrophic. Early warning, early planning, and great intelligence are the best ways to lessen the impact of a downward demand cycle.

Analyzing sales of mature market divisions

Over the years, business theorists have adopted the term *frame-breaking change* to describe tsunami-like moments in a business area. When frame-breaking change occurs, all the old rules of the game (and success factors) cease to apply and the existing product families or industries generally cease to exist.

Mature markets tend to be more susceptible than other types of markets to frame-breaking change. Just think of the record industry. Thanks to the digitizing of music and the storing of tunes as digital files, the need and usefulness of records and record players all but disappeared. When you see a competitor trying to extend the life of a mature product line, dig deeper to make sure you understand what's happening and the reason or strategy behind it. Conduct additional research to answer the following three questions:

✔ **Is the competitor number one or two in the market?** If not, any efforts on its part to extend the life of a mature product line are likely to fail. Generally, lower-ranked companies have higher costs due to lower volumes, which leads to lower economies of scale when applying fixed costs per product. If a back-of-the-pack competitor tries to extend the life of a declining product, that usually means they're limited on cash or have bad strategy. Only the leaders (who are usually the low-cost producers because of historically high volumes) can afford to try to stretch out a dying product (their cost is much lower in most cases).

Additionally, as the phenomenon of *experience curves* reveals, the manufacturer that has produced the most products can usually produce them at the lowest costs. (To find out more about experience curves, check out *Perspectives on Experience* by the Boston Consulting Group.)

✔ **Is the competitor extending the life of the product to take advantage of economies of scope?** *Economies of scope* involve multiple products that utilize many of the same components. For example, if a company makes a camera and a projector and is using the same lens in both, the combined volume of the lenses may keep its costs lower than those of competitors in each product area.

✔ **Is the competitor extending a product beyond its normal life cycle so it can hold off on developing new products to keep short-term profits higher?** This type of strategy is high risk and may indicate that the competitor has other problems you may need to investigate.

Spotting Opportunities and Avoiding Pitfalls in Declining Markets

Declining markets (or more precisely, decreasing demand for specific products) involve high risk, so you need to be able to recognize when you're competing in one. An obvious tell is when you see a competitor engaging in the following:

✔ **Rebranding its declining products:** Your competitor may try to tweak the product and introduce it as something new and improved to extend its life. (See the earlier section "Product life cycles" for details.)

✔ **Setting up smoke screens:** A company may increase its marketing and sales efforts around an aging product as a smoke screen to obscure its plans to introduce an innovative new product to the market.

Why would your competitor be doing such things? Well, competitors whose products reach the mature stage have almost always recovered their development and launch costs, so they have everything to gain and nothing to lose by extending the product's life. What you really want to watch for is a competitor's research and development expenses as a percentage of sales. An unexplained jump in the percentage tells you that while the company is pushing its old product, it may have a new and improved one in the pipeline.

Remain vigilant for any signs that your competitors are about to introduce something to the market that represents a revolutionary change. Such changes can result in long-term loss cycles while your company tries to catch up. Your stealth CI team (sales people, those who attend industry conventions, and so on) often get wind of such changes when a competitor engages in a little bragging. See Chapter 5 for details on gathering intel from your CI stealth team and others within your organization.

Expanding to the Global Marketplace

Global markets can offer both sales and sourcing opportunities. The CI team can help your organization's leaders by being aware of some key issues through the following ongoing tasks:

- ✔ **Track barter sales.** Often, a country has a cash shortage but significant capabilities in producing a product (often a raw material resource or a food product). Recognizing a barter situation — for example, one company trades vodka for a foreign company's computer systems — may give your company the opportunity to be the first to profitably enter an entirely new market before your competitors know about it.

  Barter sales can be difficult to track, but they can reveal golden opportunities for your company to wisely open new markets.

- ✔ **Maintain comprehensive intelligence information about political trends, legislative trends, joint-venture laws, and other areas that can involve very high levels of risk.** For example, some countries have laws that require 51 percent ownership by a national if a U.S. company wants to expand to the country. Sometimes, the U.S. company puts $50 million into the new company, and the 51 percent partner seems to disappear and end up retired and wealthy in Mexico. The U.S. company has no way to get its money back because its partner owned 51 percent and had the final decision-making power.

In the following sections, I wave the red flag to warn you of a couple serious risks often overlooked when doing business in other countries.

Avoiding the technology licensing nightmare

When doing business abroad, beware of *patent flooding* — the practice of other companies in a particular country filing patents on every part of your product when you import it into their country (for example, the on/off switch, the handle on the side of the product, the metal enclosure, and so on) and then suing you for patent infringement.

In many cases, the courts never allow you (the foreign company) to prevail in court. The only option you're given is to license your product to a company in that country and have them pay you a commission for every product sold. There's just one problem: By the time your licensed product rolls off their production line, their copy of your product is simultaneously rolling off another product line, and they have no interest or intent in paying you a royalty or licensing fee for those products.

The only way to avoid the technology-licensing nightmare is to be aware that it exists and avoid doing business in countries that have a bad reputation for patent flooding.

Acknowledging that if it sounds too good to be true, it probably is

Be careful setting up shop in a foreign country that requires 51 percent or more domestic ownership. History is loaded with stories of joint-venture opportunities involving millions of dollars in which the domestic partner simply took the money and ran.

Numerous companies have been willing to take on large financial risk due to the financial opportunity that a market in a particular country offers. Regardless of political connections and assurances, giving up a majority ownership of the organization abroad rarely turns out well for the company. Taking such risks where others before you have consistently failed isn't prudent.

Monitoring Mergers and Acquisitions

Regardless of the type of market you're analyzing, you're likely to see mergers and acquisitions as companies jockey for position. Keep a close eye on both because the type of merger or acquisition often reveals what a competitor is planning for the future. Here's a breakdown of the types of mergers and acquisitions you may see:

- ✔ **Market share merger:** Some companies merge simply to expand market share, which may involve merging regions or product lines.

- ✔ **Critical mass focused merger:** In some industries, advantage can be gained from size; for example, allocating fixed costs to more product units. In others, purchasing raw materials in greater quantities lowers production costs.

- ✔ **Pure acquisition buy:** One company may buy another to form a new company that's capable of growing market share and generating more profits than the two original companies working separately. The goal of a pure acquisition buy may range from improving the product portfolio to acquiring new product pipelines to expanding the talent pool.

- ✔ **Strategic buy:** Companies typically execute strategic buys to purchase capabilities they don't already have, which are key to remaining competitive and are expensive to develop from scratch. Strategic buys are common among some of the new technology companies, when buying a technology costs less than trying to develop a competing technology from scratch.

- ✔ **Technology buy:** A company acquires another firm that has a technology they want. Japanese companies often buy American companies to acquire technology.

  If you observe a company paying significantly higher than market price to acquire a company, you're usually looking at a strategic or technology buy.

Part IV
Getting Support for Intelligence Dissemination and Implementation

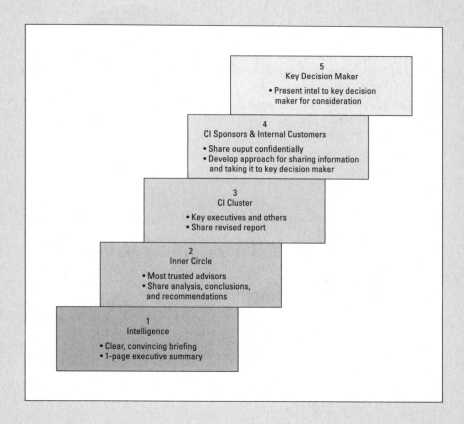

CI can't succeed without support from the people at the top of the ladder. Improve your odds of getting their help with the tips I provide at www.dummies.com/extras/competitiveintelligence.

In this part . . .

- ✔ Perform a strategic readiness assessment to find out just how receptive your organization's leadership and personnel are likely to be to innovation.

- ✔ Discover the ten values that almost all top-performing companies share.

- ✔ Brush up on best practices and approaches that help in communication, consensus building, and ultimately the execution of CI initiatives.

- ✔ Find out about the most common barriers that prevent companies from changing, and develop strategies and techniques to overcome them.

- ✔ Promote CI throughout your organization to improve everyone's willingness to cooperate and to get buy-in for your recommendations.

- ✔ Defend your company against competitor counterintelligence and other potential security breaches.

Chapter 15

Overcoming Barriers to Change

In This Chapter

▶ Performing a strategic readiness assessment

▶ Recognizing corporate values that lead to success

▶ Identifying change-averse personalities among leadership

▶ Banishing the enemies of innovation

▶ Overcoming interpretation bias to open minds

Most organizations resist change. They're so comfortable doing what they've always done that they're willing to do it for as long as it takes to go out of business. Many leaders are so stubborn and narcissistic that they reject brilliant ideas and even fire the creative souls who have the nerve to fight for those ideas. The sad fact is that roughly 80 percent of the time, companies fail to move from actionable intelligence to strategy and execution. They simply don't do what they *know* they must do to succeed.

As a competitive intelligence (CI) professional, you're likely to find yourself on the front lines in the battle against the enemies of change. When you do, you may need to fight that battle and win in order to help your organization succeed. In this chapter, I explain how to do just that by approaching obstacles in a number of ways. You can conduct an assessment to evaluate how ready your organization is for change, consider the change personalities of executives so that you know what reactions to expect, combat destructive narcissism, and more.

Always maintain your role as trusted advisor. As a member of the CI team, you may find yourself teetering on the line between trusted advisor and policy advocate. Advocating for a certain course of action that's unpopular could get you in trouble and compromise the CI team's ability to do its job, so be careful. Work though the proper channels diplomatically to get buy-in for a change. Present the facts in as convincing a manner as possible, without stepping on the often sensitive toes of the people leading your organization.

Administering the Strategic Readiness Questionnaire

A few organizations operate like clockwork. CI reveals an opportunity, management formulates a strategy, and everyone works together to capitalize on that opportunity. In most organizations, however, CI gets caught in the middle. It has intelligence that's critical to the future of the company but has little power to overcome a culture that's highly resistant to change. Even worse, an organization's leaders are often totally unaware of how resistant to change they and others in the organization are.

If you're an old hand at CI, you can see it, and you know that strong resistance to change puts your organization on a downhill sled to disaster. The most valuable service you can provide at this point is to issue a wake-up call by using the strategic readiness assessment (SRA), shown in Figure 15-1. The SRA provides an objective view of just how agile your organization is (or isn't). It quantifies change resistance in terms of numbers, which executives are often more willing to accept. The assessment isn't CI's opinion or what the people down in the organization feel. It's an accurate representation of the organization's resistance to change as a whole.

Because of the sensitive nature of the output, don't let the CI team sponsor the SRA. In fact, it's actually better if you get the CEO to hire an outside consultant to distribute and collect the assessment and calculate the organization's strategic readiness score. In any event, the CEO must champion the assessment and take full responsibility in the eyes of the organization for wanting the answers.

CI's role must be clearly understood as nothing more than handling the paperwork and passing the results to the CEO. Before distributing the assessment, prepare your organization's executive team and your own CI cluster so as to avoid stepping on any toes and to garner support for what you're doing. Here's how:

1. **Explain the purpose of the strategic readiness assessment to the executive team and explain that it's being done at the request of the CEO.**

   Ask your CEO whether she wants the first (CEO) question included, and remove the question if directed to do so. Also, never show the CEO score to anyone other than the CEO. In most cases, you're better off omitting the CEO question, but some really humble leaders (a good thing) want to know how they're doing and will respond by making changes. In any event, whether to include the question is the CEO's call.

Strategic Readiness Assessment

This questionnaire is totally confidential. Please put your unsigned response into a sealed box in the CI office that will be opened only after the survey is completed by all parties.

Below are 14 statements. In the blank to the left of each statement, please write the number from 1 to 5 that most accurately reflects your opinion:

1 = Strongly disagree

2 = Disagree

3 = Neither agree nor disagree

4 = Agree

5 = Strongly agree

Statements:

_____ Our CEO values subordinates and encourages them to be creative.

_____ Our managers value subordinates and empower them.

_____ Our culture is best described as "challenge everything."

_____ We reward people for developing creative solutions for problems.

_____ Our corporate structure can best be described as cross-functional and flexible.

_____ Our organization is capable of making decisions at the speed of light.

_____ We operate around a set of unchanging values that include integrity and taking care of our stakeholders, including employees, vendors, and customers.

_____ Our leadership operates around a value of transparency (no hidden agendas).

_____ Everyone is accountable to our corporate values, and the penalty for violating those values may include termination.

_____ Our company lives its values 100%.

_____ Our company's ethical standards are clear and unwavering.

_____ When it comes to employees, we are a company that "seeks the best for others."

_____ The standard of all activities within our company is "excellence." ("Excellence" includes how people are treated and the quality of all work.)

_____ We take pride in allowing people to fix what's wrong with processes.

Figure 15-1:
The strategic readiness assessment.

Illustration by Wiley, Composition Services Graphics

2. Brief your CI cluster — that is, the CI team and people who support the team's efforts — on the questionnaire and its purpose.

Your CI cluster consists of everyone on the CI team (which includes sponsors; see Chapter 2) along with key internal customers. For more about the CI cluster, see Chapter 16.

Employees need to be confident that their responses are confidential; otherwise, the accuracy of the results will suffer. If you're concerned that employees won't be honest, consider hiring an outside confidential-survey service to administer the questionnaire.

Have all employees complete and submit the questionnaire; then tally the scores as follows:

1. **Total the scores for each answer.**

   For example, the scores for the question "Our managers value subordinates and empower them" are 3, 2, 3, 2, 1, 2, 1, 2, 4, and 2, which add up to 22.

2. **Divide the totals from Step 1 by the total number of scores to determine the average score for each answer.**

   The scores came from a total of ten assessments, so you divide 22 by 10 to get an average score of 2.2 for that question.

3. **Divide the average score for each answer by 5 to determine the percentage score for each answer.**

   In this step you calculate where the average answer falls on a scale of 20 percent (indicating that employees strongly disagree with the statement) to 100 percent (indicating that employees strongly agree). Continuing the example, you divide 2.2 by 5 to get 0.44, which is 44 percent.

To determine your organization's total strategic readiness score, add up the percentages for each answer and divide by the total number of answers (14 if you included the CEO question or 13 if you omitted it). For example, suppose you're looking at the following scores:

CEO	42%
Managers	44%
Culture	37%
Rewards	48%
Structure	52%
Decisions	38%
Values	32%
Transparency	27%
Accountability	43%
Values Actualized	45%
Ethical Standards	48%
Value of Employees	39%
Excellence	54%
Process Flexibility	46%

The total is 595 percent. Divide by 14 to get 42.5 percent, which rounds up to a total strategic readiness score of 43 percent.

Aim high: The sky's the limit

If your strategic readiness score is less than stellar, consider setting goals to match the scores of one of the world's most successful airlines:

CEO	90%
Managers	95%
Culture	88%
Rewards	78%
Structure	87%
Decisions	90%
Values	95%
Transparency	90%

Accountability	98%
Values Actualized	92%
Ethical Standards	91%
Value of Employees	90%
Excellence	91%
Process Flexibility	87%
Strategic Readiness	**90%**

This airline consistently has been the top performer in a highly competitive market. Most of its competitors in the airline industry have a strategic readiness score between 30 and 60 percent.

Here's what the scores generally indicate regarding the ability of an organization to execute change or strategic initiatives:

20% to 35%: Incapable of executing change or strategy

36% to 50%: Highly diminished ability to execute change or strategy

51% to 70%: Moderately capable of executing change or strategy

71% to 85%: Fairly adept at executing change or strategy

86% and above: Highly adept at executing change or strategy

After performing your calculations, send the results and your interpretation of them to your organization's CEO *only*. Hopefully, the CEO is willing to lead the charge on correcting any glaring deficiencies in the organization. If the CEO discounts the report, take the following steps:

1. **Make sure that others within the organization never see the report.**

2. **Use the report to help you plan ways to use your CI support network to get your intelligence initiatives presented in such a manner as to gain buy-in from the executive team.**

See Chapter 16 for details on building and collaborating with supporters.

One of the best ways to impress upon an organization's leadership the importance of any given intel is to engage in scenarios and war games, as explained in Chapter 11. When leaders see how a situation plays out or the consequences of inaction, they're more likely to accept the current reality and the need to formulate and implement a response.

Adopting the Ten Values of High-Performing Companies

Companies are like families. Some are harmonious and always seem to excel, others have theirs ups and downs but seem to do okay, and some are clearly dysfunctional. For your organization to have any hope of surviving and thriving in an ever-changing environment, it must be exceptional. As I've discovered in consulting with both exceptional and dysfunctional organizations, the top performers share the following ten values:

- Unquestioned integrity.
- We are a team.
- We value humility (ego trips are not allowed).
- Innovation is the rule.
- You are empowered to fix what's broken.
- Everyone is accountable to our values.
- We have fun!
- Seek the best for others.
- Transparency.
- Exceptional is always the goal.

The ten values can greatly enhance your organization's ability to implement meaningful change, and one of the greatest services that you can provide to your organization is to help it adopt these values. Start by posting them in your office or whatever space is designated for the CI's use and discuss them with the CI team. The senior executives typically define the overall company values, so you need their stamp of approval to take it farther. If you have the opportunity to influence one of your organization's senior executives, share these values and their importance with him and ask for support to spread them throughout the company.

Everyone is accountable for adopting the values. You need 100 percent compliance to succeed.

What's the origin of the ten values?

In 2003, I was given access to some of most admired and successful companies in the United States along with their CEOs and others in key leadership positions. These companies included Southwest Airlines, Mary Kay Cosmetics, LensCrafters, Agilent Technologies, and Kingston Technologies. As my research progressed through all the different companies, I began to realize that they shared a common set of values. In fact, in many cases they even used nearly the same words to describe their values.

I've also done consulting for numerous companies that were not doing well. Almost across the board, they violated the ten values of top-performing companies. Furthermore, when the leaders of these companies faced critical changes that could save or drastically improve the future of their companies, almost all of them rejected the changes. They lacked the one value that they needed to listen to reason and implement changes that would improve their organizations: humility. Humility, from the CEO on down, is *always* a critical factor in achieving organizational success.

Sizing Up Key Decision Makers: The Five Personalities Assessment

Most people can be incredibly resistant to change, as revealed by Thomas Kuhn in his classic book, *The Structure of Scientific Revolutions* (University of Chicago Press). That resistance is why critical competitive intelligence often fails to translate into action and why companies often fail.

Thirteen years after Kuhn's book came out, Everett M. Rogers authored *The Diffusion of Innovations* (The Free Press), which examines hundreds of research projects on the topic of change and describes five types of people who deal differently with change. Based on Rogers's work, I developed the five personalities of change. I discuss them briefly in Chapter 2 where I guide you in building your CI team with the most helpful personality types, but I describe them here in more detail. You can use this info to assess the personality types of your organization's leaders so you know what you're up against when trying to promote change.

Describing the personalities

The following sections offer insights into the five personalities, as well as personality blends. Use the tips I share throughout this section to more accurately identify each type of personality among your company's leadership — or your competitor's.

A proven approach

A few years ago, I received a call from a senior manager who had attended one of my seminars. He was a research-lab manager in Ottawa, Canada.

He explained that they had been having a lot of problems in getting projects delivered on time, and he believed that the problem might relate to the five personalities approach I had taught in my seminar. He asked me if I would teach him how to evaluate people, link them correctly, and use the five personalities approach to help him get the right people at the right stages in the process from beginning to end. I worked with him, and he decided to use the approach.

About a year later he called to tell me that aligning people in the right order, with pathfinders and listeners (along with a few organizers) early in the process, and then building momentum for change to the 25 percent point of no defeat had worked incredibly well. It had turned the research lab around.

Pathfinders

Pathfinders are your friends. They embrace change and are key allies in promoting change in an organization. They serve well in creative and discovery roles and love to help anyone who's gathering information on special projects. Unfortunately, they comprise only about 2.5 percent of the population.

When evaluating CEOs and others in leadership positions, look for the following characteristics to determine whether you're dealing with a pathfinder:

- ✔ **Early adopter:** Pathfinders are the first in any societal group to adopt a new technology, approach, process, or other improvement.

- ✔ **Unbiased:** They're the only personality type that can see change (or the future) without bias. They're able to observe facts without reading anything into them.

- ✔ **Rarely found in senior management:** Pathfinders ruffle feathers. As a result, they may have trouble getting promoted.

- ✔ **Multi-networker:** Pathfinders are likely to network in two or more very different circles. For example, they may belong to a professional association and the same time be involved with the World Future Society.

- ✔ **Unsettling:** They tend to make people uncomfortable because they can see future threats so clearly, but their assessment is usually correct.

Listeners

Listeners (13.5 percent of the population) are receptive to what the pathfinders say and have the organizational credibility to move the intelligence forward. They're your quiet diplomats, respected by everyone in the organization. Listeners are great at presenting CI findings and mustering support for new ideas and initiatives.

You can identify the listeners in a group by looking for the following characteristics:

- ✔ **Early adopters:** Listeners are second only to pathfinders in adopting new technologies, ideas, and approaches.

- ✔ **Open minded:** They tend to be the only personality that listens to pathfinders.

- ✔ **Diplomatic:** They tend to be great facilitators between different personality groups.

- ✔ **Go-to guys and gals:** Listeners are often recognized in an organization as the people to go to with new ideas.

- ✔ **Leadership quality:** They often climb to fairly high levels in an organization but usually not to the level of CEO.

Organizers

Organizers, representing about 34 percent of the population, typically run the company. Although they tend to be highly resistant to change, they can serve as valuable members of the extended CI team by taking the lead in pushing CI information and initiatives, especially if they're in leadership roles.

To identify organizers, look for the following personality traits:

- ✔ **Highly resistant to change:** After all, change tends to be messy, which isn't appealing to organizers.

- ✔ **Highly driven perfectionism:** Organizers may come across as being obsessive compulsive.

- ✔ **CEO track:** CEOs of companies are often organizers.

- ✔ **Enemies of pathfinders:** Organizers tend to dislike pathfinder personalities, which is probably why pathfinders are rarely found in the ranks of senior managers.

Followers

Followers, who represent about 34 percent of the population, are the people who get things done — if you can convince them to do it. Their tenacity makes them highly qualified to handle discouraging or challenging research assignments.

Followers exhibit the following qualities:

- ✔ **Late adopters:** Followers are reluctant to adopt change, doing so only after the organizers reluctantly lead the way.

- ✔ **Tenacious:** When presented with a challenge, they never give up.

- ✔ **Faithful:** Followers comprise the group that's most loyal to the organization.

- ✔ **Enemies of pathfinders:** They hate change and pathfinder personalities.

Diehards

Diehards (about 16 percent of the population) patriotically defend the status quo, but when you have a seemingly impossible task, the diehard is probably your go-to guy or gal. They simply never give up.

To identify the diehards in your organization, look for the following personality traits:

- ✔ **Last adopters:** Diehards adopt change only after they've exhausted all other options.

- ✔ **Saboteurs:** They tend to undermine change initiatives.

- ✔ **Bitter enemies of pathfinders:** Given the chance, they would fire the pathfinders.

- ✔ **Highly faithful:** They're highly faithful to the organization — even as they work to sabotage its future success.

Blended personalities

Some people don't fit neatly into one of the personality categories. Certain individuals exhibit a mix of personalities. For example, engineers tend to test out as 40 percent pathfinder and 60 percent organizer. That means they possess the typical curiosity and data-driven insight that's characteristic of the pathfinder, but they have a lot of the organizer's drive and perfectionism.

Here are some of the more-common blended personalities I've encountered:

- ✔ **40/60 pathfinder/organizer:** Typical of engineers, researchers, and some marketing professionals. These people are often good leaders for CI initiatives or even as the head of CI. They possess the required inquisitiveness, drive, and organizational skills.

- ✔ **60/40 pathfinder/organizer:** Typical of advertising and marketing professionals who make it to middle- and senior-management areas in their field. These folks work really well in research and development (R&D) areas and are great in leading creative enterprises. On the CI team, they can serve well in both leadership and contributor positions.

- ✔ **40/60 listener/organizer:** Typical of inspirational leaders, who may be difficult to compete with if the individual is a competitor's CEO. A 40/60 personality can be an incredible member or leader of the CI team. They're great at managing the demands of a highly driven organization.

> ✔ **20/20/20/20/20 all personalities:** The typical jack of all trades and master of none, this type of person is the ultimate multitasker, easily bored with single-task jobs but great at problem solving. This blended personality type generally can't hack it as CEO and rarely ever reaches that level. If you have a 20/20/20/20/20 personality on your CI team, remember that this individual loves to multitask. He's also great at handling unexpected challenges, complaints, or urgent requests from senior management, but he's likely to get bored on long-term projects.

Conducting the five personalities assessment

You can use the five personalities of change to size up people in your organization and in organizations you compete against. Simply select the individual you want to assess and then assign the person to one or more of the five personalities categories based on the information you have about her.

If you created CEO profiles in Chapter 13, use those profiles to help you conduct your assessments.

You can usually develop a fairly accurate five-personalities profile simply by observing a person's behavior and the decisions she makes. You can then use the profile to predict future behavior and decisions. Personality profiles are particularly helpful in predicting a CEO's behavior and how she's likely to react in any given situation. A personality profile can help you predict how enthusiastically your CEO is likely to receive a recommendation for change or how likely a competing CEO will decide to adopt a new technology.

Dealing with the Ego and Bureaucracy That Destroy Companies

Big egos and bureaucratic tendencies transform organizations into dinosaurs destined for extinction. Unable to evolve in response to changes in an industry or in specific markets, the organization loses ground to its more agile foes. If conditions persist, the organization eventually experiences the same fate as its prehistoric ancestors.

To be honest, unless you're a member of a company's board of directors or the CEO, you don't have much power to execute change, but you can take some practical steps to overcome the ego and bureaucracy that stand in your way. In the following sections, I explain how best to work around and through these obstacles with and without assistance from the executive team.

Here's a note for all of you CEOs out there reading this book. Research shows that almost all leaders deal with some level of personal narcissism. In fact, that drive for excellence is what makes you push yourself to be exceptional and to lead exceptional organizations. At the same time, narcissism can blind you to opportunities and threats and eventually drive an organization into the ground. This section is really for you. You're the only person who can lead the meaningful change that must take place to maintain or reestablish your organization's ability to capture and act upon ideas that are new, different, and potentially profitable.

Purging narcissism: The enemy within

Narcissists can destroy organizations. They drive key contributors to leave the company and ultimately have a direct negative impact on customer relationships. If performance is the objective, then these performance destroyers must be eliminated.

At the heart of a narcissistic personality is an overwhelming need to control everything and command unquestioned obedience. An added dimension to many narcissists is a tendency toward sociopathic behavior: They see no right or wrong except as it relates to what they want. They can be incredibly brutal toward any perceived threats, even if those "threats" hold the promise of improving the organizations they lead.

Recent research reveals that some degree of narcissism is present in almost all leaders, so your concern should center on the degree of narcissism. A mild case of narcissism isn't a concern, but organizations need to deal with moderate or severe narcissism so that it doesn't hinder change and progress.

To purge narcissism, encourage your organization to establish a clear no-ego-trip policy and enforce that policy consistently, meaning that no one gets a free pass. If a senior executive breaks the rules, he must face the consequences, which may ultimately involve termination. Any standard short of that is a waste of time.

Establish the CEO as the accountability agent for the company's no-ego-trip policy. For personnel to take the policy seriously, they need to hear a clear and forceful message from the CEO that ego trips will not be tolerated.

A narcissistic CEO can ultimately destroy an organization. While CI may have no power to stop such a CEO, sometimes the board of directors or a private equity firm will take the reins to dissemble the bureaucracy and destroy the narcissism that accompanies it. Clayton, Dubleir, and Ross, one of the most successful private equity firms, has made its money by doing just that and transforming failing companies into success stories.

Why bureaucracy is bad

The most accurate predictor of an organization's decline or failure is whether the organization is a bureaucracy. Bureaucracy damages an organization in the following ways:

✔ Organizations become internally focused, making them incapable of innovation and creativity.

✔ As bureaucratic calcification builds, the intellectual capital of the firm drops. You're likely to witness an exodus of the best and brightest.

✔ From a CI perspective, ego-driven bureaucracies undermine the organization's ability to convert critical intelligence into action.

Confronting a declining level of entrepreneurialism in an aging company

As companies mature, the level of entrepreneurial behavior tends to decline, as shown in Figure 15-2. They begin to lose sight of many of the ten values of top-performing companies, including humility, innovation, individual initiative, creativity, and generosity. They're so caught up in *doing* business that they forget about *generating* business.

Entrepreneurial Activity:
New Company versus Mature Company

Figure 15-2:
As a company ages, it becomes less entrepreneurial.

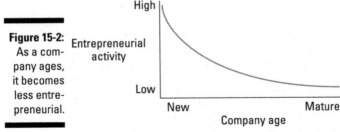

Illustration by Wiley, Composition Services Graphics

One of the most difficult challenges any company encounters is that of fostering entrepreneurialism on a long-term basis. Companies fail not because they lose focus on historic competencies and their supposed sustainable competitive advantage but for the following five reasons:

✔ Inability to create or discover the next little thing (short-term profit drivers).

✔ Inability to create or discover the next big thing (long-term profit drivers).

✔ Inability or unwillingness to manage the organization as a financial portfolio. Decisions are based more on what the firm has historically done well rather than on which opportunities have the most potential.

Corporate leaders need to think like portfolio managers. They need to know when to divest of a mature or declining product division and reinvest into a segment with high-growth, high-profit potential. This is where corporate leaders must be capable of thinking in terms of unrelated diversification. For example, if the buggy-whip division is dying, sell it and try to find a high-growth technology opportunity.

✔ A change in culture from challenging everything to maintaining the status quo.

✔ Forgetting that the people make the profit. (One of America's top-performing companies claims that 99 percent of all innovation comes from its people, not from senior management.)

Depending on your position or status, you may or may not have the power to breathe entrepreneurial life back into your organization. If you're just a working stiff, the most you can hope for is to convince your organization's CEO or board of directors that an attitude adjustment is necessary. If your organization has deteriorated into a calcified, stupefied bureaucracy, all new ideas are shot on sight. More often than not, the messenger gets shot as well.

If you do have the power to reinvigorate your organization or at least influence those who have that power, here's a strategy to get your organization back to its entrepreneurial roots:

1. **Perform an informal audit of your CI team and its internal customers and sponsors regarding their attitude toward change.**

   Pay special attention to the executive-level sponsors. Spotting highly resistant people is easy; they use phrases such as *don't rock the boat.*

2. **Pick out areas of future weakness, maturity, or decline in your product families.**

3. **Convert information about problem segments into financial projections by using your internal intel resources.**

4. **Share your observations with the CI team, especially if you have senior executives as sponsors on the team.**

5. **Try to discover targets of opportunity that may generate growth as a replacement for the loss areas you discovered.**

Embracing change for big rewards

In the early 1990s, a Fortune 500 company's executive team was confronted with some realities about its existing product portfolios. Almost all of them would produce slow, dependable profit in the future, but they were all mature segments.

When confronted with almost certain limited growth potential, the senior executive team began thinking about alternatives. They discovered a new technology called *digitization*. After careful study, they concluded that ultimately the world was approaching a tsunami-like shift that would change everything, from cellphones to televisions.

The firm's leadership and board made a dramatic and bold decision: They decided to systematically sell off all the old-line businesses (billions of dollars) and invest in this new digital area.

As a result of the company's ability to engage in *unrelated diversification* (expansion outside of current industry and supposed competencies and resources), the company became a global leader in the new, digital age. The company is living proof that you don't find your future in the rearview mirror.

Battling Interpretation Bias

People like to think of themselves as rational human beings and objective thinkers. A few actually are. The rest of us are more selective. A majority of the population is receptive only to information that confirms their existing views, a phenomenon known as *confirmation bias*. If something doesn't fit into their existing matrix of understanding, they reject it. For example, conservatives gravitate toward conservative media and reject liberal views, and liberals tune in to liberal media and reject conservative ideas and ideologies regardless of whether a certain view has any merit.

In addition, people tend to interpret facts in a way that supports their existing point of view. Congressmen, for example, have been known to completely change their views on raising the debt ceiling depending on which party is residing in the White House. In the world of business, the CEO may dismiss a serious threat posed by a new competitor simply because that competitor hasn't yet claimed a significant market share. That's not objective thinking. That's *interpretation bias*.

Interpretation bias is the result of emotional thinking, which almost always overrides logic. Any change in thinking from a familiar paradigm is rejected roughly 80 percent of the time.

Many of the analytical tools I describe in this book, including see-mean-do (SMD), observe-orient-decide-act (OODA) loops, scenarios, and war games are designed to diminish interpretation bias and lead to evidence-based thinking. In the following sections, I describe additional ways to increase awareness of interpretation bias and overcome it.

Developing an awareness of interpretation bias

Interpretation bias is a lot like alcoholism in that those who have the condition are the most likely to deny having it. Also, as with alcoholism, the first step in overcoming interpretation bias is to admit that you have it. You probably have interpretation bias if you do any of the following:

- ✔ Have strong opinions on certain issues that are unlikely to ever change
- ✔ Actively seek out information that confirms your viewpoint
- ✔ Have strong reactions to any information or perspectives that challenge your beliefs
- ✔ Hang out exclusively with people who share your views
- ✔ Often dismiss or ignore the suggestions of others

Observe yourself and others (specifically the leaders in your organization) to look for signs of interpretation bias. As you witness the signs on a daily basis, your awareness of your bias and others' begins to grow.

Training resources for overcoming interpretation bias are readily available. Joel Barker is one of the leading thinkers on paradigm blindness, and any of his books can increase your awareness and understanding of this issue. In addition, "Gunfire at Sea: A Case Study of Innovation" by Elting Morison (The MIT Press; you can read the case study at http://cs.gmu.edu/cne/pjd/TT/Sims/Sims.pdf) reveals just how counterproductive interpretation bias can be. Another good case study is "The Lab That Ran Away From Xerox" by Bro Uttal (originally printed *Fortune* magazine, viewable at www.auburn.edu/~boultwr/9xerlab.pdf).

Tap the power of your CI cluster, which should have a number of pathfinder and listener personalities who can be very helpful in exposing and overcoming bias, especially if some of the guilty parties are senior-level executives. If the culture is politically charged, your sponsors may not be willing to go public with their support, but they may be willing to counsel you and help move information to the right people. (I explain pathfinder and listener personalities in the earlier section "Describing the personalities.")

Anticipating interpretation bias so you can nip it in the bud

One way to battle interpretation bias is to always assume that you're going to encounter it and plan accordingly:

✔ **Whenever you're presenting an issue, point out how it's likely to affect the bottom line.** Whenever possible, show a five-year breakout of the impact an issue is likely to have on the bottom line. Revealing possible outcomes may help those with interpretation bias look at the intelligence from a different perspective.

✔ **Include a scenario or other information that focuses on the potential success that a competing company would likely achieve by acting on the intel.** In other words, pose the question, "What if our organization doesn't do this but one of our competitors does?"

When presenting intel and possible outcomes, you need to present a compelling case for implementing a change. Otherwise, you're unlikely to overcome the natural resistance to change.

Sidestepping bias

Sometimes the best way to overcome interpretation bias is to step around it by starting with people who are less likely to be blinded by bias and more likely to see the opportunity and urgency of your intel. Here are a few paths that may help you avoid the pitfalls of bias:

✔ **Take it to the top.** Assuming that your CEO is open minded, he's always the best sponsor.

✔ **Enlist the assistance of your CI supporters.** The CI team and its sponsors and internal customers can rally around the intel and possibly make suggestions on how to present it and to whom to improve its chances of being accepted.

✔ **Involve internal customers whenever possible.** A division leader who realizes that an issue can create success or failure for his or her division may become your strongest ally.

For more about drumming up support for a call to action, turn to Chapter 16.

Chapter 16

Shepherding CI Information through Your Organization

You did your job. You collected information, analyzed it, and identified an amazing new opportunity or an ominous threat. Now it's time for the decision makers to act and for you to pass the baton to someone else and pat yourself on the back for a job well done. Right?

Not so fast.

Although the responsibility for executing strategic initiatives and setting policy clearly rests on the shoulders of your organization's executives and managers, you still have a role to play in encouraging them to take action. In this chapter, I offer guidance as your role shifts from analyst to trusted advisor.

Don't assume that just because you hand your organization a golden egg on a platinum platter that everyone will rally enthusiastically to capitalize on that opportunity. People often get so caught up in performing their daily duties that great opportunities fall between the cracks. One of your jobs as a member of the CI team is to make sure that doesn't happen.

Progressing to Implementation

Your role in implementing strategic initiatives is to serve as trusted advisor to the executive team and your internal customers. You're uniquely qualified to serve in this role because of your work leading up to this point and your position in the organization. How so? Consider that

✔ Your research and analysis has made you the one person in your organization who fully understands the implications of the intel and the urgency in which change must be implemented.

✔ As a member of a team that serves all areas of the organization, you may have the connections and influence necessary to help the decision makers deal with internal political obstacles and other barriers they face — or that they perceive they must overcome in order to implement the recommended changes.

Here's what you can do at each stage of the process leading up to implementation to help your company's leaders take action on your analysis. (For a visual representation of the following steps, check out Figure 16-1.)

1. **Prepare a clear and convincing intelligence briefing.**

   Include a one-page executive summary that clearly identifies the opportunity or threat. Use plenty of white space and avoid extensive detail. (For additional pointers on crafting an intelligence brief, turn to Chapter 10.)

2. **Share your analysis, conclusions, and recommendations with your inner circle — CI team members and sponsors who are trustworthy and can help you identify risks or political land mines in the organization that you may encounter.**

   People in your inner circle support your efforts but often feel the need to remain anonymous due to internal politics or sensitivities. They won't take a bullet for you, but they'll do everything they possibly can, short of that, to contribute to the success of the CI team.

3. **Brief each member of your CI cluster (key executives and others) individually, obtain feedback about your conclusions, and try to gauge how strongly each person feels about the need for action.**

   Members of your CI cluster generally work openly with the CI team, primarily by helping them gather intel at trade shows through their participation in groups that set industry or technology standards. They may also support the CI team's efforts overall.

4. **Extend your intel sharing (confidentially) to sponsors and internal CI customers who are likely to benefit most from it and collaborate with them to develop an approach for sharing the intel with the key decision maker.**

   CI sponsors, typically senior managers, are generally part of your intelligence support network. They see the value in your work (as do your internal customers) and are usually willing to support the CI mission openly. They probably know whether the intel is going to ruffle feathers and why and how to communicate it in a way to make the key decision maker more receptive to it.

As a member of the CI team, you can't push a solution, but you must make sure that your sponsors and customers really have a grasp on what you present to them. If you have additional information that allows you to estimate opportunity cost related to the issue, explaining that is probably okay, but stop short of making policy. (*Opportunity cost* reflects the potential profit to be made from an opportunity or the loss from not responding to an opportunity.) By running the numbers, you can show the financial impact of an opportunity or threat more objectively without telling the decision maker what to do.

If you've done your job effectively, you now have a group of key stakeholders who buy into your intel long before you present it to the final decision maker. Always keep your CI sponsors and internal customers in the loop; you never want them to find out about your intel by surprise.

5. **Present your intel to the key decision maker for consideration.**

See the later section "Working on Your Delivery" for details.

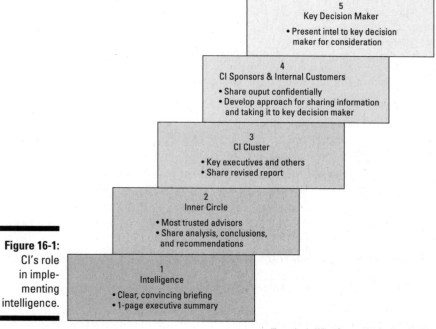

Figure 16-1:
CI's role
in imple-
menting
intelligence.

Illustration by Wiley, Composition Services Graphics

Serve as a consultant, providing internal customers and sponsors with resources and advice, as explained in the following sections.

Making the case for the F-15 fighter jet

As U.S. military planners began trying to discover what the next fighter jet should look like, a lot of opinions were on the table. As the CIA's intelligence people began studying the problem, they began asking the planners to describe the different aspects of the mission that the fighter had to satisfy. The analysts wanted to know what the fighter needed to do.

Almost always they were given the same answer: It had to exceed the capabilities of the MIG-21 (USSR). In doing their intelligence, the CIA team set about to create a detailed profile of the MIG-21 and its capabilities. With this extensive laundry list of MIG-21 capabilities, the planners had everything they needed to create the successful F-15.

Building an intelligence support network

Don't try to fly solo when you're shepherding intel through your organization. Start with an inner circle of trusted advisors and work together to form a support network — a group of allies who team up to overcome internal resistance and other hurdles standing in the way of change. Your support network should include representatives from the following three groups:

- ✔ Interested executives who are willing to sponsor initiatives.

  If you can involve the CEO in your network, overcoming resistance to change becomes much easier.

- ✔ Pathfinders and listeners, whom you can always rely on for support. (I describe the pathfinder and listener personality types in Chapter 15.)

- ✔ Internal customers, including department heads, who have a stake in making sure that issues are correctly dealt with from a strategic standpoint.

Using your support network to develop a plan of attack

Convincing someone that action is necessary often comes down to how effectively you communicate your case. A good rule of thumb is to approach communication with humility. Don't assume that you know the best way to convince people to take action. Seek the counsel of others who may have a better sense of how to approach people and build consensus in your organization. Your support network is a good place to start:

- ✔ Get the support network's help in identifying any potential areas of resistance or political pitfalls.

✔ Ask members for advice on how to present the information to decision makers most effectively. Some decision makers prefer audio/visual presentations, others prefer single-page briefings, some may expect in-depth data dumps, and so on. Consider your audience and its preferences.

✔ Investigate the possibility of getting a senior manager or an internal customer to serve as sponsor for taking the information forward. (Consider approaching the CEO directly, especially if the issue is extremely urgent. Of course, this meeting is much easier if CI has been briefing the CEO all along.)

If your organization's strategic readiness score is below 50 percent, or if you've discovered very high levels of internal resistance, your CEO will probably need to spearhead the initiative in order for it to succeed. (Not sure what your organization's strategic readiness score is? Chapter 15 can help you figure it out.)

Consult with your support network and internal customers to develop an effective way to introduce the intel and your recommendations to the organization. Your plan of attack should account for the following:

✔ **Who, what, and when:** Whom do you tell, what do you tell them, and when do you include them in the process? Also consider which individual(s) you ultimately need to convince in order to move the intel forward.

If your organization has a formalized process in place for communicating intel, start with that process.

✔ **Politics:** Office politics often change with any given situation, so consider how the dissemination of the intel is likely to play to the intended audience.

✔ **Urgency:** Consider how quickly your organization needs to act in order to take advantage of an opportunity or avoid a threat. Urgency may influence how quickly you need to pass along the information and how assertive you need to be.

Building Up Buy-In for Your Intel Incrementally

When you're trying to gain acceptance within your organization for the reality of a situation, one approach is to gather support gradually until you have enough backing and enough steam to blast through the barriers of any internal resistance.

The role of the CI team is to help leadership understand the facts and appreciate the urgency of taking action so that leadership can formulate and implement a response. Although you can present a range of options, the final decisions are ultimately in the hands of your organization's leaders.

Here's an incremental method for overcoming inertia in a bureaucracy that has worked in many companies:

1. **Consider who in the organization has impact and categorize them based on the five personalities of change (described in Chapter 15) so you know who your allies and adversaries are.**

   Your CI support network should already be populated with several allies.

2. **Start to familiarize pathfinders, listeners, and perhaps very few organizer personalities with the intel through a series of briefings or orientation meetings.**

   Familiarizing a small group of CI supporters with the intel helps ensure that you're on the right track before you decide to move the intel up the ladder. If you can't convince your supporters of the importance or urgency of the intel, then the intel probably isn't strong enough to convince your organization's decision makers.

   Don't include followers or diehards at this stage of the process. You may want to set up your briefings offsite and after working hours so these folks don't get a whiff of what's going on.

3. **Continue reaching out to pathfinders, listeners, and a few organizers until you have buy-in from 25 percent of the people in your organization.**

   Research indicates that somewhere between 10 and 25 percent acceptance creates enough momentum to carry a change through an organization; 25 percent acceptance is the point of no defeat.

   Never pitch your intel with a Monday morning announcement. Such actions only serve to motivate any dissenters to dig in their heels. Calls for change often trigger knee-jerk reactions against it.

According to the Ansoff power formula of $P \gg R$, the power (P) you apply must significantly exceed the resistance (R) you encounter. Power comes in the form of status (power from sponsors who hold higher positions in the organization) and numbers (the number of people who buy into the intel and the need for a response).

Beating down bureaucracy

Although you should never cross the line into the policy-making arena, sometimes you need to find a creative way to communicate what you know in a convincing manner. If a bureaucracy reaches the point of calcification, initiating change while keeping your job may be quite a challenge. You need to be persistent and may have to invest some of your own time and effort. Consider the case of a team that took the initiative to execute change and won.

Motorola, a global technology leader, had been on a decade-long decline. The once-innovative organization had been replaced by a politically driven, change-resistant culture, all the way up to the CEO.

A new product development team came up with a breakthrough concept for a phone and tried to get the idea up to the decision makers.

They were met with threats and rejection. They then took the intelligence (and creativity) and formed a stealth team that worked nights and weekends to create the new phone. Finally, the product was ready to see the light of day. The team, en masse, walked into the director's office holding a mockup of the new phone. It was clearly so good that no reasonable human being could reject it, especially because it had already been built.

The new phone (remember the Razr?) was accepted and became an undisputed success. Motorola was able to use the new product to regain its previously lost number-one position in the industry. A creative and persistent team of product developers was able to establish enough momentum to push the idea through to the top.

If the resistance to the intel or its urgency is extremely high, no effort may be sufficient in overcoming it. This isn't necessarily a defeat for the CI team. Sometimes the CI team is wrong, and sometimes it's through no fault of its own. The CEO or others in the executive suite may have rock-solid information that you simply don't have access to. I was once given an assignment involving a highly technical and obscure issue. I actually found information that wasn't included in any of the mainstream information sources. As it turned out, my superiors knew about the information. What they wanted to know was whether I could find it, because they knew that if I found it, others could, too. So never forget that your job is to provide the most accurate and insightful information you can. Sometimes, you may not even be given all the information available . . . on purpose!

In the following sections, I describe various techniques for employing this incremental strategy to build support for your intel and the need to formulate a response.

Conducting an informal poll

Taking a poll is a great way to get a feel for how receptive people are likely to be to intel and the need for a response without hitting them with the full force of it. In an informal way, approach all the people in the organization who can support your efforts and ask them the following questions:

- How important (or unimportant) is the information?
- Do you think our conclusions are accurate, based on your knowledge?
- What misgivings or questions do you have about the conclusions?
- What level of support for this conclusion would you expect to receive from decision makers in the organization?
- Where (or from whom) would you expect to encounter resistance to this intel and the need for a response?
- Do you have any suggestions on how to present the intel to overcome any resistance to it?

Taking trips into the organization

According to one study about managers who were consistently successful in pushing through new initiatives, the managers took little trips out of their office and into the organization. They would carefully choose a few people to introduce the idea to and then give them time to process it. Then the managers would make another trip and talk with a few more people. They would repeat their impromptu meetings until they felt they'd developed critical mass for initiating the proposed change (around 25 percent buy-in).

To increase receptivity for your intel in your own organization, take a few "trips" to different areas of the organization that are likely to be on the front lines of implementing any required changes. Start with people you know you can trust to keep the information confidential. Assuming that your informal poll involved a limited number of highly trusted associates (see the preceding section), you're now ready to broaden your evaluation of attitudes. In this case, you probably want to visit with the entire CI support network. Ask your sponsors and internal customers the same questions presented in the preceding section.

Although you're gathering valuable information and insight on how to present your intel and the need for a response, you're also warming people up to the information and its implications.

Overpowering resistance with overwhelming CI

Cliff Kalb has distinguished himself over the years as the consummate CI professional. In one situation he received a call about a sign that had gone up across the street from one of his company's major manufacturing centers located in a Central American country. The sign simply said, "X Corp. will be building a new factory on this site." The problem was, the company building the factory was a large competitor of his company. The manager of the manufacturing center called Cliff for advice.

Cliff immediately sent a request for information to all of his company's global managers, asking if that situation had ever happened to them before. Within hours, he had three replies from three different managers in other foreign countries. It turns out, the same competitor had done exactly the same thing across from their manufacturing facilities. After the factory was built, the company then proceeded to offer salaries 30 percent higher than his company was paying. In every case, the managers lost more than 100 of their key employees to the competitor.

Armed with that information, Cliff went to the financial executive who prepared the budgets for the country in question. He gave him the intelligence and suggested that the company consider budgeting 30 percent salary increases at the beginning of the next fiscal year. When the competitor opened shop and started offering their salaries, none of the company's existing employees opted to cross the street.

What Cliff understood was that proposing a 30 percent increase in a budget would always be a hard sell for the CI unit. However, when he packaged his intel with the probable loss of 100 key employees, the acceptance was immediate.

Interviewing middle managers

Sometimes you get a better feel for how an organization will respond by interviewing middle managers. Frequently, middle managers are caught between the desires of customers and the directives of upper management, so they can provide more insight into how your intelligence will be received. Ask the same questions you asked during your informal poll.

Determining intensity of resistance

After you complete your internal investigation, summarize the input you received from all the different interest groups. Put all the different opinions together and develop a solid understanding of the resistance you should expect to encounter. You can then formulate a strategy for moving forward based on the intensity of that resistance.

Working on Your Delivery

As you prepare to present your intel to your organization's leaders, you need to spend some time working on your delivery. What you say and how you say it are equally important in improving the chances of having your intel put into action. In the following sections, I offer several suggestions on how to present your message to make your audience more receptive to it.

As momentum builds, change spreads more easily through the rest of the organization. By the time you have 10 to 25 percent buy-in, your intel is almost assured of eventually achieving full acceptance. Your briefings should clearly be focused on building those numbers; in other words, your briefings need to be convincing.

Focusing on the positive

If the chief issue of your briefing is a threat that the organization must take action to avoid, you certainly need to describe the threat in order to talk about it. But don't dwell on it. Focus most of your presentation on possible ways that your organization can respond to the threat and the positive outcomes that are likely to result.

If your initiative instead calls for pursuing a newly discovered opportunity, avoid any mention of past mistakes or failing products. Instead, talk about the opportunity you discovered and the potential revenue gains and other potential benefits.

Avoiding imperatives and ultimatums

As you transition from collecting and analyzing intel to convincing decision makers to take action, your role as analyst transitions into the role of diplomat. In this role, avoid using imperatives, such as *must* and *should,* as well as ultimatums, which convey arrogance and tend to put people on the defensive.

If you start feeling the need to be more forceful, ask a question instead. That person may have a very good reason for his lack of enthusiasm over your intel and what it entails related to his own position and interests. You might say something like, "I'm getting a sense that you're hesitating here. May I ask what your concerns are?" Be humble. Others may know something you haven't considered.

Offering alternatives, prioritizing issues, and remaining detached

One of the best ways to lessen resistance among decision makers is to do most of their work for them. Here are some suggestions for developing a presentation that preemptively addresses any concerns or objections and is likely to make your audience more receptive to your intel and its ramifications:

- **Anticipate and address any objections.** By addressing possible objections upfront, you demonstrate that you thought carefully about the issue and the ramifications of possible responses.

- **Offer alternatives.** If alternatives exist, present those alternatives so the decision makers have a choice other than a simple "yes" or "no."

- **Prioritize issues.** When prioritizing issues, try to align your priorities with those of the decision makers — or at least recognize their priorities so you can establish some common ground.

- **Remain detached.** Don't engage in emotional or political battles. Focus on the facts and what's best for the organization. Opposition is usually driven by emotion. The best way to overcome opposition is through logic, so keep the dialogue focused on facts and figures.

Clearing the pitch with your intelligence cluster

Before you deliver your pitch to a decision maker who can shut it down, rehearse with your CI cluster and make sure everyone approves. Your cluster can not only help you polish your presentation but also engage key executives prior to the presentation for the purpose of gauging and anticipating resistance.

You have to win over your CI cluster in order to have any hope of winning over the rest of your organization, so work on convincing your cluster first. New ideas get shot down roughly 80 percent of the time. Great intelligence may be useless if you fail to manage the process of convincing key decision makers. Your organization only wins when you're able to conquer internal resistance.

Communicating critical information in change-resistant environments

If you ever get the feeling that senior management just isn't listening, it's probably because it's not. Senior managers have been known to treat CI with a certain degree of passive aggressiveness, letting the CI team gather and analyze data but ignoring the resulting intelligence. To alleviate this problem, try the following approaches:

- ✔ When submitting your intelligence briefing, mark the urgent status in red to call attention to the high level of urgency. Just be sure to use the urgent status sparingly, only for truly urgent matters, so it maintains its impact. When submitting urgent items, marked in red, explain why those items are marked in red — because the information appears very accurate and the impact may be significant. In this way, you're signaling the urgency of taking action without telling a superior what to do.

- ✔ After submitting an urgent competitive intelligence briefing or memo, send a separate e-mail message to reinforce the urgency of the situation. You may even want to call leaders on the phone or stop by their offices.

- ✔ If you can arrange it, give the briefing at a meeting of senior management and your internal sponsors (especially the senior executives who are part of your CI team) or internal customers.

Conducting executive briefings

When presenting to anyone on the executive team, including the CEO, you need to bring your A game. A shoddy presentation not only undermines the CI team's efforts to persuade the executive team of the need to take action but can also cause long-term harm to CI's reputation. To craft and perform a quality presentation, follow these suggestions:

- ✔ **If you're doing a PowerPoint presentation, keep it succinct and use lots of white space.** Slides should include only key ideas — no sentences or paragraphs. You flesh out the presentation when you deliver it through what you say.

- ✔ **Rehearse, rehearse, rehearse until you feel comfortable delivering your presentation.** After all, the goal is to establish yourself as a knowledgeable expert. If you find yourself hesitating or stumbling at certain points in the presentation, you may need to revise it or rehearse more.

Never read aloud to your audience. It often annoys and offends people (they can read faster than you can talk), plus it usually indicates that you haven't prepared for your presentation and probably don't really have a good working knowledge of it.

- ✔ **Practice in the same venue (and the same room, if possible) prior to your presentation and in front of an audience.** Ask your CI team members to serve as your practice audience and provide constructive feedback.

- ✔ **Capsulize your information to make it easy to swallow.** Executives have little time and even less patience to process information. You need to digest it for them and present the highlights. If they want details, they can ask for more.

  Condense your entire presentation into a one-page (max) executive summary. Include an additional page of detail for each of the key points highlighted.

- ✔ **Control handouts.** Don't distribute your executive summary or any other documents prior to your presentation. You don't want people reading while you're speaking. You can distribute copies of slides for note taking, but hold on to support documents until after the presentation.

- ✔ **Always have a backup.** Bring printed copies of slides in case your technology fails.

- ✔ **Use less time than you're allotted to leave some time for questions and discussion at the end.**

- ✔ **Wear professional attire.** Dress like an executive.

- ✔ **If more than one person from CI is involved in the presentation, only one of you should be standing at any given time.**

- ✔ **Have a timekeeper to alert you of time limits.**

- ✔ **Be serious and professional.** No jokes or mannerisms (such as clicking a pen, tapping on the conference table, or leaning on the podium).

- ✔ **Match the volume of your voice to the size of the room.**

Responding to the "We already knew all that" response

If you've been in the intelligence business for a while, you've heard the "We already knew that" response many times. Sometimes it's even true; the person really did already know what you told him. Other times, that response is merely a defensive maneuver; the person doesn't want to appear ignorant. Either way, you need to get past the natural tendency that most people have when they encounter new information or old information with new calls for change. The best approach is preemptive. Here are a few options:

- ✔ **If you expect a negative response, try a pre-briefing to explain to key attendees (ideally including the CEO) why you think the information is important.** Doing so helps remove ego from the equation.

- ✔ **Include a "We Already Knew That" slide and explain why this information is different or why the situation is now a matter of urgency.**

- ✔ **Ask one of your internal customers who "gets it" to spell out the potential impact of the issue on your organization.** Another voice reinforces the urgency of taking action.

- ✔ **Seek out people who've already tried to communicate the same information.** Find out what they've tried and how you may help their cause (and yours) in moving the issue forward.

- ✔ **Make your issue new.** Focus on a specific outcome that hasn't been considered in the past; for example, if the concern previously was on how the issue could affect sales, present it anew in terms of its possible impact on market share or competitor success.

- ✔ **Take a "just the facts" approach to shift the focus from emotional opinion to look at the issue objectively and in terms of its potential impact.** Moving the discussion to numbers is one way to focus on facts.

- ✔ **Anticipate emotional reactions.** Dissonant information (that is, material that's new, novel, or different) threatens a person's power. Most people see change as a threat to their position as an expert in some area. The simplest illustration of this perceived threat is software conversions. People who become adept at using a specific software almost always oppose the migration to a new version or a different software package altogether. Remembering that you're dealing with emotional factors rather than facts tends to make you more successful in dealing with the emotional resistance upfront, which then simplifies the task of eliciting the desired action from others.

Chapter 17

Perfecting and Promoting CI

. . . .

In This Chapter

▶ Pitching CI as a service

▶ Building strong relationships internally

▶ Raising CI's profile through effective communication

▶ Spotlighting CI's contributions

▶ Improving CI to earn respect

. . . .

CI often flies so far below the radar that only a few people in the organization are aware of its existence or what it does. Even worse, some may consider CI unnecessary or even an expensive indulgence that consumes resources and drags down the company's bottom line.

Regardless of whether such a perception is accurate, it can hinder CI's effectiveness in collecting data as well as implementing strategic initiatives. Personnel won't contribute to the information pool or draw intel from it to drive innovation. And some may even try to sabotage recommended changes.

To improve CI operations and effectiveness, you need to prove and then publicize CI's value and its achievements on an ongoing basis. In this chapter, I explain how to accomplish these goals.

Positioning CI As a Service Center

One of the best ways to convince anyone of the value of CI is to prove it. Position CI as a service center, and then take steps to serve the decision makers in a way that improves their success. Here are several ways you can prove CI's value:

> ✔ **Be a servant.** Operate as an internal customer service center, where decision makers can go to have their questions answered and their concerns addressed. Make serving others in your organization your priority — don't let your ego get in the way.

✔ **Stick to the facts.** Present data and your analysis of it without developing an emotional attachment to any point of view.

✔ **Build strong collaborative relationships with the CEO and internal sponsors and customers.** You earn allies, especially your internal customers, by helping them become more successful.

Being able to communicate openly and effectively with the CEO is most important. Just as internal audits generally flow through the CEO, you should route your intel through the CEO. Reporting directly to the CEO and having her sponsor CI's work helps you circumvent power struggles and political issues.

✔ **Stay on top of changes.** Keep abreast of the ever-changing needs of your internal customers — typically executives and managers who have the power to act on the intelligence you provide. Consider maintaining a watch or needs map, as explained in Chapter 5, and notifying your internal customers of any developments in areas they've asked the CI team to monitor.

✔ **Keep everyone in the loop.** Distribute regular intelligence briefings to all personnel to increase awareness of key events in the industry or particular markets and to encourage personnel to share any information they discover with CI. See Chapter 10 for more about creating and distributing briefing sheets.

At the beginning of every year, create a contact/briefing calendar to remind yourself to keep your internal customers posted. (See the later section "Creating a contact calendar" for details.)

✔ **Act professionally.** Be confident, firm, and professional — in other words, conduct yourself the way a trusted advisor should. Embrace and embody the values of unquestioned integrity, transparency, and altruism (seeking the best for others).

Don't get caught up in political battles or power struggles. Always propose that internal customers communicate directly with each other (rather than through you) when addressing areas of potential conflict.

✔ **Share the accolades.** Wherever possible, give public credit and recognition to people who help you do your job better, including other members of the CI team and individuals who share valuable information with the team.

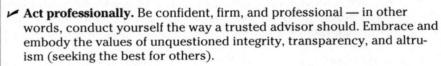

Even if you succeed in positioning CI as a service center, CI faces several potential internal threats — namely the ones I present in the following list. An awareness of these threats improves your ability to avoid them.

✔ **Turf battles:** CI and marketing may bump heads when their responsibilities overlap. A senior marketing manager may perceive CI as pulling personnel and other resources that should be allocated to the marketing department. Careful coordination between marketing and CI can help avoid this problem.

Challenging the urge to downsize and eliminate CI

A big mistake companies commonly make is to replace good strategy with downsizing. Downsizing is a no-brainer way to boost short-term profits because when you slash expenses, you get an immediate bump in profits. Unfortunately, the bump is usually short lived and followed by drops in earnings, market share, and profits. Research shows that downsizing rarely, if ever, results in medium- and long-range earnings increases.

Unfortunately, downsizing initiatives usually target low-profile departments, including training and CI. In the training area, you can use "training ROI" to link the training department with the bottom line in order to demonstrate the value of training to senior executives. Although a comparable "CI ROI" approach doesn't yet exist, you can use the various strategies described in this chapter to prove and publicize the value of CI to those responsible for making downsizing decisions.

Additionally, CI may reveal weaknesses in someone's pet project. If the person isn't humble enough to accept the CI team's input and implement changes to address its concerns, conflict may arise, not least of which is that certain individuals or departments may try to keep any future plans secret from CI.

✔ **Empire building:** *Empire building* occurs when an individual attempts to achieve power by adding functions, such as CI, to his area of responsibility. It may dilute CI's role and result in conflicted messages being sent to the CEO or other senior executives.

✔ **Downsizing:** Organizations often target CI in their downsizing efforts, which is usually a big mistake, as explained in the nearby sidebar.

Achieving and Maintaining a Connection with Key Players

One of the most brilliant aspects of the work done by Steve Jobs at Apple was his use of *pull marketing,* which involves attracting consumers to a product rather than trying to advertise products to people who may not need or want them (push marketing). As you position CI as a service center, consider using a pull approach rather than a push approach. Find out who your internal customers are and what they need in terms of intelligence, and then deliver information and insights that meet those needs. In the following sections, I explain how to employ this pull approach with CI.

Keeping your internal customers and sponsors engaged

In the process of conducting CI, especially when you're immersed in analysis, becoming isolated is easy. After all, good analysis requires a great deal of concentration. However, isolation undermines your ability to rally the troops. You need to stay engaged with everyone in the company through the following activities:

- ✔ Conducting regular briefings
- ✔ Performing periodic needs assessments (see the later section "Updating needs assessments" for the scoop on these)
- ✔ Requesting information, opinions, and insights on an as-needed basis

  Asking people to share their information, insights, and opinions (with sincere interest) to keep people engaged

Pathfinders and listeners are typically much more open to receiving information and supporting CI's efforts than are organizers, followers, and diehards. If you keep them engaged, they can help you make others feel involved and supportive. (For more about the five personalities of change, see Chapter 15.)

Creating a contact calendar

If you're like most people in the workforce, your work runs you when you should really be running your work. With CI, a contact calendar can put you back in the driver's seat and ensure that you maintain periodic contact with your internal customers and sponsors. A contact calendar offers two major benefits:

- ✔ It allows you to plan ahead so you can make appointments with key people well in advance (to get on their calendars).
- ✔ It ensures that you never let the battles of the day override a critically important aspect of your job — maintaining continual contact with your key resources.

To create a contact calendar, start with a spreadsheet or table with 13 columns (one column for contact activities and the remaining 12 for the months of the year). In the left column, list the contact activities that you must perform regularly, as shown in Figure 17-1. Place an X in the column for each month you plan to perform each contact activity.

CI Contact Plan for 2014

Activity	Jan	Feb	Mar	Apr	May	Jun	Jul	Aug	Sep	Oct	Nov	Dec
Mgr-Marketing	X			X			X			X		
Mgr-Finance Dept	X			X			X			X		
Sales Director	X			X			X			X		
Key Sales Resources	X	X		X			X		X		X	
Advertising Director	X						X					
Exec Team Sponsor #1		X			X			X			X	
Exec Team Sponsor #2	X	X	X	X	X	X	X	X	X	X	X	X
CEO (if possible)	X						X					
EVP	X			X			X			X		

Figure 17-1: Sample contact calendar.

Illustration by Wiley, Composition Services Graphics

Consider the following schedule:

- ✔ Monthly briefing for the CEO, or more frequently depending on the CEO's preference and the velocity of change.

- ✔ Monthly executive team briefings.

- ✔ Quarterly face-to-face meetings with the senior executive team to confirm CI's value contribution.

- ✔ Quarterly (or more frequent) briefings for CI sponsors and internal customers.

- ✔ Periodic reminder to the CEO to express some gesture of recognition to publicly celebrate CI wins. (The best way to get this done is to prepare the vignette for the CEO and request approval. For example, if someone in the sales department gathers some important information for you, ghostwrite an article by the CEO saluting that person in sales and ask for approval to publish it in the company newsletter.)

Rather than keeping your contact calendar on your computer, consider using a whiteboard or poster board and hanging it in a prominent location in your office or in the CI area. This tactic keeps your CI to-do list front and center and makes adding notes easy and convenient.

Always work by appointment rather than on a drop-by basis to convey the message that your work and time is high value, and always do the following:

✔ Confirm each appointment at least one day prior to your meeting so the person has ample time to prepare.

✔ In your reminder, describe the purpose of the meeting.

✔ Remain on schedule; arrive on time and use only the allotted time.

✔ Find out what you can do for the person prior to your next meeting. After all, your objective is service excellence.

Maintaining a calendar is a good practice, but sharing the CI team's time and resources fairly with all constituencies can still be quite a challenge. In the real world, what often happens is that the squeaky wheel gets the grease. In other words, certain groups that know about the value and capabilities of the CI team (usually sales, marketing, and product development) try to monopolize the CI team's time and resources. Sales teams always seem to be in "capture" mode, marketing always in "business development" battle stations, and product development always pushing the latest widget.

Don't inadvertently ignore an important constituency. One solution is to look for opportunities to repurpose intelligence products you created for tactical consumers to create briefings for your executive (strategic) consumers. Sometimes, just rewriting intel reports with a different consumer prospective is sufficient.

Updating needs assessments

Keeping CI on everyone's radar is only one of the purposes of regular contact. You also need to get information from the people you meet with about what they need from the CI team and how useful prior CI analysis has been to them. And you need to remember that information and the source, because executives, managers, and working grunts alike will be annoyed and less interested in helping CI if you never remember what they tell you. So to keep track of what you learn, prior to and during meetings with internal customers, sponsors, resource people, and other personnel, complete the internal resource/customer needs assessment shown in Figure 17-2. Fill in the information at the top, as well as the Briefing summary section, before the meeting and complete the rest of the form during the meeting.

Periodically update your needs assessments and needs map (see Chapter 5) to maintain the focus of your efforts on the needs of your internal customers and sponsors.

Internal Resource/Customer Needs Assessment

Date: ____________

Contact person: ______________________ Title: ______________

Area of Responsibility: ____________________________________

Phone: ____________________ Email: ______________________

Purpose of visit: ___ Briefing ___ Needs assessment ___ Update areas of focus

Briefing summary:

Review of needs/areas of interest:

Emerging/new areas of interest:

Are any of the above to be considered sensitive or confidential? ____Yes____No

Follow-Up Information (dates, information to be provided, etc.):

Notes:

CI contact completing interview ______________________________

Figure 17-2: Maintain an updated needs assessment.

Illustration by Wiley, Composition Services Graphics

Enhancing CI's Value Proposition and Image

Most organizations don't have a value proposition for each of their internal functional units. (A *value proposition* simply states how the unit or department contributes to the organization's ongoing success.) With CI, creating and living a value proposition can help the team serve the organization in a significant and meaningful way and earn the respect it deserves. I encourage you to develop a value proposition for CI along the lines of the following example:

> *We will gather, analyze, and distribute meaningful, actionable intelligence to our internal constituencies by*
>
> - *Focusing foremost on serving our internal customers*
>
> - *Operating with integrity, transparency, and altruism (seeking the best for others in the organization)*
>
> - *Keeping our internal clients informed of unexpected, discontinuous events that may be developing in our future*
>
> - *Ensuring that our only goal is to be a trusted partner in helping our internal clients succeed*

After establishing your value proposition, look for ways to enhance the CI team's value proposition. In the following sections, I offer a few suggestions.

Applying continuous improvement to the CI function

Many Japanese companies operate according to a business philosophy they call *kaizen,* which means continuous improvement. CI should embrace and embody kaizen in the following ways:

- ✔ **Query internal clients regularly to identify their CI needs, any concerns they may have, and any competitor initiatives they're aware of.** See the earlier section "Achieving and Maintaining a Connection with Key Players" for more on this.

- ✔ **Continually upgrade intelligence analysis and methodologies.** Continuing education is key. Active membership in Strategic and Competitive Intelligence Professionals (SCIP), *the* organization for CI professionals, can help you keep abreast of developments in the profession. For more about SCIP, visit www.scip.org.

- ✔ **Track changes and advances in internal and external analytics applications.** Make sure you're getting the most out of your technologies.

- ✔ **Use internal client questionnaires and brainstorming sessions to measure their perception and how much they value CI services.** I explain these sessions in the following section.

As part of an integrated *kaizen* effort, the head of the CI team should follow up each intel briefing with the internal customer who's been briefed to obtain the customer's unvarnished impression of the intelligence that's been delivered. Doing so continues the dialogue and enables the CI team leader to ask about other information needs.

Brainstorming to enhance CI services

Brainstorming with a mixed group of individuals from different areas of the organization is a great way to come up with ideas on how to more effectively serve your internal customers. Your brainstorming session should focus on identifying the next little things and the next big things that are likely to appear in the market or a specific sector. The idea is to engage participants in an "over the horizon" exercise that will help you better serve them.

You can brainstorm through a questionnaire or online discussion, but results are usually better if you meet in person.

To conduct a brainstorming session, perform the following steps:

1. **Gather a group of internal customers (a mixed group representing different areas in your organization).**

2. **List your organization's major product offerings.**

3. **Ask participants to envision what the next little thing in each product area is going to be.**

   Have fun. Encourage participants to be creative and suggest ideas that are really out there. Consider drawing a mind map on a whiteboard to track the path of ideas or have participants come to the front to write their ideas.

   Leave enough room for summaries at the end of your discussions.

4. **At the end of the discussion, ask participants to summarize the group's thinking with a list of conclusions or key points.**

   Don't just jot down the conclusions or key points as you see them. Your job as facilitator is to encourage participant interaction and lead the group to consensus.

5. **Repeat Steps 3 and 4, shifting the focus to identifying competitors and what they're likely to introduce as their next little things.**

6. **Repeat Steps 3 to 5, asking participants to give their thoughts about the next big thing in each area.** Use the same exact format, discussing products first and then competitors.

7. **Conduct an out-of-the-blue exercise: Ask the group to discuss possible issues that could arise in reference to products and competitors that would surprise them.**

   Ask participants to also consider potential competitors from other markets or sectors that may try to expand into your organization's space.

8. **Wrap up the meeting, thank everyone for their contributions, and set them free.**

9. **When you return to your office, create a mind map for each segment of the discussion and send a copy of the mind maps, including the group's conclusions and comments, to each participant.**

   You can draw a mind map in nearly any graphics program or even using Microsoft Word's drawing tools. If you want something that's more sophisticated and can perform some of the work for you, consider using a dedicated mind mapping software, such as XMind. Visit www.xmind.net for more information and to download a shareware copy of the program.

Fostering innovation in CI offerings

CI is just as susceptible as other departments to experiencing stagnation and resistance to change. To keep members of the team sharp and foster innovation within the CI team, engage in the following activities:

- ✔ **Reward people who create or discover novel approaches to doing CI or approaching certain issues.**

- ✔ **Create opportunities with other departments (such as information technology and the marketing department) that foster creative thinking and discovery.**

- ✔ **Routinely move CI people out of CI to other departments for exposure to other disciplines.** Use these opportunities to bring fresh perspectives back into the unit.

Rotating personnel from other departments into CI to expand awareness

Just as CI can benefit from rotating personnel into other departments, it can benefit from rotating personnel from other departments into CI to build awareness of what CI does and its value. Here are a couple ways to expand awareness of CI by involving more people in its operations:

Lessons from the Citizen's Police Academy

Neighborhood watch programs are one way that law enforcement tries to engage the community in policing the streets. In a relatively new initiative called the Citizen's Police Academy, law-enforcement agencies are trying to increase community involvement. These agencies take citizens through a series of classes that focus on the law, police procedures, and even how citizens can function as the eyes and ears of the police department on the front lines of fighting crime.

Through this approach, law enforcement has discovered that as citizens complete the training, they develop a newfound appreciation for the job and the challenges that officers encounter on a daily basis. As a result, this program builds support for local law enforcement that further improves its effectiveness.

Follow this same model to engage your entire organization in CI. After all, when everyone in the organization is on the lookout for potential threats and opportunities, the potential for innovation is unlimited.

✔ Set up a program that brings key departmental personnel into short-term assignments in the CI department.

✔ Develop a plan that involves rotating potential sponsors and internal customers into the sponsor group.

Communicating to Maintain Visibility

Great companies that walk the talk understand the value of symbolism and storytelling. They don't just say that they value CI; they demonstrate it in a meaningful way. If your organization views CI as a key factor in its future success, leadership must have a clear plan for using symbolism and storytelling to ingrain CI's value in the DNA of the company. In the following sections, I describe various ways to acknowledge the value of CI.

Using your sponsors to elevate your CI communication

The first rule in credibility is that you never publicize your own accomplishments. Instead, you let others to do it. That's where your internal sponsors come in. Here are the keys to making sure those folks do what you need them to do:

Going topsy-turvy

When building Southwest Airlines, Herb Kelleher wanted to stress the importance of what I call the *inverted structure:* the important people (customers, employees, and vendors) at the top with the least important (senior executives) at the bottom.

Kelleher became Southwest's messenger for that principle. He would often show up on a flight and serve coffee. When he needed to make an important decision about baggage handling, he would call in a team of first-level employees (who actually did the job) and get them to help make the right decision. After a key decision was made, Kelleher would give credit for the new procedure to the first-level people who were integral in the decision.

In the same way, the CI team needs to involve people on the front lines in the process of gathering information and putting the resulting intel to good use. And the CEO and others on the executive team must acknowledge the contributions of these front-liners in very public and meaningful ways.

✔ **Serve your sponsors.** Provide exceptional service and information.

✔ **Orient your sponsors.** During your periodic visits with your sponsors, make sure they understand the importance of their role in publicizing some of the CI wins that you helped them achieve.

✔ **Return the favor.** Make sure you publicize your sponsors for their role in helping you capture and analyze intelligence.

✔ **Always focus on team.** In CI, sustainable success is the result of a team approach. For example, your sales people are invaluable resources for gathering CI. Publicly saluting individuals for their contributions reinforces their commitment to your mission.

Expanding the communication circle

As the CI team becomes firmly established in an organization, it often becomes the point "person" for issues that involve more than one department or function in the organization. In some cases, a department manager may not know that someone in another department has the skills or knowledge that can help her solve a problem or deal with a particular issue.

By establishing close relationships with everyone in the organization, you may find yourself uniquely qualified to refer people to one another and expand the communication circle. Just make sure you don't step on any toes in the process. Here's an approach that's safe:

1. **If someone needs help and you know of someone inside (or outside) the organization who's uniquely qualified to provide assistance, ask the person who needs help if you can have the person you know contact her.** If she says no, end of story. If she says yes, proceed to Step 2.

2. **Ask the person who's uniquely qualified to help if she would be willing and able to provide assistance.** If the answer is no, let the person who needs help know that the person you thought could help is unable to. If the answer is yes, then proceed to Step 3.

3. **Provide contact information to the person who's uniquely qualified to help (or serve in some other way to bring the two people together).**

In some cases, expanding the communication circle simply means looping another person — perhaps the CEO or other higher-level sponsor — into the conversation you're having so you have additional input. However, sharing information can sometimes involve political nuances or power struggles that you're unaware of, so before looping someone in, make sure everyone already in the loop is okay with it.

Jumping on unforeseen opportunities or threats

The CI team is often able to increase its impact by jumping on opportunities or threats it discovered through its research but that nobody else in the organization saw coming. Giving an internal customer an impromptu heads-up lets the person know that you're covering his back and committed to his success. Here's a good way to approach unexpected opportunities and unforeseen threats:

1. **Schedule a short meeting with your internal customers who hold a stake in the information for a briefing about the emerging issue.**

2. **Use the meeting to convey new information and gauge the level of need or deficiencies in current knowledge that require additional research.**

3. **Ask questions to develop an understanding of the timeline/urgency of getting the information back to the internal customer.**

4. **Follow up with your internal customers according to the agreed-upon timeline.**

Publicizing CI's Value and Achievements

Internal memos and newsletters usually do a pretty good job of celebrating the achievements of sales and marketing with headlines such as "Middle Market Team Lands $500 million Tennessee Project!" What's usually missing from those headlines and the stories that accompany them are the valuable contributions from CI that enabled the big event to happen. For the CI team to maximize its effectiveness, your organization needs to publicly acknowledge and perhaps even celebrate its contributions to the organization's success. In the following sections, I describe a few ways to publicize the CI team's contributions.

Enhancing CI's image through your intelligence cluster

Make your intelligence cluster (the CI team, internal customers, and sponsors) aware of the importance of publicizing CI wins. Ask them for suggestions on how to diplomatically promote CI within the organization. You don't want to steal the stage from others who certainly deserve some of the spotlight, but you do need to find ways to share the stage in order to increase CI's visibility and credibility.

Don't boast. Nobody likes a braggart. Try to find ways to share the stage and give shout-outs to others in the organization who played a key role in executing successful initiatives.

Promoting CI through a newsletter

Team up with the person or team in charge of communications in your organization to determine the best way to publicize CI's work internally. In most cases, you have the following options, but always make sure that the CEO approves before pursuing any of these options:

- ✔ **Add a CI column to an existing newsletter.** Your organization's newsletter editor would probably be more than happy to include whatever you choose to contribute.

    Consider a "Competitive Corner" column that presents key issues and challenges that your organization will face in the future. Such a column enables you to soft sell the value of CI.

- ✔ **Claim some space in the CEO's monthly newsletter.** While space may be limited, any association with the CEO boosts CI's credibility.

✔ **Create your own CI newsletter.** This option gives you the most free[...] and space.

Whichever option you choose, consider adding "attaboy" and "attagirl" recognition to reward employees who contribute to CI's success and make everyone aware of CI's role in helping the organization remain competitive. You can also use your monthly newsletter content to keep everyone up-to-date, highlight key issues, and reinforce the role that everyone in the organization plays in gathering information and passing it along to CI for analysis.

Using recognition to create a "pull effect" for internally generated intel

Symbolic gestures of recognition are powerful tools for sparking radical change within an organization and establishing CI as a key component for success. In particular, recognition from leadership and peers is a powerful motivator. To inspire people in your organization to pass information to the CI team, reward them with recognition from the executive level on down.

Using symbolic recognition to build interest in CI is similar to pull marketing. Rather than pushing CI onto individuals who may resist it, you're drawing individuals to engage in it. This technique is incredibly powerful in motivating desired behaviors.

Compare the following two scenarios to determine the recognition approach that's most rewarding and likely to motivate the entire organization to contribute to CI's success:

✔ Management has selected you as CI Sleuth of the Month for passing along information to the CI team that helped the organization land a multimillion-dollar contract. As a result, you're awarded a steak dinner for you and your guest at a fancy restaurant. Your boss gives you the award and the gift certificate in an envelope and shakes your hand as she thanks you.

✔ You are selected as CI Sleuth of the Month for the aforementioned reasons. As a result, you're awarded a steak dinner for you and your guest at a fancy restaurant. As you enter the office one morning, your boss and the CEO of the company greet you. They call 50 or so of your fellow employees together, the CEO personally recognizes you for your work in front of everyone, and he hands you the envelope and thanks you for your contribution.

The power of symbolism is evident when you read the second scenario. Such an event would create an immediate desire on the part of others in the organization to do something that gets them recognition for a job well done, and the story would spread all over the company in less than 30 minutes.

Part IV: Getting Support for Intelligence Dissemination and Implementation ____

Chapter 18

Defending against Competitor Intelligence

....

In This Chapter

▶ Developing prudent paranoia

▶ Dodging common intel traps

▶ Tightening your organization's security

....

Knowledge is power. You know it, and so do your competitors. Like you, your competitors are probably engaged in competitive intelligence (CI) to some degree. After all, you're not the only one seeking to gain a competitive edge. They may be reading this book, and some of them may choose to ignore the advice I give in Chapter 4 and engage in unscrupulous behavior. They may hire some of your key employees in the hopes of getting trade secrets or engage in industrial espionage by stealing sponsored research or planting electronic surveillance devices or software inside your organization.

 Regardless of whether your competitors play by the rules, you should never let down your guard. You need to protect your organization and prevent any sensitive information from falling into the wrong hands. In this chapter, I give you the information and tools you need to guard against competitor intelligence.

Assuming Everyone's a Liar until Proven Otherwise

These days, you can't trust anybody . . . not that you ever really could, but lying and deception seem to be at an all-time high, maybe because the Internet has made it so easy. To protect your organization, you, as the gate-keeper of CI, and really all your fellow personnel need to operate with a heavy dose of skepticism. Start by believing none of what you hear and only half of what you see. Healthy skepticism ensures that you follow up on issues that may give you small hints about the unethical nature of a competitor or even a supplier, distributor, or future partner.

When sizing up a competitor — and before establishing a close relationship with another organization — ask and answer the following questions:

- ✔ **What is the culture of this company's country of origin?** In some cultures, anything goes when competing with companies outside of their country, so it may engage in unethical business practices.

- ✔ **What's the company's track record of working with other companies similar to yours?** If an organization has been dishonest with another company, that company will be most happy to tell you the truth about how the organization in question does business.

Additionally, you can employ the triangulation technique I present in Chapter 11 to confirm the information you have about an organization from at least two other sources.

Many organizations list customers and partners on their websites and in other promotional materials. In addition, companies often connect on LinkedIn and other social networking sites. (Social-network analysis — finding out who's connected to whom — is a growing field of interest.) Consider contacting these third-party sources to find out more about how the organization does business and to evaluate its reputation among its peers.

Know whom your friends are friends with

Sharing highly confidential information, including very sensitive trade secrets, with key suppliers seemed innocent enough to executives of a certain company. After all, these key suppliers were well-established U.S. firms that had long-standing, lucrative relationships with the company that was sharing its secrets. On the surface, they had no motivation to pass sensitive information along to competing firms.

Over time, however, the company's major international competitor seemed to be beating them to market consistently. The company's leadership couldn't figure out what was happening until one day, a former U.S. government official asked if he could meet with the company's executive team. They agreed. What he revealed was shocking.

The international competitor had used a complex web of holding companies to acquire all the company's key suppliers. Much to their dismay, the company's leaders realized that they had been handing all their most sensitive new product information to their biggest competitor!

The moral of this story is to be careful, even when sharing information with entities you believe are your allies. They may not be as careful with your sensitive information as you are, and you probably have no control over their internal security systems.

Recognizing Shady Competitor Intelligence Tactics

Some organizations are willing to engage in shady schemes to access the intellectual capital of their competitors and any other firms that may be able to give them a competitive advantage. Developing an awareness of these practices enables you to become more vigilant and protect your organization against them. In the following sections, I describe several of the more common devious ploys.

Acquiring intellectual capital through acquisitions

Many global competitors work through domestic equity capital firms — former Wall Street financial firms with extensive backgrounds in acquisitions — to buy the intellectual capital they need to beat their competitors, many of which are U.S. companies. These financial firms engage in the following acts to help their international clients:

✔ Searching for suppliers, competitors, and other entities that may have unique information about how to manufacture your product

✔ Searching for individuals and organizations that can plug the gaps in the international competitor's technology portfolio

✔ Assisting in the acquisition of companies that have the technology needed by the international competitor in a way that evades government oversight

As you can probably guess from this list, such acts can often be compared to treason.

Keep an eye on your competitors' acquisitions. By knowing which companies a competitor works with and the type of companies and technologies it's acquiring, you can usually figure out what your competitor is up to and what its true motivations and goals are.

Stealing your research

Tapping the intellectual power of university research labs for help in developing new products is a savvy and legitimate way to gain a competitive advantage. Some companies, however, take it a little too far by paying big bucks for the right to set up an office in the lab that essentially serves as a spy center. You end up paying for the research, which is likely to reach your competitor long before it's delivered to you. International companies are particularly adept at using their laboratory presence as a key intelligence-gathering base.

Here are three precautions you can take to protect your company from such tactics:

✔ Before agreeing to pay a university team to do research, make sure no competitor companies or countries have access to the lab premises or to any ongoing research.

✔ Ask for a written contract that ensures that no researcher from a competitor country or company is allowed access to your research.

✔ Make sure your organization has the ability to visit the lab periodically and review the lab's access and security situation.

Penetrating organizations

Some organizations prefer a direct approach to stealing information. They get inside their competitor's operation and extract information in a variety of ways. They may bribe someone on the inside, get one of their own people hired on, plant listening devices in conference rooms or executive offices, infect computers with spyware, and so on.

Following are some ways to defend against these and other similar tactics:

✔ Routinely assess key executive personnel or others who have access to critical information. Watch for any unusual activity or access to sensitive information that may indicate potential problems.

✔ Allow no one, including delivery drivers and cleaning crews, access to company premises without an escort.

✔ Be especially alert to any electronic gadgets that appear anywhere on your company premises. Some competitors have been known to put radio transmitters on fax machines or plant audio bugs in competitor premises.

✔ Work with IT to scan computers regularly for spyware and to prevent unauthorized access to the company network.

Watch the pillow talk, too

In one of the largest trading scandals in recent years, an IBM executive was discovered to have revealed critical insider information over a period of months to his mistress. She allegedly became a co-conspirator with the head of a hedge fund in making millions of dollars based on the insider information she obtained.

The moral of this story: Don't confuse shop talk with pillow talk.

Hiring key people and then dumping them

One way companies get the goods is to hire a competitor's key employees and ask them to share their insider knowledge. If an employee left your organization bitter, she's even more likely to share what she knows. No foolproof method can protect you from rogue ex-employees, but you may be able to mitigate some of the damage caused by such leaks if you follow these suggestions:

- ✔ If you're hiring or promoting a person to a position in which the individual has access to sensitive information, require that the person sign a nondisclosure agreement prior to taking the job.

- ✔ Track people who leave your company to find out where they land. Is the company that hired the person a competitor? Does anything make you suspect that the person is sharing confidential information?

    Social media, including LinkedIn and Facebook, are great tools for tracking former employees and finding out where they're employed.

- ✔ Ask the person's friends who are still employed at your company how things are going with their friend. Often, former employees maintain relationships with current employees, who may be willing to share what their friend is up to.

- ✔ If an employee is hired by a competitor and then leaves, consider asking him what his former employee asked about your organization when he was first hired. This may give you some insight into the way your competitor conducts CI and the type of information it looks for.

Looking for juicy information at trade shows and conventions

If you think you're the only company gathering intelligence at a convention or trade show, think again. Trade shows are like CI conventions; everyone's gathering information and listening in on conversations, which is fine as long as nobody in your organization shares confidential information.

Here's how to avoid falling victim to unscrupulous intelligence gatherers while at trade shows and conventions:

- ✔ Provide your employees with training to help them recognize and deal with competitors who try to get intelligence about your company.

- ✔ Give your sales team extensive training to make sure they avoid getting drawn into a "who's got the best product" discussion that could end up leading to the sales person's revelation of your next big product release.

- ✔ Always enforce a two-drink rule for all your trade-show attendees. Liquor loosens lips . . . and if you can't say that without tripping over your tongue, you've probably had too much already.

Creating a Security Perimeter around Your Organization

Any information left in plain view is fair game for your competitors, so you need to take reasonable precautions to secure sensitive information. The best place to start is outside the company property. Securing the perimeter ensures that no unauthorized personnel get close enough to access the information. In the following sections, I offer some suggestions on recommendations you can make to senior management about how to secure your company's perimeter.

As a CI professional, you serve as trusted advisor. Your role on the security team is to point out vulnerable areas and perhaps offer your opinion on how to tighten security, but formulating and implementing security measures must start with the CEO and other members of the executive team.

Conducting a counterintelligence audit

When you want to test just how secure your organization is, attack it by conducting a counterintelligence audit. Create a *red team,* a group of your own people assigned the task of acting like an outside aggressor to penetrate your security and reporting any areas of vulnerability. Here's how:

1. **Assemble your red team, choosing people in the organization who are likely to be clever and persistent in finding and testing vulnerable areas.**

   Consider including one or more individuals who have the technical savvy to test network security and dig up information about your organization online.

2. **Instruct the team to pretend it's working for your biggest competitor and try to gather information from outside the physical perimeter of your organization.**

   Here are some examples:

   - What can they see from the perimeter of your firm? Customer names on shipments? Customer pickups of product?

   - If you have a gated entrance, what information can they gather from watching the traffic in and out of your property?

   - What can they learn if they follow your company vehicles when they leave your property?

3. **Instruct the team to evaluate external access points or other entry modes that may allow unauthorized, undetected access to the property.**

   In other words, the team needs to find out how easy it is for just anyone to walk in off the street and gain access to internal information or for people inside the company who don't have security clearance to access areas that require such clearance.

4. **Instruct the team to conduct CI on your company to find out what information is publicly accessible and see if any sensitive information is already out there.**

   Use the same techniques that the CI team uses to dig up intel on competitors. See Chapter 6 for details. If sensitive information is being leaked, you may need to conduct an internal investigation to identify the source of the leaks and plug the holes.

5. **Challenge the team to dig up any potentially sensitive information it can find on your organization's website and by searching the web.**

   This step often reveals a critical need to de-thatch corporate websites of older presentations, white papers, and information brochures that can be accessed by using simple search algorithms in Google and other search engines.

6. **Instruct the team to examine all external touch points of your organization — investor relations, marketing, sales, engineers, and so on to identify any departments or individuals that are vulnerable to information leakage.**

   For example, by design, industry user groups and trade associations are excellent for information exchange, but any employee who participates in these groups can become a source for leaks. They need to be advised on what to say and what's strictly off limits. The same holds true for people in marketing and sales who attend trade shows.

After the team has wrapped up its work, debrief the team and create a detailed report of any security weaknesses. Present the report to the executive or department head who's in charge of security.

The CI team should continue to monitor Slideshare, Twitter, Facebook, Pinterest, and other social sharing sites for presentations, pictures, and potentially revealing corporate information and work toward removing any such content from the web. Remember, if your CI team can find it, so can your competitors.

Controlling internal physical access

In order to conduct business, you probably need to allow people to freely enter and exit the building, but you shouldn't allow them to freely roam the halls and offices. To prevent unauthorized access to sensitive areas of your organization, implement the following security measures:

- ✔ **Never allow uncontrolled access to your organization.** Make sure that visitors are always accompanied by an employee.

- ✔ **Set up secure entry points in key areas of the building to limit access to authorized personnel.**

- ✔ **Be especially observant of individuals who bring cameras into your facility or are using their cellphones in sensitive areas.** You may want to establish a policy of having all visitors turn off their cellphones or leave them in a personal locker before they're allowed access to sensitive areas.

- ✔ **Require that all sensitive information be secured (locked) before an employee leaves his or her work area.**

- ✔ **Make sure that no new product information, sales projections, or strategic planning documents are visible on walls or whiteboards in public view.**

Controlling social-networking access to your information

Social networking is a valuable tool for connecting personally with current and prospective customers, but it also poses some risks. You don't want just anyone posting on behalf of the company, engaging in flame wars with disgruntled customers, or sharing information about the organization's future plans. The flow of information and how it's presented publicly needs to be controlled internally.

Establish a social-media policy that addresses the following points:

- ✔ Who's allowed (and not allowed) to post content on behalf of your organization.

- ✔ Who must approve content before it's posted.

- ✔ What types of information can and can't be shared via social media.

- ✔ How much freedom your organization has in monitoring social media use internally. Many companies are now requiring that employees allow them to routinely look at personal social-media sites as part of the firm's ongoing security program.

Using analytics to detect internal leaks

A new generation of analytics tools now enables an organization to keep very close tabs on a lot of what is really going on in their organization. Here are some of the things that analytics can do:

- ✔ Track themes and attitudes in the flow of information on the company's e-mail.

- ✔ Track file transfers into and out of the internal network.

- ✔ Track phone traffic into and out of the organization and pick up on the themes and content of those calls.

CI and IT should work closely to develop systems that automate the process of preventing and detecting security leaks.

Protecting against global industrial espionage

When doing business in the global economy, you're often competing against companies that don't follow the same rules and may be backed by government-sponsored intel agencies that arose out of military intelligence agencies or are even integral parts of those agencies. In other words, your global competitor may have access to intelligence capabilities that far exceed your own.

Expecting the worst and planning to defeat such capabilities may be your best defense against such actions. Here's what you need to keep in mind when dealing with international competitors:

- ✔ In most cases, international competitors throw ethics out the window when competing against companies in other countries. The company's allegiance is to its country. You're working for the enemy.

✔ Numerous countries around the world have adopted the original government-industry model of Japan (described in the nearby sidebar). Even the United States is beginning to wake up to reality and use government intel to help U.S. companies stay competitive.

✔ International competitors have access to highly technical and sophisticated resources that probably surpass your internal capabilities.

Exploring the roots of Japan's government-industry model

In most industrialized nations, business is war. Many people in the United States recognize this fact, but few U.S. businesses fully grasp how brutal these global battles can be and how closely certain governments and the businesses within their countries collaborate on waging war against their competitors. To gain a better understanding of how international companies compete and how they justify what many business owners in the United States would view as unethical, turn back the pages of history to World War II.

One of the most well-run agencies of the Japanese government during the war was the Ministry of Munitions. At the end of the war, the Ministry of Munitions wasn't disbanded. It remained with the same people in place in the same facilities. Its name was changed to Ministry of International Trade and Industry (MITI), and its mission was altered to focus on helping Japanese companies compete in the global economy.

MITI became the dealer between government policy and major corporations in Japan. In effect, it began coordinating government actions, tariffs, and legislation in accord with the country's global economic objectives. One thing that this new hybrid government-industry organization brought with it was the traditional military approach for intelligence gathering. This approach continues in Japan and has spread to many other industrialized nations, including France and China, the two countries with perhaps the worst reputations for not playing by the rules.

Before government-sponsored industrial espionage became an international issue, an essay coauthored by Shintaro Ishihara, then minister of transport and future governor of Tokyo, and Sony cofounder and chairman Akio Morita shed a lot of light on this issue. The essay entitled "The Japan That Can Say No," first published in Japan, suggests that World War II never ended; it simply shifted from military to economic warfare. Much of the essay criticized U.S. business practices as focusing too much on money, such as mergers and acquisitions, while not paying enough attention to delivering quality products to the marketplace. While many of Morita's claims were accurate, the essay caused a great deal of controversy in the United States, where it was not well received.

When countries begin to view themselves as engaged in economic warfare, as more and more countries do these days, they're more open to the idea of restructuring their intelligence networks to support their own business communities as they compete in the global economy.

As a CI professional, you need to realize that when your organization competes globally, it's often competing with organizations that think and act as though they're engaged in world war and have their country's global intelligence network to support them.

Part V
The Part of Tens

the
part of
tens

Head to www.dummies.com/extras/competitiveintelligence for a list of the ten forces that affect all businesses. Being aware of and monitoring these forces regularly can help you stay ahead of the competition.

In this part . . .

✔ Get an idea of how effective and efficient CI is within your company by asking and answering ten critical assessment questions.

✔ Find out how to fully bring your organization's CEO onboard with all things CI. (After all, if the CEO doesn't clearly support and welcome CI's recommendations, other decision makers aren't likely to either.)

✔ Identify the ten warning signs that indicate your company is heading for the cliff. The good news is that by spotting them early enough, you may be able to turn your organization around.

Chapter 19

Ten Questions to Help You Assess CI's Effectiveness

In This Chapter

▶ Determining whether your organization has the right mindset

▶ Evaluating CI's ability to predict future events

▶ Gauging the support of your organization's leaders

Auditing CI is an ongoing process with the ultimate goal of achieving and maintaining best-in-class CI capabilities. In this chapter, I lead you through the process of answering ten questions that you need to consider when gauging how effective and efficient your CI program really is.

Do Your Leaders Have a Healthy Case of Intuitive Paranoia?

Intuitive paranoia is a sixth sense that enables an individual to immediately recognize potential threats without having to gather a bunch of information and analyze it. If your organization's leaders aren't intuitively paranoid, they should be.

Although the definition of *paranoia* technically refers to an irrational and unsubstantiated fear of being harmed, not being afraid of threats in an ever-changing competitive environment is truly irrational. Although your competitors may not specifically set out to destroy your company, your organization needs to continually adapt to changes in the industry or in specific markets — or else suffer certain extinction.

Intuitive paranoia keeps everyone on their toes and on the lookout for opportunities and threats. Find out more about it in Chapter 1.

Has Management Adopted a Momentary-Advantage Mindset?

As a consultant, I often encounter two types of organizations: those that adopt a momentary-advantage mindset and those that attempt to build a strategy based on their historic competitive advantage — what they've always done well and succeeded at doing. For CI to be successful, decision makers need to adopt the *momentary-advantage mindset,* which is an awareness that the playing field is in a constant state of change that continually produces new opportunities and threats. They need to lead the organization to take advantage of opportunities and respond to potential threats in ways that increase profits and market share incrementally.

One way to function with a momentary-advantage mindset is to operate the organization the way a portfolio manager buys and sells investment vehicles. Monitor the marketplace for opportunities and reinvest resources intelligently to capitalize on those opportunities. See Chapter 1 for more about the importance of operating with a momentary-advantage mindset.

Are You Confident in the Quantity, Quality, and Depth of Your Data?

Analysis is sort of like cooking. In cooking, if you don't have all the ingredients or if some ingredients are poor quality, the end result is probably going to taste pretty bad. In CI, if you start with insufficient or inaccurate data, you're probably going to end up drawing faulty conclusions.

Before moving from data collection to analysis, you need to be confident that your data is valuable in relation to the following qualities:

✔ **Quantity:** Do you have a sufficient amount of data to analyze? If you're not confident that you can draw accurate conclusions from the data, you need to do additional research.

✔ **Accuracy:** Triangulate to verify the data you have against at least two other reliable sources. If three reliable sources say something's true, then you're probably on the right track.

✔ **Breadth:** Cast a wide net to catch anything on the fringe of an issue that may impact it.

✔ **Depth:** Interrogate the data, as explained in Chapter 6, to make sure that you've investigated all relevant factors.

✔ **Time relevance:** Is your data future focused? That is, does it enable you to predict an opportunity or threat far enough into the future to capitalize on the opportunity or avoid the threat?

✔ **Clarity:** How certain are you of the conclusions you've reached? If clarity is low, you're dealing with ambiguity, which requires additional research and perhaps more time to clarify.

See Chapter 9 for additional advice on evaluating the quantity, quality, and depth of data.

Do Your Intelligence Analysts Have the Right Stuff?

Although skilled analysts may seem to have psychic powers, they actually have a combination of innate abilities and training that uniquely qualifies them to conduct analysis. To ensure that you're getting the most bang for your buck from your analysts (the people on your CI team who analyze the information or the specialists you hire), make sure they exhibit the following qualities (which you can read more about in Chapter 10):

✔ Natural curiosity

✔ Hypervigilance

✔ Tendency to notice things in information that others overlook

✔ Ability to see the big picture as well as the details

✔ Skeptical attitude toward information

✔ Capacity for skimming large volumes of information

✔ Logic and critical thinking

Is CI Systematic?

Although CI is valuable for answering a specific question, solving a problem, or double-checking whether a certain decision is best, it's more valuable when it's continuous and systematic. As explained in Chapter 1, CI is a continuous four-step process:

1. Planning

2. Gathering

3. Analyzing

4. Executing

All four steps are essential, but Step 4 seems the most difficult because people tend to be change averse. In Chapter 15, I offer some suggestions on overcoming common barriers to change.

Is CI Future Focused?

Companies often get bogged down in sales numbers, profit estimates, and a host of other data that's historical or focused on present conditions. None of this data is of much use in formulating a strategy that's likely to lead to success one to three years down the road.

CI needs to be future focused. Your organization must spot opportunities and threats months or even years down the road so you can plan and prepare to take advantage of changes while your competitors miss out.

Do Senior Managers Test Their Conclusions?

Executives and senior managers are often driven more by ego or emotion than by fact and reason. Organizations that embrace humility rarely encounter problems in this area, because leaders actively seek out input and insight from others and test their conclusions against reality. If your organization's leaders tend to formulate strategy out of thin air, your organization may achieve some temporary success . . . if it's very lucky. However, it's probably doomed to fail over time.

Is Your CI Team Adept at Predicting Future Outcomes from Foggy Data?

Every once in a while, you may encounter a single piece of information that reveals a golden opportunity, such as an unmet customer need that all your competitors have overlooked. In most cases, however, you pick up weak signals that provide only a foggy glimpse of what may be an opportunity or threat. These weak, ambiguous signals are what really test your CI team's predictive prowess.

To transform weak signals into strong signals, interrogate the data and follow your leads. Interrogating the data often leads you in different directions that ultimately reveal an opportunity or threat.

Do You Have Solid CI Support from Executives and Managers?

Three of the four stages of the CI process require support from executives and managers — planning, gathering, and executing. Analyzing not so much, but even that step can benefit from management and executive input. After all, without leadership support, you may not get all the information you need to conduct analysis, and you won't have the support you need to put your intel in action. In short, before you try to engage in any heavy-duty CI, get some influential leaders on board.

Is Your CEO Active and Visible in Supporting the CI Mission and Team?

The single most influential member of your organization is your CEO. The CEO has the power and visibility to engage everyone in the organization in CI activities and to drive the engine of change in the direction that CI points. If your CEO also serves as your CIO (chief intelligence officer), CI's achievements can far surpass anything it can possibly accomplish without the backing of the CEO.

Although the CEO can play a powerful role in establishing the importance of the CI team and in putting intel into action, the CEO doesn't necessarily make or break the CI team's efforts. If the CI team has at least one (preferably more) influential champion throughout the organization, it can still succeed, with or without support from the CEO. In fact, having one or more senior managers sponsoring the CI team is key to establishing continued success if the current CEO departs for whatever reason; these sponsors can sing the CI team's praises to the next CEO.

Chapter 20

Ten Actions a CEO Can Take to Bolster CI's Impact

. . . .

In This Chapter

▶ Grasping why a CEO's support is so essential

▶ Encouraging cooperation between the intel team and management

. . . .

*Y*our organization's CEO is its figurehead representing the company's values and serving as the engine that drives positive change. If your CEO doesn't support the intel team and publicize its achievements — or, even worse, if he or she rejects the intel team's insights and recommendations — then your competitive intelligence efforts will fall short for the following reasons:

- ✔ The CEO won't share information freely with the intel team.

- ✔ Other people in leadership or decision-making roles won't be as eager to collaborate or share information with the intel team.

- ✔ The intel team won't have the reputation and respect required to overcome resistance to change.

- ✔ Everyone who initially supported the intel team will get discouraged, and innovation will grind to a halt.

Your CEO may not be a pathfinder, but if her personality of change is at least an organizer with some listener mixed in, you have a good chance of bringing your CEO on board and up to speed on the value of CI. (See Chapter 15 for more about the five personalities of change.) This chapter describes ten concrete ways your CEO can contribute to CI's success and, consequently, the success of the entire organization.

The success or failure of an organization hinges on the ability of the firm to capture the future and to act on that information. The CEO–intel team partnership is the most effective way to keep your company ahead of the curve and in the game. However, keep in mind that having the CEO on board doesn't necessarily make or break your CI program. Regardless of whether the CEO is on board, encourage and recruit other senior-level managers to sponsor your organization's CI efforts. This chapter provides concrete ways that your CEO and other influential leaders in your organization can show their support.

Serve As Chief Intelligence Officer

If your organization has no official chief intelligence officer (CIO), then your CEO may want to claim that title, too. As CIO, your CEO must take over the following duties:

- **Sponsoring CI:** Communicate CI's value to the rest of the organization and encourage everyone in the organization to share information with the intel team and take advantage of what it has to offer.
- **Publicizing CI's achievements:** Nobody carries more weight in singing the praises of CI than the CEO.
- **Helping identify strategic areas that are most likely to benefit from CI:** The CEO probably has a fairly clear vision of where CI can benefit the organization most.

Your CEO is probably very busy and has little time to serve both as CEO and CIO, so take as much of the burden as possible off her plate. For example, you can do most of the heavy lifting in publicizing the intel team's achievements (for example, by writing articles for the company newsletter) and simply ask your CEO to sign off on what you're doing and put her name behind it.

Feed Information to the Intel Team

Your CEO probably has a great deal of knowledge and insight about the industry, competitors, suppliers, technologies, processes, and the markets that your organization serves. He knows which potential threats keep him up at nights and is (or should be) always on the lookout for potential opportunities. In addition, the CEO often has exclusive access to special briefings, reports, or conferences where industry or technology trends are discussed. Your CEO needs to pass this information and insight along to the intel team systematically to ensure a constant flow of time-relevant data.

Formalize the intelligence-gathering process by department, including the CEO, so all employees are aware of the role they play and have an easy method to enter fresh information into the system. If it's too complicated, people won't do it, and that includes the CEO.

Battle Resistance to Change

A few organizations are built on their ability to execute change. Whenever a potential opportunity or threat arises, everyone is energized and eager to formulate and implement initiatives in response to the situation. Most organizations, however, especially those that have been around for several years and have been successful doing things a certain way, are change averse. They operate by the motto "If it ain't broke, don't fix it," and they don't realize anything is broken until it's too late — after a more agile competitor puts them out of business.

Your organization's CEO is in the best position to spearhead change. If you can convince your CEO to enthusiastically support a proposal, that support is usually sufficient to overcome any resistance in the organization. (For further ideas on overcoming resistance to change, see Chapter 15.)

If you're unsure whether your CEO will support a proposal, then work with your intelligence cluster, as explained in Chapter 16, to gradually introduce an initiative and build some momentum. If you can gain buy-in from 10 to 25 percent of your organization, that should be enough to overcome any resistance to change.

Cheer On the Intel Team

As a group of professionals, the intel team doesn't need cheerleaders for motivation, but when the CEO cheers on the intel team, she communicates her support for CI and encourages others in the organization to support the team by sharing information with it and taking advantage of the intel that's produced.

While the CEO cheers on the intel team, the intel team should cheer on the people within the organization who help it succeed. When someone feeds a key piece of information or a clever idea to CI, be sure to give that person a shout-out in a meaningful way, perhaps by adding an "attaboy" or "attagirl" mention of the person's contribution in an article in the company newsletter. Or you may decide to set up an award for CI Contributor of the Month. See the next section for details.

Communicate Support through Moments of Symbolism

Public recognition is one of the most effective ways to reinforce an individual's importance to the community, and your organization's CEO is the prime source for that public recognition. To reward valuable contributions to the intel team and motivate employees to continue to help the organization achieve success, your CEO should celebrate their achievements in front of the entire organization, if possible, or in front of an entire department. He should acknowledge contributions and innovation, thank the people who are responsible, and present them with a valuable token of appreciation (perhaps a gift card for a fancy dinner out) on behalf of the entire organization.

A reward given in private has little, if any, motivational impact. An award given publicly as a big deal is the ultimate motivator.

Conduct Executive Team Intel Briefings

Your organization's entire executive team should support the intel team's efforts, gather information and pass it along to the intel team, and take advantage of the intelligence that the intel team produces. To encourage the executive team's support and engagement with the intel team, the CEO should either conduct or host executive team intel briefings on a regular basis — quarterly or monthly.

Conducting executive team intel briefings is not only good practice for keeping everyone on the executive team in the loop but also serves as a symbolic gesture expressing how much the CEO values the intel team's role in the organization's success.

Circulate and Support CI Briefs

Although the intel team may be responsible for distributing intel briefings to your organization's decision makers, another option may be for the intel team to route all or some of its intel briefings through the CEO. When briefings come from the CEO, they're likely to carry more weight.

Broker Partnerships between the Intel and Strategy Teams

Because the CEO sits at the top of the mountain, figuratively speaking, she has a big-picture view of how all the pieces of the organization work together, and she has a greater influence than anyone else in the organization over how each department functions. The CEO is also uniquely positioned to pull people and departments together to work on strategic initiatives.

As the CEO builds strategy teams in response to perceived opportunities or threats, she needs to broker partnerships between these teams and the intel team. For example, if the CEO assembles a team to pursue an acquisition, the intel team needs to be brought in to provide the strategy team with the information and insight it requires to make well-informed strategic decisions, such as whether or not to move forward with an acquisition.

Encourage Product and Sector Leaders to Leverage Intel

Although a CEO may be wise not to micromanage product or sector divisions, he should encourage the decision makers in those divisions to leverage the power of CI in making informed decisions, identifying opportunities, and spotting potential threats. Without such encouragement, product or sector divisions may start to operate as silos (that is, act independently) and become vulnerable to the same stagnation and bureaucracy that can infect the organization as a whole.

The CEO should also encourage product and sector leaders to pass along any relevant information to the intel team for processing, analysis, and distribution.

Feature the Intel Team in Company Communication

A great way to communicate the CEO's support for CI is to feature the intel team and its accomplishments in internal communications from the CEO, which may include the following:

- ✔ Internal memos celebrating the intel team's contributions to key strategic initiatives

- ✔ A CI column in the company's internal newsletter reporting on the intel team's accomplishments and current projects

- ✔ An internal CEO blog that regularly mentions the intel team's contributions to the organization's success

Chapter 21

Ten Signs Your Organization Is in Trouble

*W*hen organizations resist change and fail to adapt to the ever-evolving marketplace, they're doomed to fail. How can you tell when your organization is falling behind? In this chapter, I list ten symptoms of companies that fail to take advantage of what CI has to offer. If you can catch the symptoms early enough, your CEO and others in leadership positions may have a chance, with the help of CI, to turn things around and save the patient. This chapter is required reading for CEOs because they're really the only people who have the power and influence to execute the necessary changes.

Although recognizing these symptoms is a great way to self-diagnose, this list of symptoms is also useful in recognizing when competitors, suppliers, distributors, or other businesses that impact your organization are headed for trouble.

Profit Margins Are Declining

Declining profit margins are an early warning sign that an organization has encountered *strategic misalignment,* which is a fancy way of saying that the organization's operations aren't in sync with its goals. Strategic misalignment usually triggers a downward spiral that goes something like this:

1. Strategic misalignment inhibits the organization's ability to compete as aggressively and successfully as its competitors.

2. Profit margins begin to decline as the organization attempts to compete on price alone.

3. Entrepreneurial behavior and creativity are replaced by an inwardly focused bureaucracy.

4. A crisis occurs that threatens the future of the organization.

Declining profit margins indicate a need to look outside the organization for new opportunities. Avoid the temptation to turn inward.

Focus Shifts from Performance to Politics

Organizations that focus on performance pay special attention to future opportunities, technological shifts, new product creation, and innovation — all performance drivers.

Organizations that focus on politics allow personal power and ego to make critical decisions. In most cases, when politics take precedence over performance, the ability of the firm to engage in continual reinvention approaches zero.

Egos Are Killing Initiatives

Egos kill initiatives and then organizations. They stifle creativity and innovation, blind executives to opportunities and threats, and bully anyone who tries to speak up. They cost your organization customers, vendors, employees, and reputation. Just think about it: How sensitive can someone be to a customer's needs if she's already certain that the organization is doing its best to meet those needs?

The most successful companies have what I call *corporate humility*. From the topmost executive down to the part-time worker bee, employees of successful companies have a commitment to "no ego trips allowed." (See Chapter 15 for more about the ten values of high-performing companies.) When you see big egos driving an organization, it's usually headed for the cliff.

Success is no accident. It must be fact based, deliberate, planned, and supported. Big egos are too irrational for the job.

You Have to Fight with Your Boss to Do the Right Thing

If you and others in your company have to fight the boss to do what's best for your company, the organization is probably in trouble. The working stiffs who deal with customers, suppliers, distributors, and competitors on a daily basis often have keen insight into what the organization can do to improve and what it must do to remain competitive. After all, they're involved in the daily operations of the company and are immersed in their respective areas of expertise.

When bosses don't encourage their underlings or, even worse, don't listen to their ideas and solutions, at some point that rejection becomes institutionalized, and moving important information up the corporate ladder becomes nearly impossible. The most creative individuals begin to feel stifled and either leave or keep their ideas to themselves. In any event, they're the least surprised when the company ultimately goes belly up.

Top Talent Starts Leaving the Company

If the most talented people start to leave the organization, sound the sirens for three reasons:

- Talent drives the innovation that's required for the organization to remain competitive.

- One of the main reasons why talented individuals leave organizations is because they believe that the organization is going in the wrong direction and they have no power to make it change course.

- Your talent may be heading straight to your competitors.

The most talented individuals are usually only the *first* to leave because they're the most capable of finding a new job. Others will follow as the wheels start to come off the company.

Engage your top talent in CI and listen to what they have to say about the direction in which the organization is headed. By getting your top talent more involved, you improve the likelihood of retaining them while simultaneously benefitting from their knowledge and insight.

Few or No New, High-Growth, High-Profit Products Are in the Works

Stall-warning horns keep aircraft pilots from making major mistakes by blaring when the angle of attack and airspeed of the aircraft are nearing a stall — when the airplane stops flying and can go into a spin and crash.

The stall-warning horn for companies should sound when the number of new high-growth, high-profit products drops off or disappears. After all, new products are the lifeblood of a company's future. As current products reach the end of their life cycles (see Chapter 14), new products *must* be introduced to take their place.

Leadership Starts Focusing More Internally than Externally

Company leadership can develop internal focus. When frame-breaking change (see Chapter 14) or overwhelming competition hits a market, turning attention toward internal operations is often much easier and more comfortable than looking at external threats and opportunities.

However, losing focus on external realities is predictably deadly for companies. The key is to never lose sight of the firm's emerging context. When you're working toward improving performance and ensuring your organization's survival, reality is your friend.

The Company Adopts Downsizing As a Strategy

One of the most flawed yet still popular "solutions" to increasing earnings has been an approach called *downsizing* — generally, cutting 10 to 20 percent of the firm's overhead (usually by laying off employees) to increase profits. Research has clearly demonstrated that downsizing is at best a momentary or short-term fix because it only serves to cover up the real problem until it rears its ugly head again within a few quarters.

 "Too many people" usually isn't the real problem plaguing companies that go the downsizing route. And when those companies downsize, often they're laying off the people who *didn't* cause the problem in order to keep the people who did.

Senior Management Forgets That the People Make the Profit

 When senior management forgets that their people make the profit, that attitude ultimately goes straight to the customer . . . on its way to the bottom line.

Case in point: A number of years ago, a certain company was known as the best in the world. It treated its people well and was renowned for its "best in class" customer service. Over the years, the company developed a by-the-numbers approach to decision making, and it took its people out of the equation. After years of turmoil, really bad relationships with key employee groups, and dwindling earnings, the company filed for bankruptcy protection. At the same time the company was voted "most hated" by the customers in that industry.

No One Focuses on Creativity and Discovering the Next Big Thing

At the root of the other nine signs that your organization is in trouble is a lack of focus on creativity and innovation. The absence of creativity usually results in the company's demise.

 Help your company maintain an atmosphere of creativity by encouraging the adoption of the ten values of high-performing companies, which I list in Chapter 15. Successful companies use these values to get on top — and then stay there. Just think of 3M, where employees are *expected* to spend a percentage of their time thinking about new concepts and products (doing so is actually in their job description).

Index

About the Author

Jim Underwood, DBA, MBA, MA, is a professor of management at Dallas Baptist University and the author of numerous books, including *More Than a Pink Cadillac* (a *New York Times* bestseller published by McGraw-Hill) and *Thriving in E-Chaos* (winner of the International Competia Award and published by Prima Venture, a division of Prima Publishing).

His clients have included IBM, HP, Sprint, and McKesson, plus numerous other organizations. Jim served as the Global Strategy Content Expert for the Nortel Learning Institute and has supervised more than two hundred Fortune 500 MBA studies — all in addition to conducting his consulting and CEO-advisory work.

Jim has used his predictive modeling and intelligence work to accurately forecast the future performance of numerous companies, including those that eventually ended up in insolvency. He has completed a number of intelligence studies dealing with future technologies, such as broadband technology, small office home office (SOHO) technologies, and technology-related industry shifts.

He is currently the vice chairman of Far Corners Missions, which operates hospitals, clinics, and educational institutions in India for victims of poverty and human trafficking.

Jim and his wife Patsy live in the Dallas-Ft. Worth area.

Dedication

To Captain John Marshall Yeatts, my former classmate, fellow officer, and friend, who lost his life defending our country on May 12, 1969.

Author's Acknowledgments

Although I wrote this book, dozens of other talented individuals contributed to its conception, development, and perfection. Special thanks to Michael Lewis, who chose me to author this book; to my agent, John Willig, for handling all the behind-the-scenes negotiations; and to wordsmith Joe Kraynak for his relief efforts. Special thanks also to the tag-team duo of Alissa Schwipps and Jennifer Tebbe, who expertly shepherded the manuscript through the editorial and production process, improving it every step of the way. Thanks to Caitie Copple, our copy editor, who read through everything — forward and backward — to identify and obliterate the many grammatical goofs and typos. I also tip my hat to the folks in Composition Services at Wiley for doing such an outstanding job of transforming a loose collection of text and illustrations into such an attractive bound book.

Special thanks to technical editor Fred Wergeles for ferreting out any technical errors in the manuscript, making sure no critical information was omitted, and helping guide its content.

Publisher's Acknowledgments

Acquisitions Editor: Michael Lewis

Contributor & Development Editor:
Joe Kraynak

Senior Project Editor: Alissa Schwipps

Project Editor: Jennifer Tebbe

Copy Editor: Caitlin Copple

Technical Editor: Fred Wergeles

Project Coordinator: Katie Crocker

Cover Image: ©iStockphoto.com/Alex

...ple & Mac

...ad For Dummies,
...h Edition
...8-1-118-49823-1

...hone 5 For Dummies,
...h Edition
...8-1-118-35201-4

...acBook For Dummies,
...h Edition
...8-1-118-20920-2

...S X Mountain Lion
...r Dummies
...8-1-118-39418-2

...ogging & Social Media

...acebook For Dummies,
...th Edition
...8-1-118-09562-1

...om Blogging
...r Dummies
...8-1-118-03843-7

...interest For Dummies
...8-1-118-32800-2

...ordPress For Dummies,
...th Edition
...8-1-118-38318-6

...usiness

...ommodities For Dummies,
...nd Edition
...8-1-118-01687-9

...nvesting For Dummies,
...th Edition
...8-0-470-90545-6

Personal Finance
For Dummies,
7th Edition
978-1-118-11785-9

QuickBooks 2013
For Dummies
978-1-118-35641-8

Small Business Marketing Kit
For Dummies,
3rd Edition
978-1-118-31183-7

Careers

Job Interviews
For Dummies,
4th Edition
978-1-118-11290-8

Job Searching with
Social Media
For Dummies
978-0-470-93072-4

Personal Branding
For Dummies
978-1-118-11792-7

Resumes For Dummies,
6th Edition
978-0-470-87361-8

Success as a Mediator
For Dummies
978-1-118-07862-4

Diet & Nutrition

Belly Fat Diet For Dummies
978-1-118-34585-6

Eating Clean For Dummies
978-1-118-00013-7

Nutrition For Dummies,
5th Edition
978-0-470-93231-5

Digital Photography

Digital Photography
For Dummies,
7th Edition
978-1-118-09203-3

Digital SLR Cameras &
Photography For Dummies,
4th Edition
978-1-118-14489-3

Photoshop Elements 11
For Dummies
978-1-118-40821-6

Gardening

Herb Gardening
For Dummies,
2nd Edition
978-0-470-61778-6

Vegetable Gardening
For Dummies,
2nd Edition
978-0-470-49870-5

Health

Anti-Inflammation Diet
For Dummies
978-1-118-02381-5

Diabetes For Dummies,
3rd Edition
978-0-470-27086-8

Living Paleo For Dummies
978-1-118-29405-5

Hobbies

Beekeeping
For Dummies
978-0-470-43065-1

eBay For Dummies,
7th Edition
978-1-118-09806-6

Raising Chickens
For Dummies
978-0-470-46544-8

Wine For Dummies,
5th Edition
978-1-118-28872-6

Writing Young Adult Fiction
For Dummies
978-0-470-94954-2

Language & Foreign Language

500 Spanish Verbs
For Dummies
978-1-118-02382-2

English Grammar
For Dummies,
2nd Edition
978-0-470-54664-2

French All-in One
For Dummies
978-1-118-22815-9

German Essentials
For Dummies
978-1-118-18422-6

Italian For Dummies
2nd Edition
978-1-118-00465-4

---

e̷ Available in print and e-book formats.

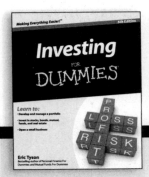

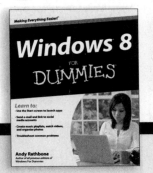

Available wherever books are sold. For more information or to order direct: U.S. customers visit www.Dummies.com or call 1-877-762-2974.
U.K. customers visit www.Wileyeurope.com or call (0) 1243 843291. Canadian customers visit www.Wiley.ca or call 1-800-567-4797.

Connect with us online at www.facebook.com/fordummies or @fordummies

Math & Science

Algebra I For Dummies,
2nd Edition
978-0-470-55964-2

Anatomy and Physiology
For Dummies,
2nd Edition
978-0-470-92326-9

Astronomy For Dummies,
3rd Edition
978-1-118-37697-3

Biology For Dummies,
2nd Edition
978-0-470-59875-7

Chemistry For Dummies,
2nd Edition
978-1-1180-0730-3

Pre-Algebra Essentials
For Dummies
978-0-470-61838-7

Microsoft Office

Excel 2013 For Dummies
978-1-118-51012-4

Office 2013 All-in-One
For Dummies
978-1-118-51636-2

PowerPoint 2013
For Dummies
978-1-118-50253-2

Word 2013 For Dummies
978-1-118-49123-2

Music

Blues Harmonica
For Dummies
978-1-118-25269-7

Guitar For Dummies,
3rd Edition
978-1-118-11554-1

iPod & iTunes
For Dummies,
10th Edition
978-1-118-50864-0

Programming

Android Application
Development For
Dummies, 2nd Edition
978-1-118-38710-8

iOS 6 Application
Development For Dummies
978-1-118-50880-0

Java For Dummies,
5th Edition
978-0-470-37173-2

Religion & Inspiration

The Bible For Dummies
978-0-7645-5296-0

Buddhism For Dummies,
2nd Edition
978-1-118-02379-2

Catholicism For Dummies,
2nd Edition
978-1-118-07778-8

Self-Help & Relationships

Bipolar Disorder
For Dummies,
2nd Edition
978-1-118-33882-7

Meditation For Dummies,
3rd Edition
978-1-118-29144-3

Seniors

Computers For Seniors
For Dummies,
3rd Edition
978-1-118-11553-4

iPad For Seniors
For Dummies,
5th Edition
978-1-118-49708-1

Social Security
For Dummies
978-1-118-20573-0

Smartphones & Tablets

Android Phones
For Dummies
978-1-118-16952-0

Kindle Fire HD
For Dummies
978-1-118-42223-6

NOOK HD For Dummies,
Portable Edition
978-1-118-39498-4

Surface For Dummies
978-1-118-49634-3

Test Prep

ACT For Dummies,
5th Edition
978-1-118-01259-8

ASVAB For Dummies,
3rd Edition
978-0-470-63760-9

GRE For Dummies,
7th Edition
978-0-470-88921-3

Officer Candidate Tests,
For Dummies
978-0-470-59876-4

Physician's Assistant Exam
For Dummies
978-1-118-11556-5

Series 7 Exam
For Dummies
978-0-470-09932-2

Windows 8

Windows 8 For Dummies
978-1-118-13461-0

Windows 8 For Dummies,
Book + DVD Bundle
978-1-118-27167-4

Windows 8 All-in-One
For Dummies
978-1-118-11920-4

Available in print and e-book formats.

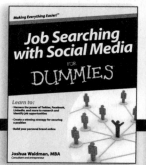

Take Dummies with you everywhere you go!

Whether you're excited about e-books, want more from the web, must have your mobile apps, or swept up in social media, Dummies makes everything easier .

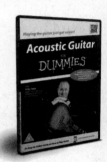